STORY AND ART BY
Sankichi Hinodeya

CONTENTS

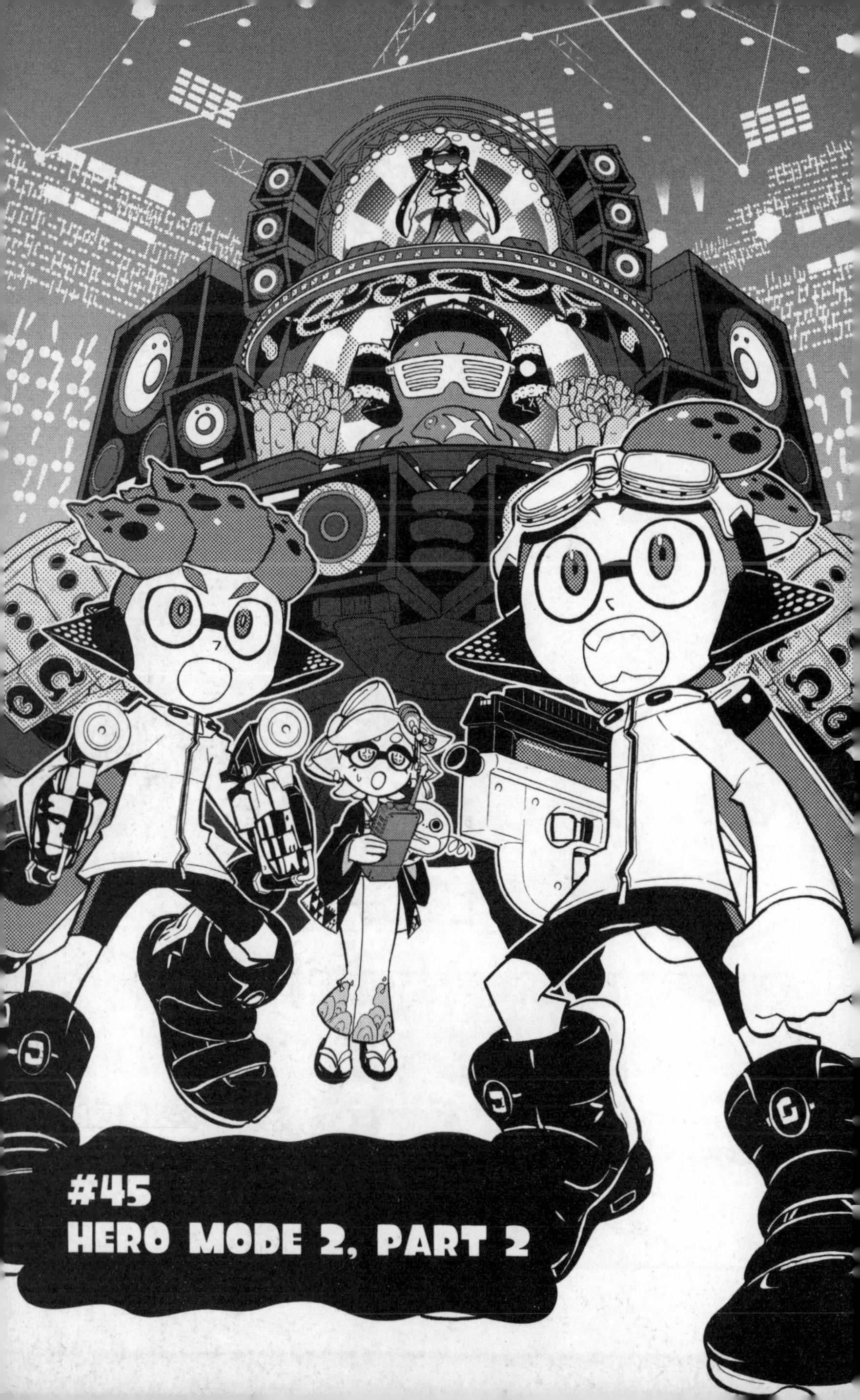
#45
HERO MODE 2, PART 2

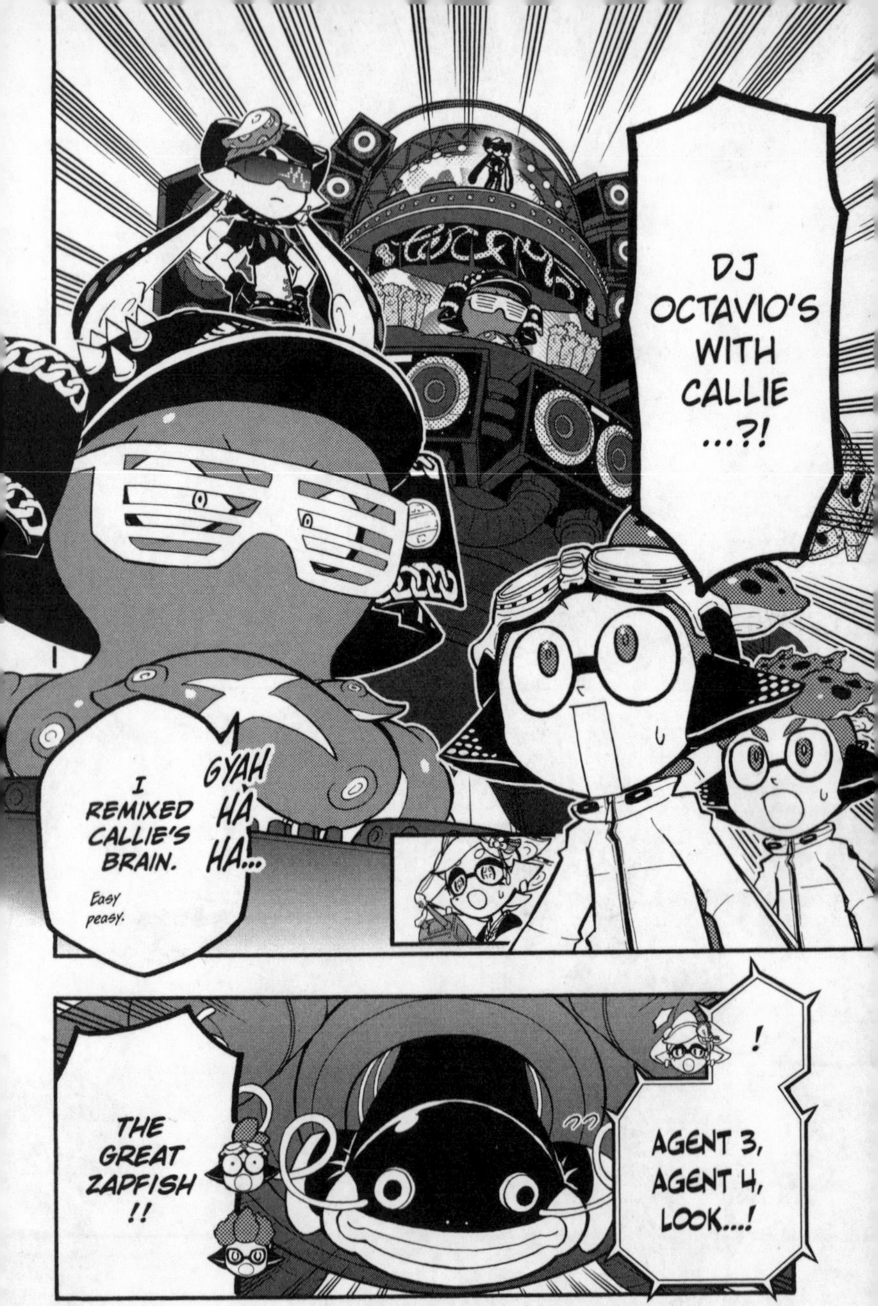
DJ OCTAVIO'S WITH CALLIE ...?!
GYAH HA HA...
I REMIXED CALLIE'S BRAIN.
Easy peasy.
!
AGENT 3, AGENT 4, LOOK...!
THE GREAT ZAPFISH !!

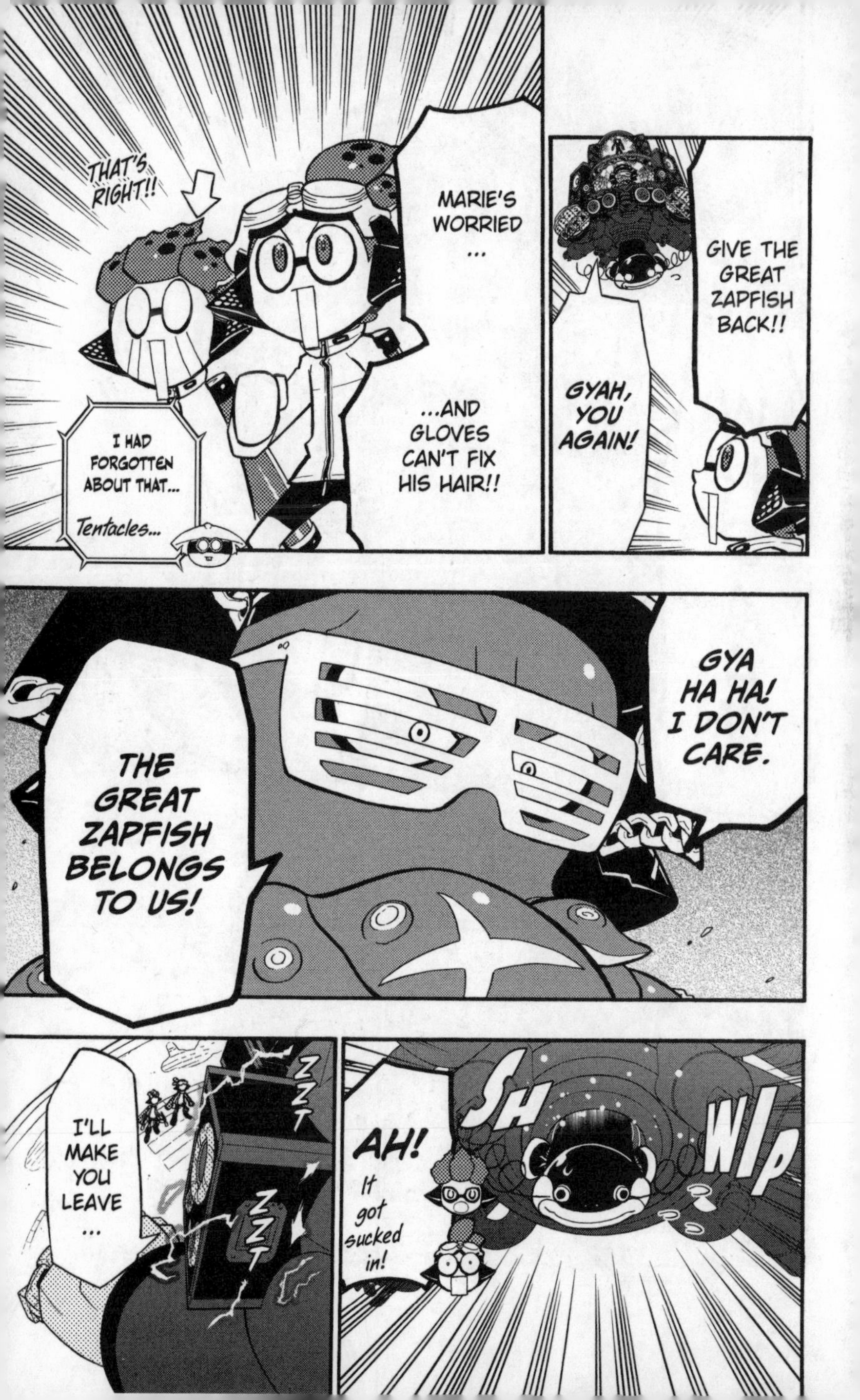
GIVE THE GREAT ZAPFISH BACK!!
GYAH, YOU AGAIN!
MARIE'S WORRIED ...
...AND GLOVES CAN'T FIX HIS HAIR!!
THAT'S RIGHT!!
I HAD FORGOTTEN ABOUT THAT...
Tentacles...
GYA HA HA! I DON'T CARE.
THE GREAT ZAPFISH BELONGS TO US!
SH
WIP
AH!
It got sucked in!
ZZZT
ZZZT
I'LL MAKE YOU LEAVE ...

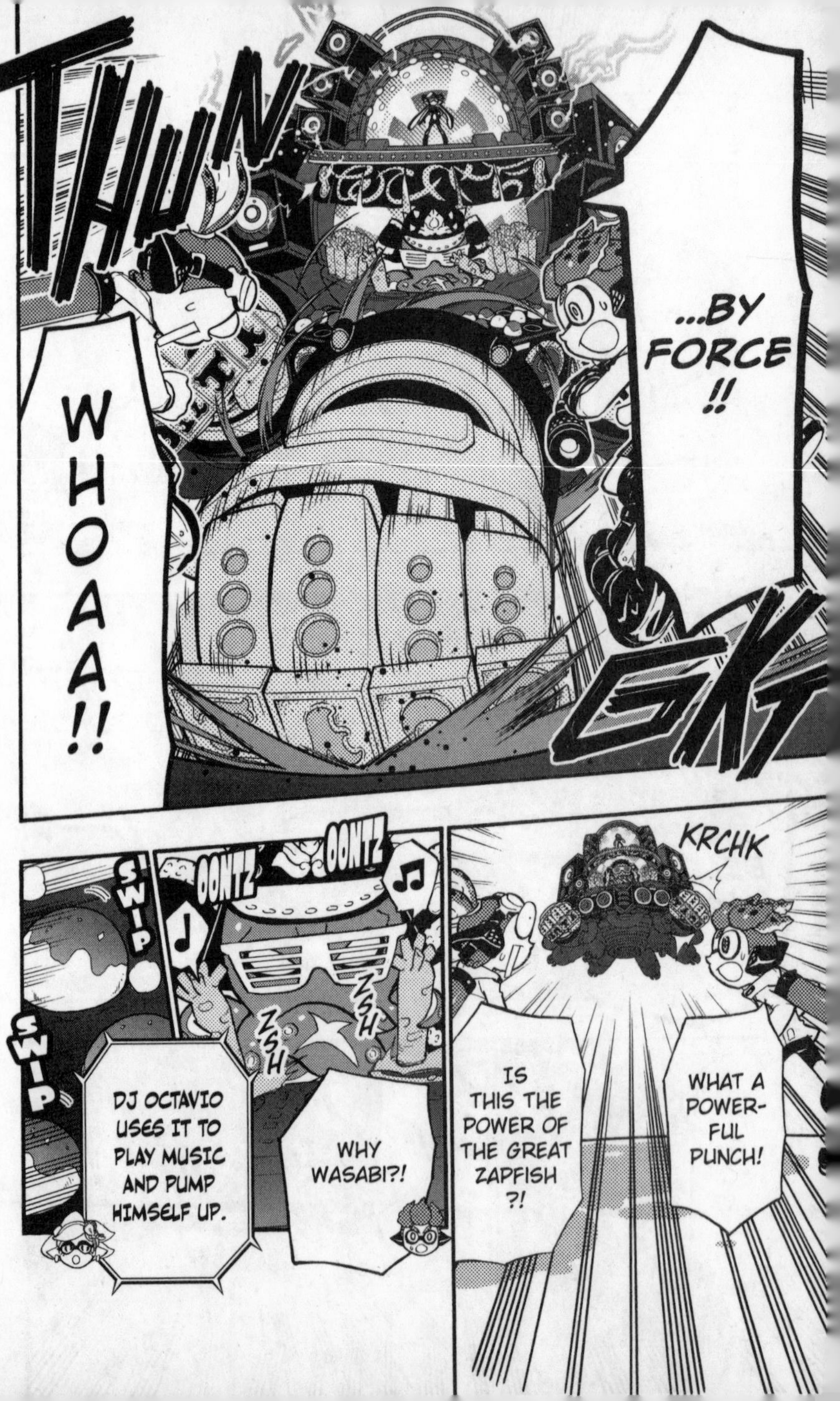

...BY FORCE!!
THWN
WHOAA!!
KRCHK
WHAT A POWER-FUL PUNCH!
IS THIS THE POWER OF THE GREAT ZAPFISH?!
OONTZ
OONTZ
ZSH
ZSH
WHY WASABI?!
SWIP
SWIP
DJ OCTAVIO USES IT TO PLAY MUSIC AND PUMP HIMSELF UP.

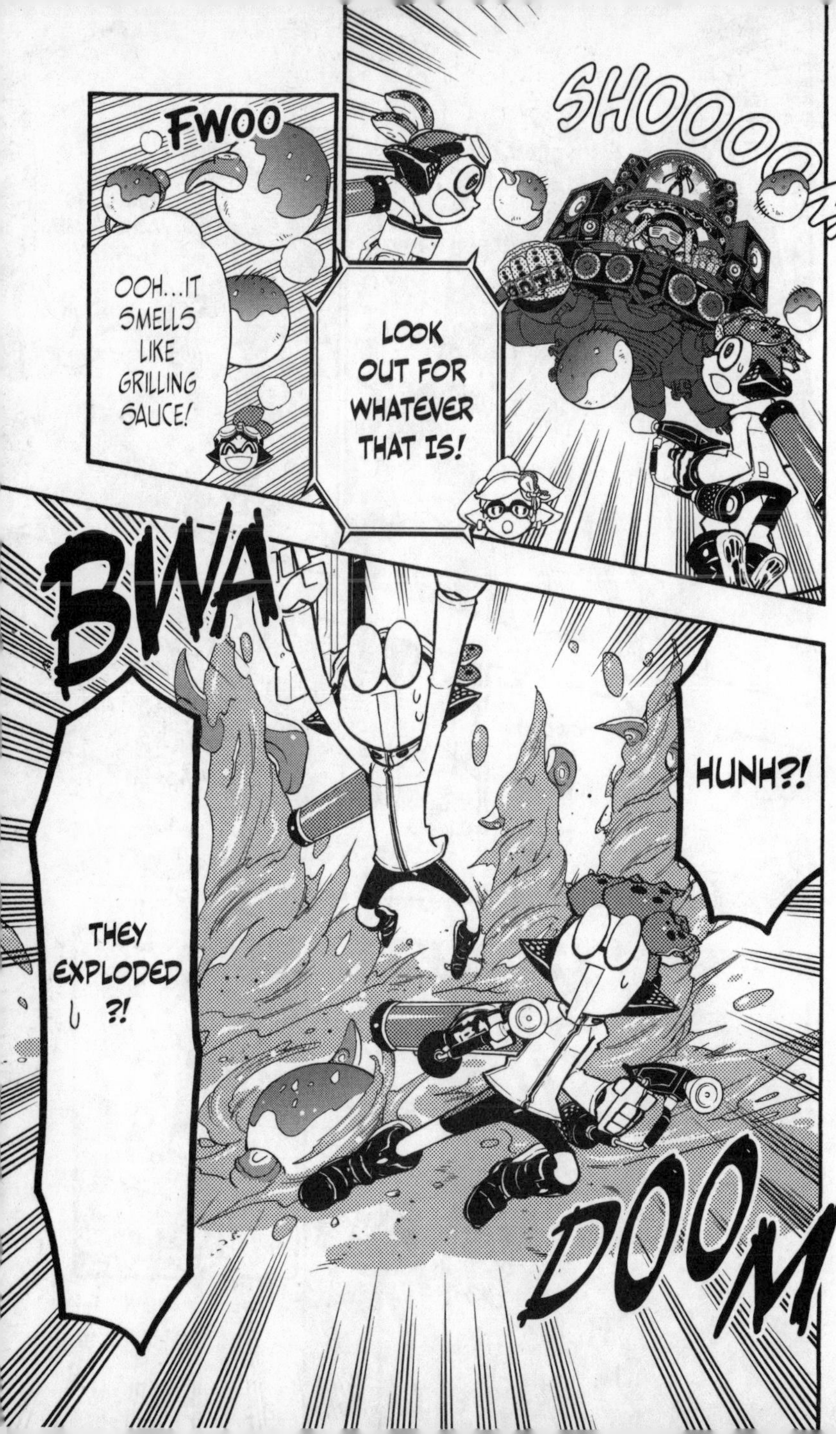
SHOOOOM
LOOK OUT FOR WHATEVER THAT IS!
FWOO
OOH...IT SMELLS LIKE GRILLING SAUCE!
BWA
HUNH?!
THEY EXPLODED ?!
DOOM

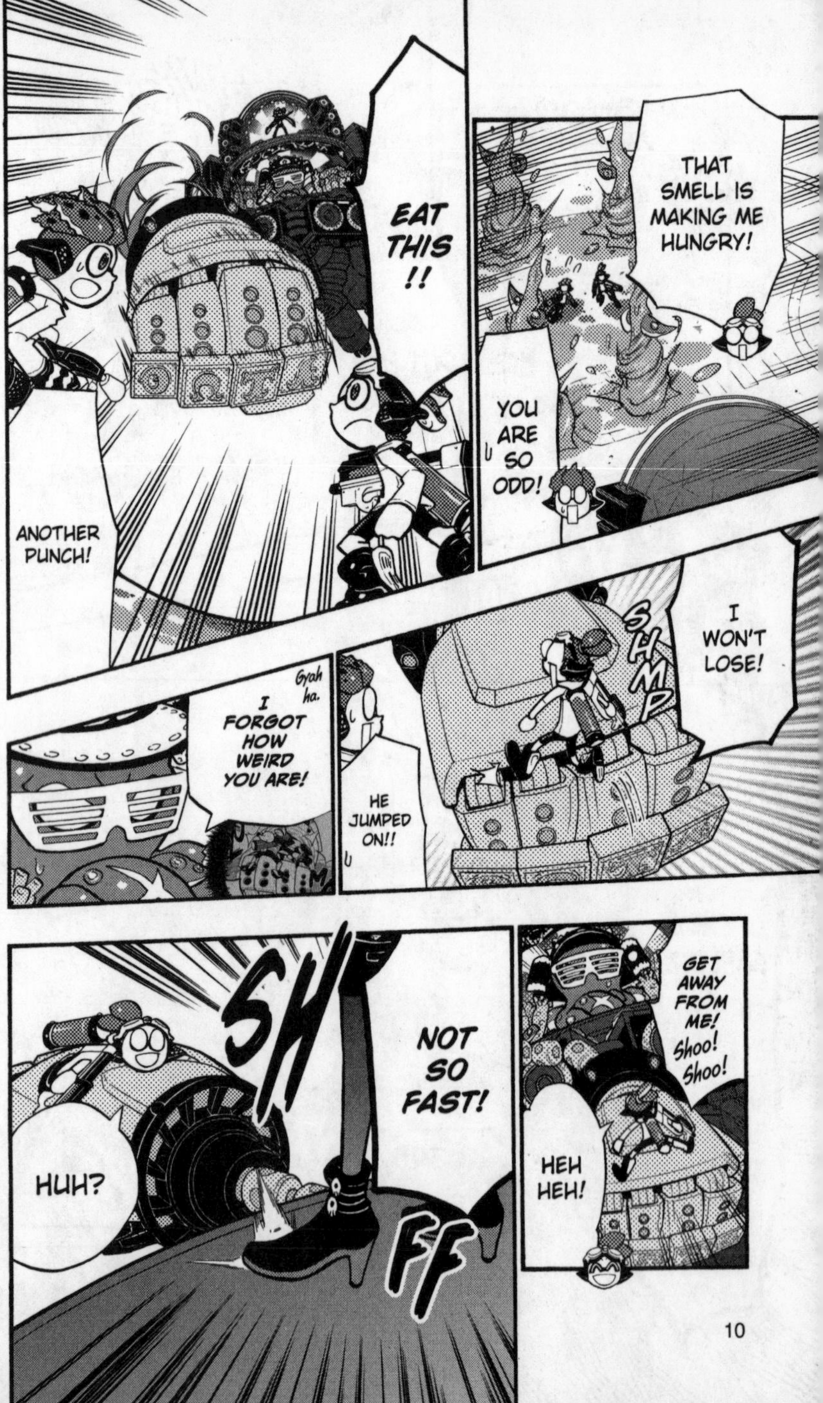
THAT SMELL IS MAKING ME HUNGRY!
YOU ARE SO ODD!
EAT THIS!!
ANOTHER PUNCH!
I WON'T LOSE!
SHMP
HE JUMPED ON!!
Gyah ha.
I FORGOT HOW WEIRD YOU ARE!
GET AWAY FROM ME! Shoo! Shoo!
HEH HEH!
NOT SO FAST!
SHFF
HUH?

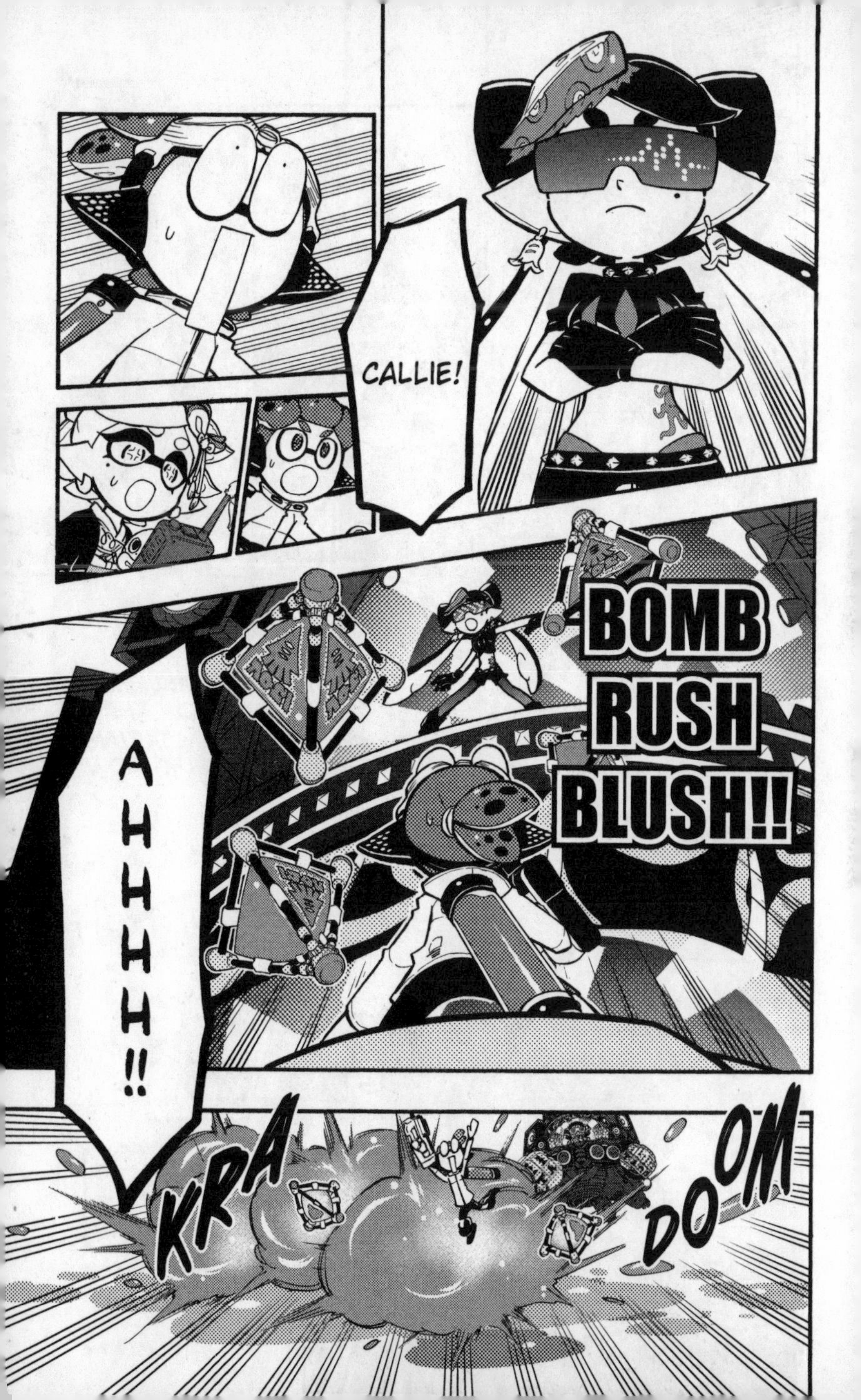
CALLIE!
BOMB RUSH BLUSH!!
AHHHH!!
KRA
DOOOM

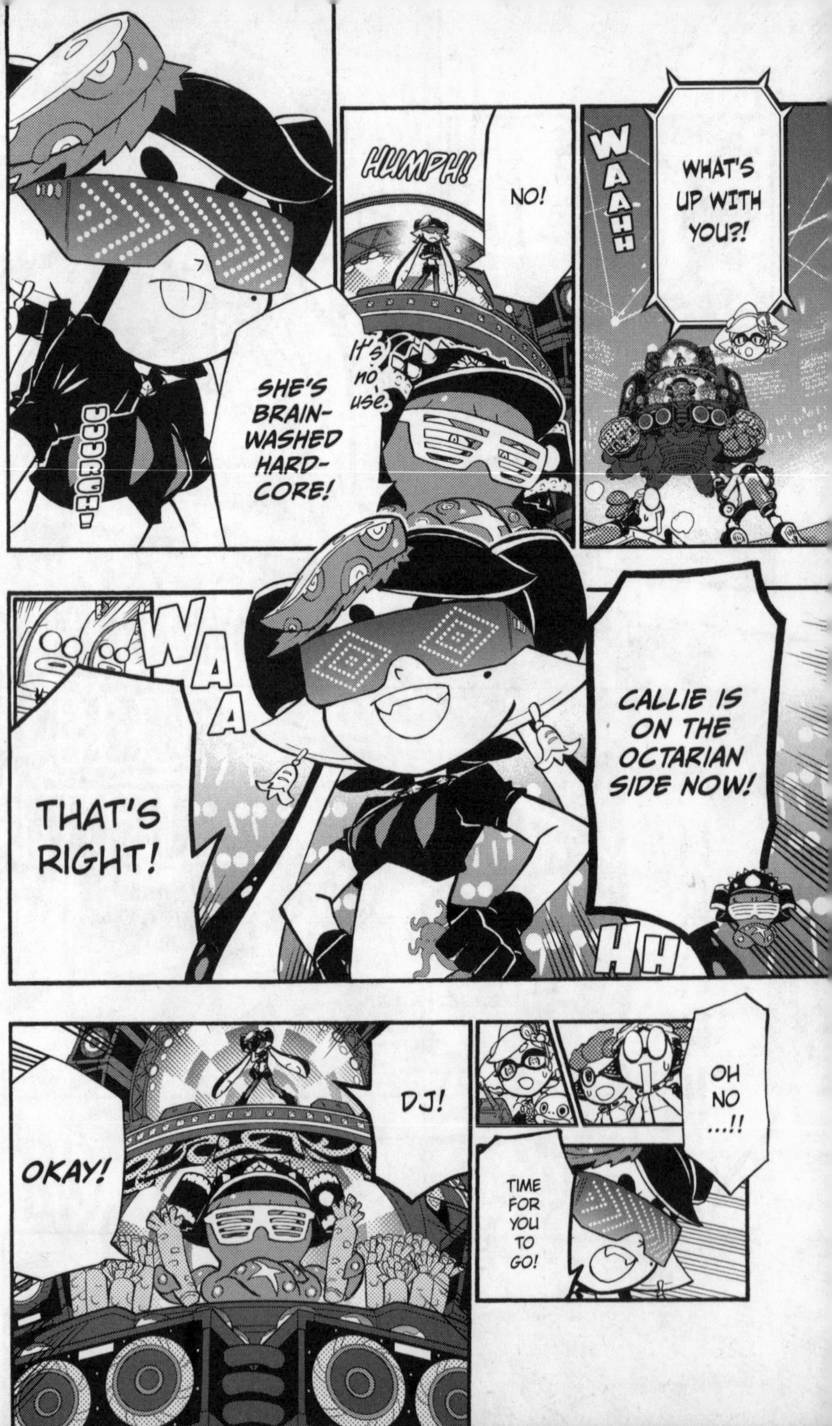
WAAHH
WHAT'S UP WITH YOU?!
HUMPH!
NO!
It's no use.
SHE'S BRAIN-WASHED HARD-CORE!
UUURGH!
CALLIE IS ON THE OCTARIAN SIDE NOW!
WAAAHH
THAT'S RIGHT!
OH NO ...!!
TIME FOR YOU TO GO!
DJ!
OKAY!

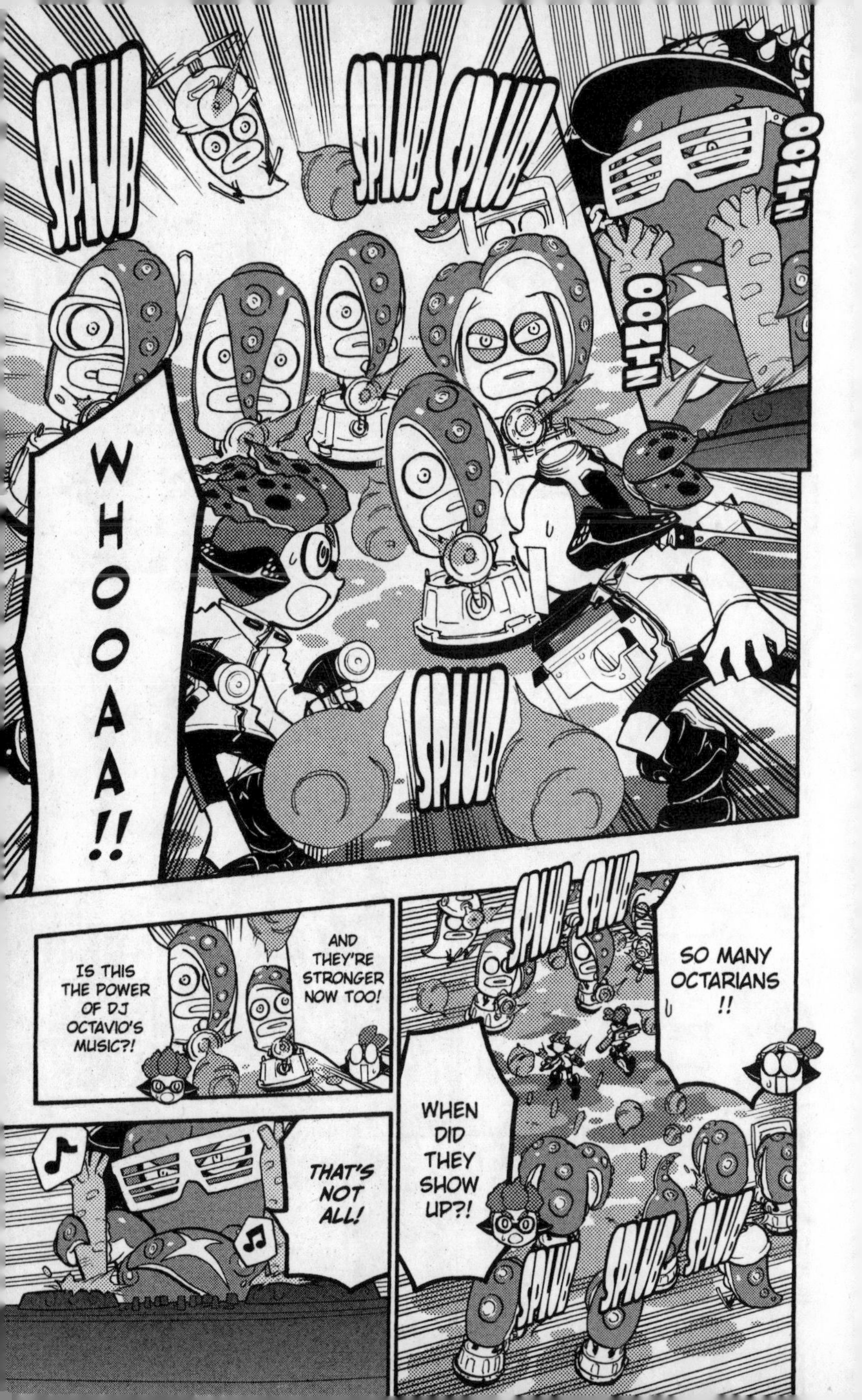
OONTZ
OONTZ
SPLUB SPLUB
SPLUB
WHOOAA!!
SPLUB
SPLUB SPLUB
SO MANY OCTARIANS!!
WHEN DID THEY SHOW UP?!
SPLUB SPLUB SPLUB
AND THEY'RE STRONGER NOW TOO!
IS THIS THE POWER OF DJ OCTAVIO'S MUSIC?!
THAT'S NOT ALL!

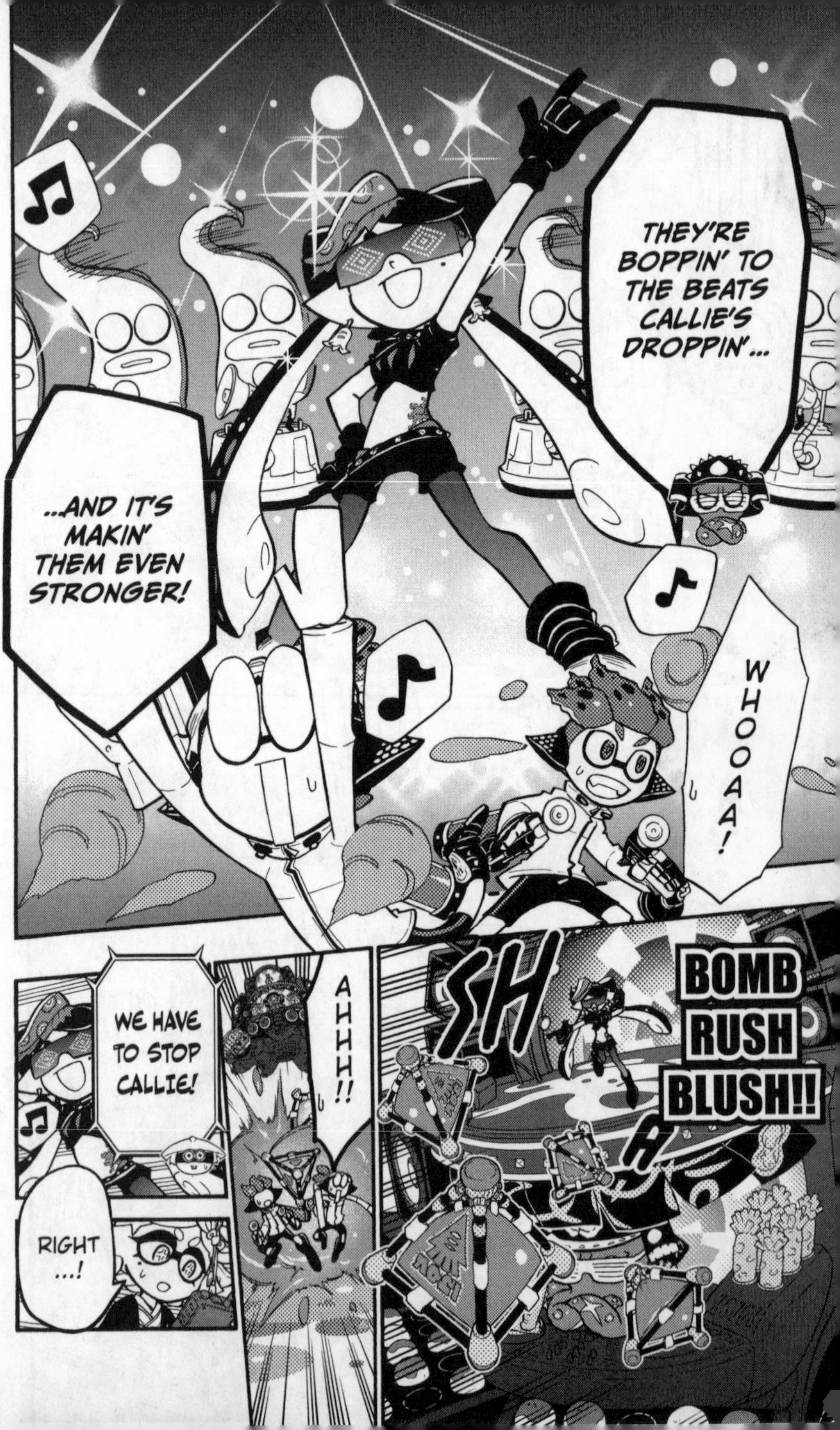
THEY'RE BOPPIN' TO THE BEATS CALLIE'S DROPPIN'...
...AND IT'S MAKIN' THEM EVEN STRONGER!
WHOOOAA!
BOMB RUSH BLUSH!!
SH
AHHH!!
WE HAVE TO STOP CALLIE!
RIGHT ...!

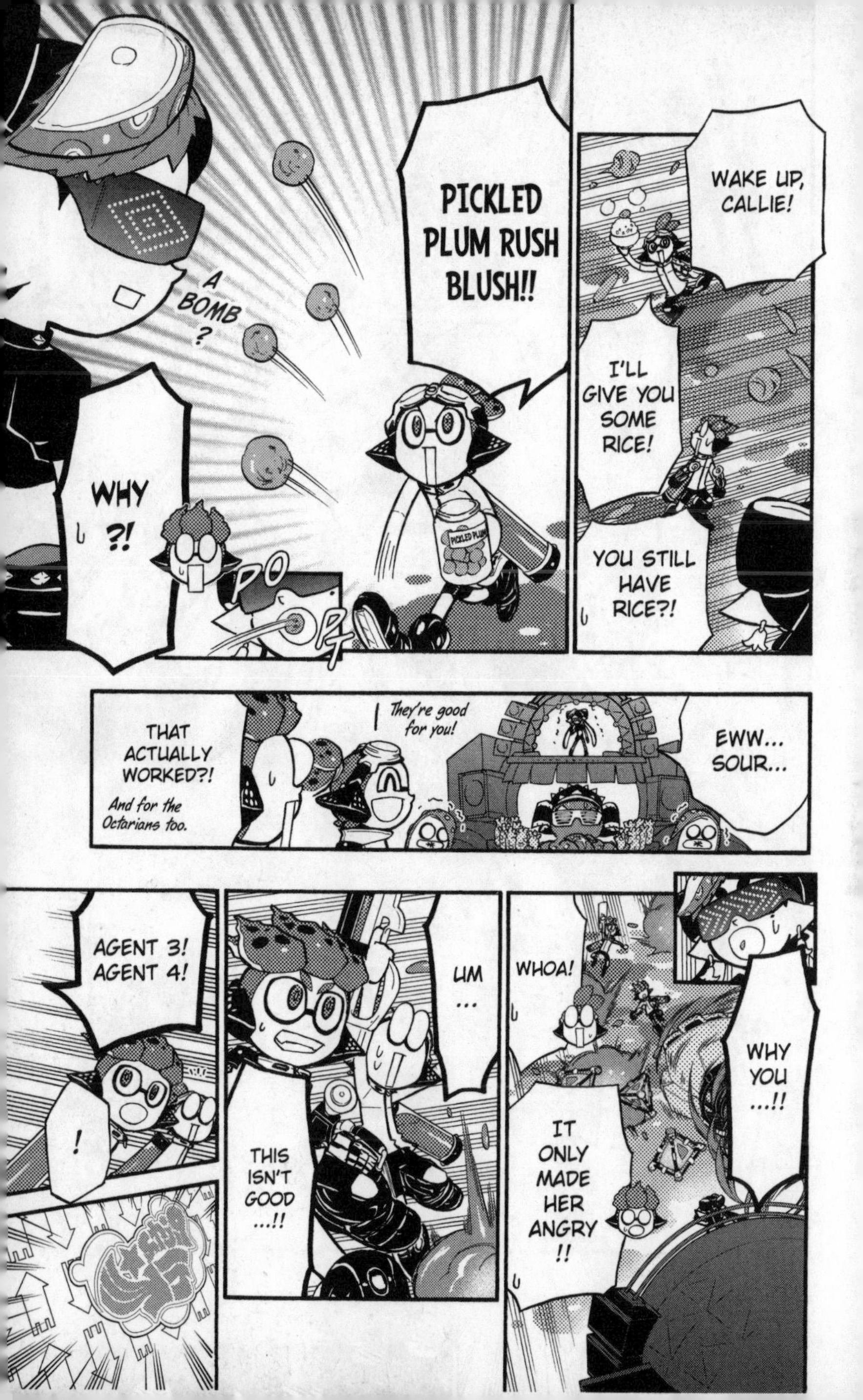
WAKE UP, CALLIE!
I'LL GIVE YOU SOME RICE!
YOU STILL HAVE RICE?!
PICKLED PLUM RUSH BLUSH!!
A BOMB?
PICKLED PLUM
WHY?!
EWW... SOUR...
They're good for you!
THAT ACTUALLY WORKED?!
And for the Octarians too.
WHY YOU...!!
WHOA!
IT ONLY MADE HER ANGRY!!
UM...
THIS ISN'T GOOD...!!
AGENT 3! AGENT 4!
!

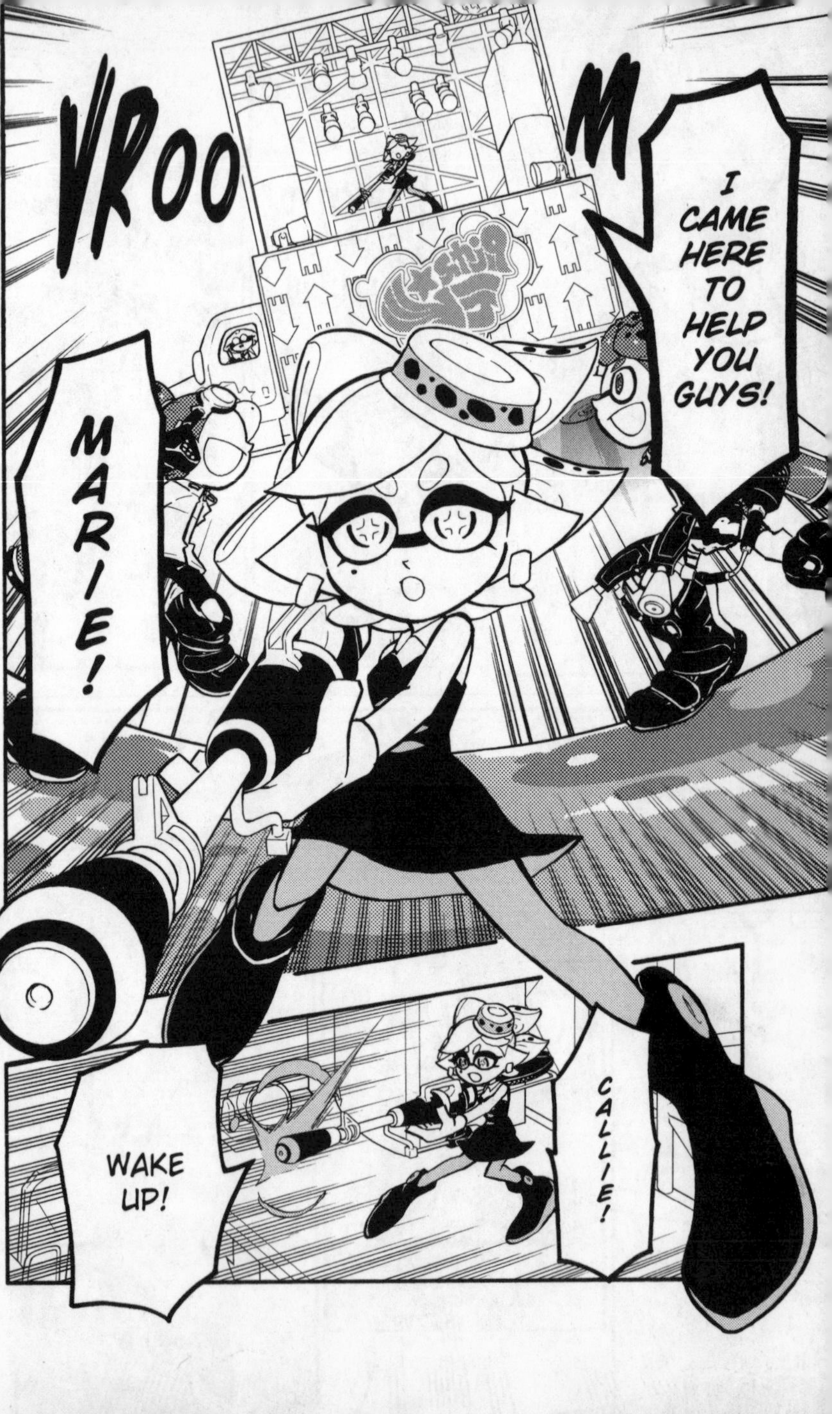
VROOM
I CAME HERE TO HELP YOU GUYS!
MARIE!
CALLIE!
WAKE UP!

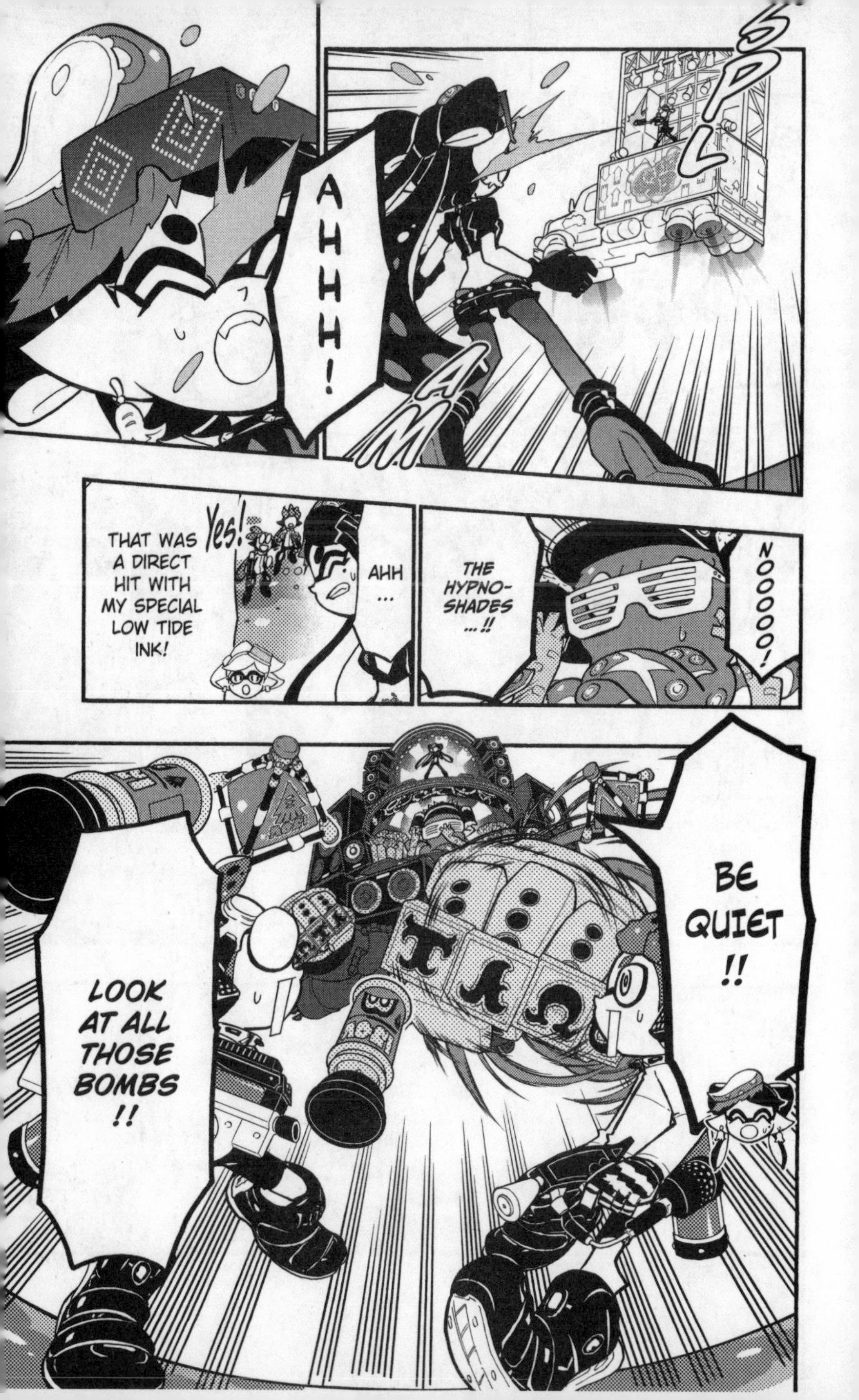
SPL
AM
AHHH!
NOOOOO!
THE HYPNO-SHADES...!!
AHH...
Yes!
THAT WAS A DIRECT HIT WITH MY SPECIAL LOW TIDE INK!
BE QUIET!!
LOOK AT ALL THOSE BOMBS!!

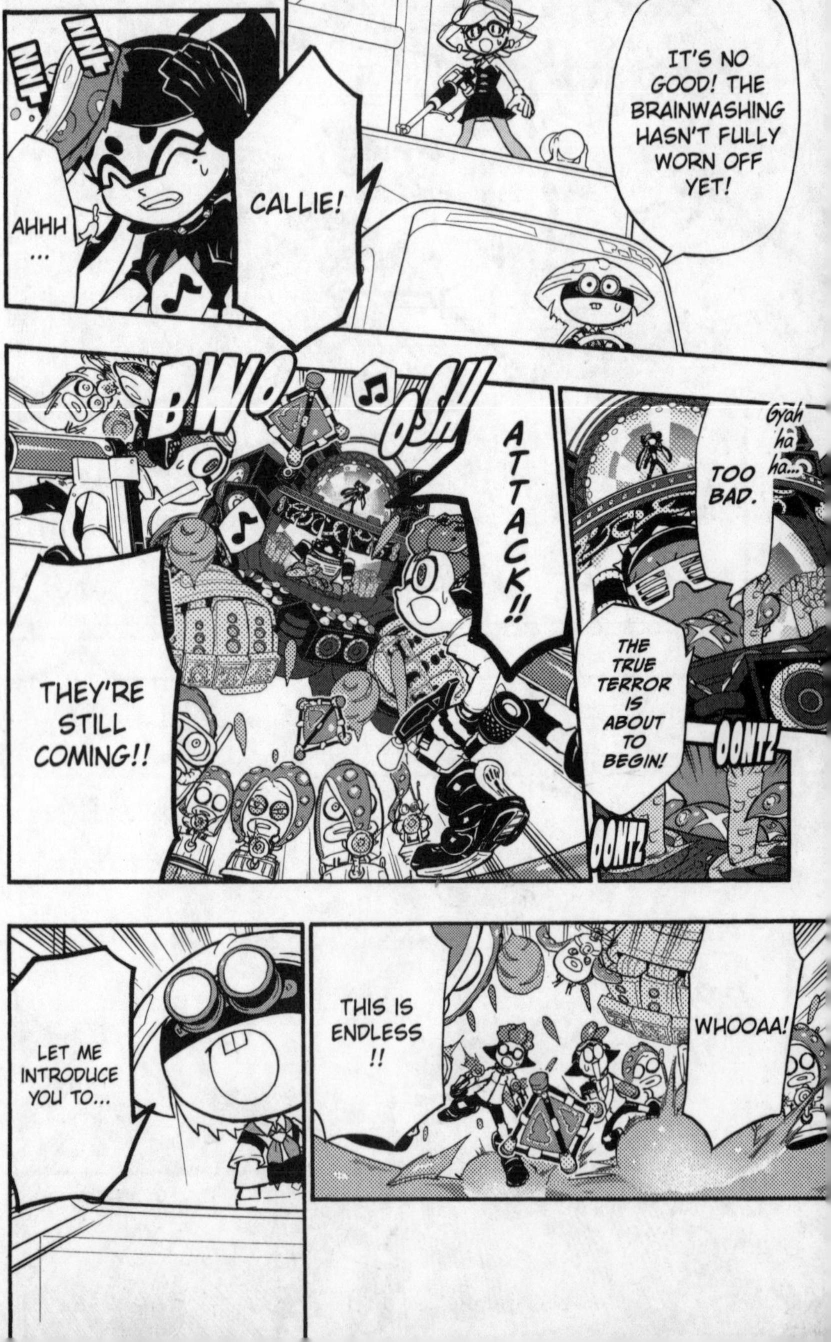
IT'S NO GOOD! THE BRAINWASHING HASN'T FULLY WORN OFF YET!
CALLIE!
NNF
NNF
AHHH ...
Gyah ha ha...
TOO BAD.
THE TRUE TERROR IS ABOUT TO BEGIN!
OONTZ
OONTZ
BWO-OSH
ATTACK!!
THEY'RE STILL COMING!!
WHOOAA!
THIS IS ENDLESS !!
LET ME INTRODUCE YOU TO...

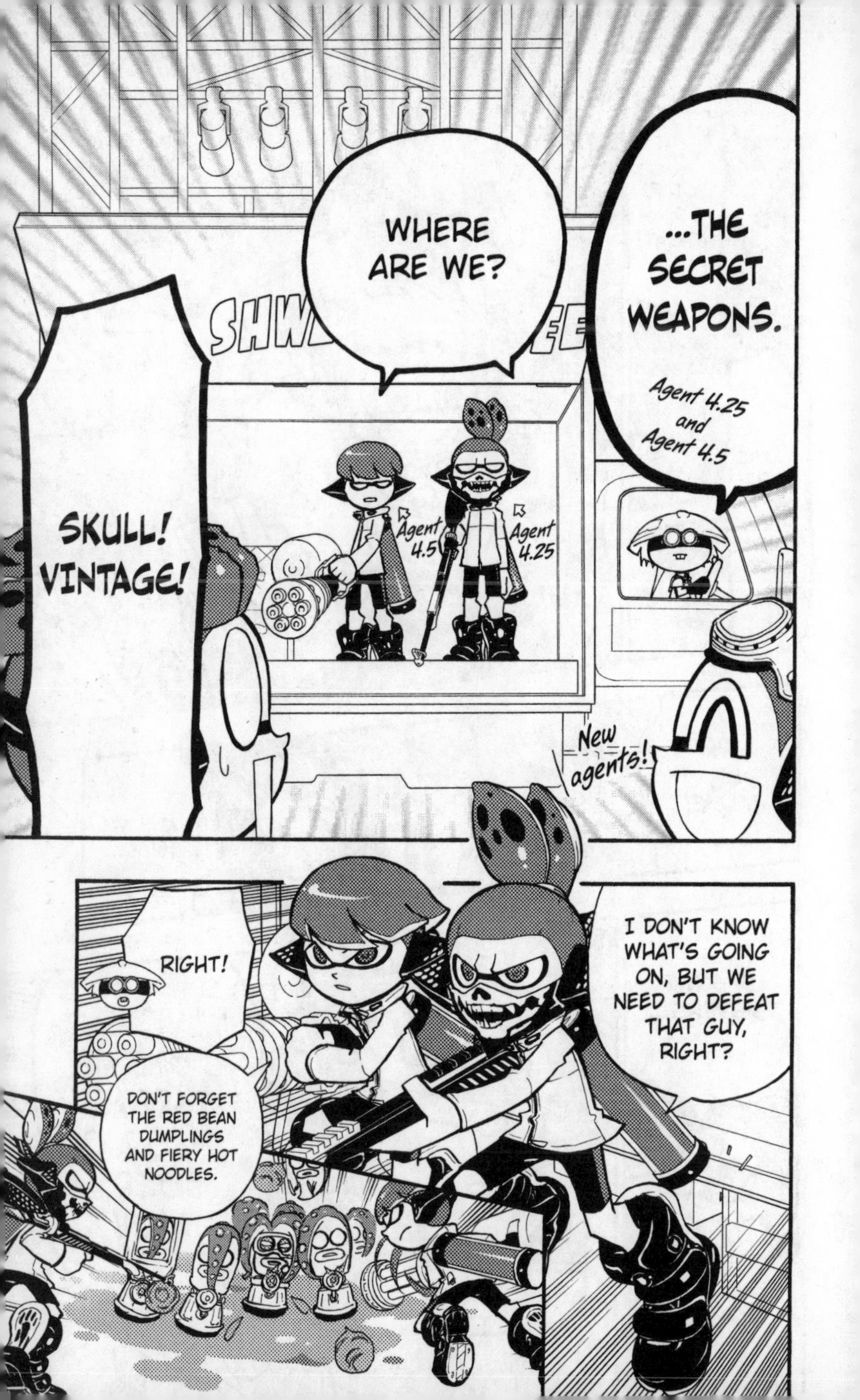
...THE SECRET WEAPONS.
Agent 4.25 and Agent 4.5
WHERE ARE WE?
Agent 4.25
Agent 4.5
New agents!
SKULL! VINTAGE!
I DON'T KNOW WHAT'S GOING ON, BUT WE NEED TO DEFEAT THAT GUY, RIGHT?
RIGHT!
DON'T FORGET THE RED BEAN DUMPLINGS AND FIERY HOT NOODLES.

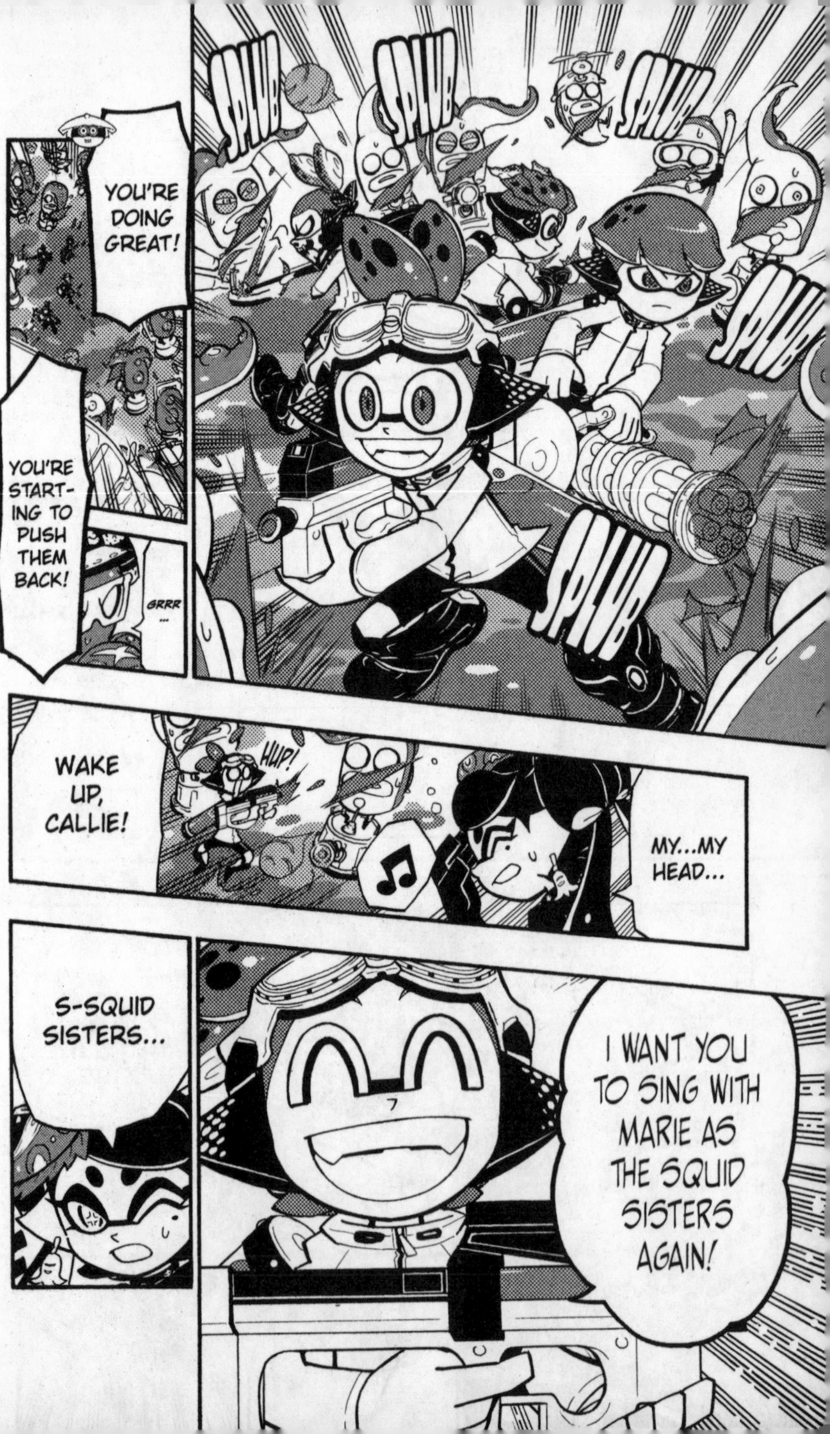
SPLUB
SPLUB
SPLUB
SPLUB
SPLUB
YOU'RE DOING GREAT!
YOU'RE START-ING TO PUSH THEM BACK!
GRRR...
MY...MY HEAD...
HUP!
WAKE UP, CALLIE!
I WANT YOU TO SING WITH MARIE AS THE SQUID SISTERS AGAIN!
S-SQUID SISTERS...

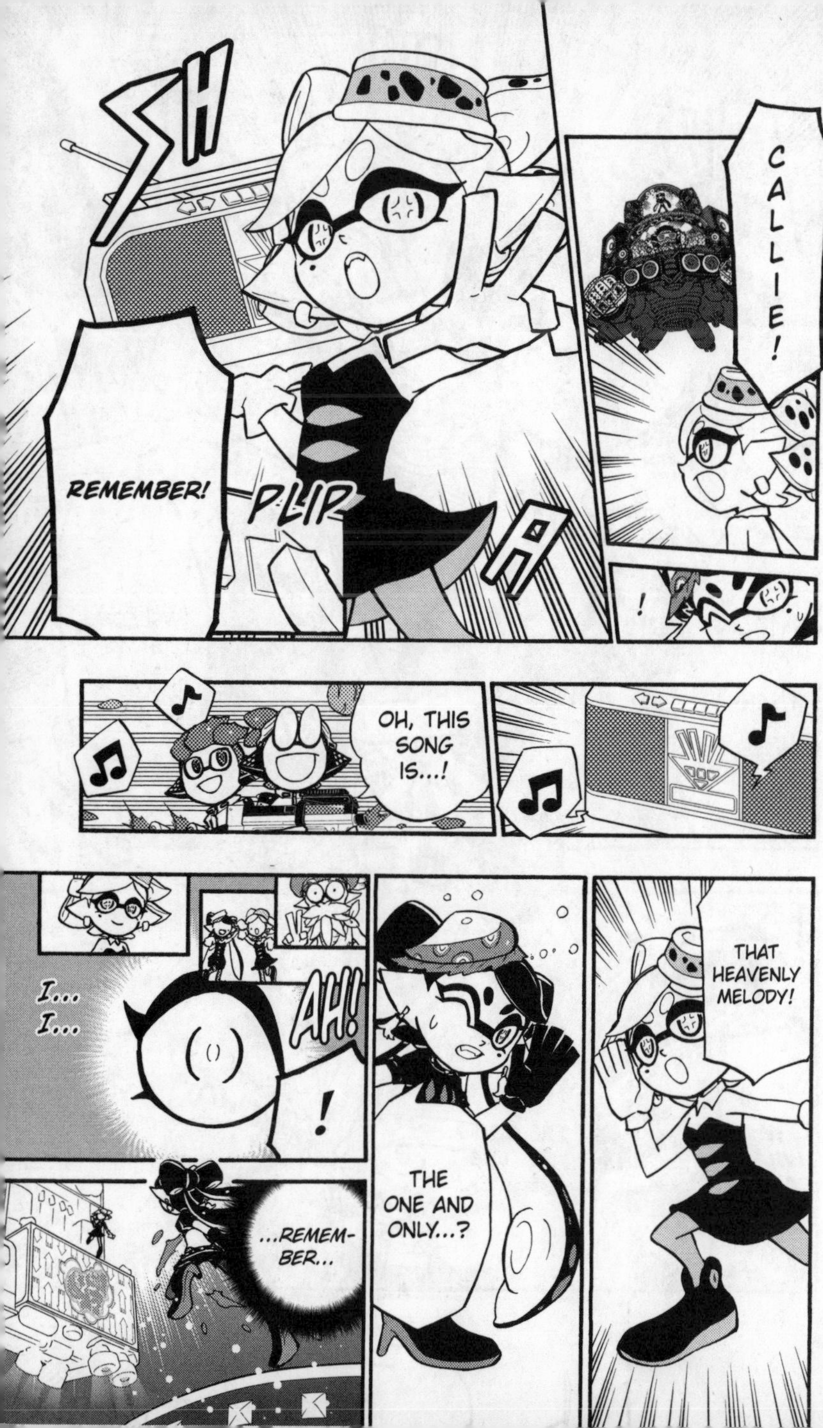

CALLIE!
!
SH
A
PLIP
REMEMBER!
OH, THIS SONG IS...!
THAT HEAVENLY MELODY!
THE ONE AND ONLY...?
AH!
!
I... I...
...REMEM-BER...

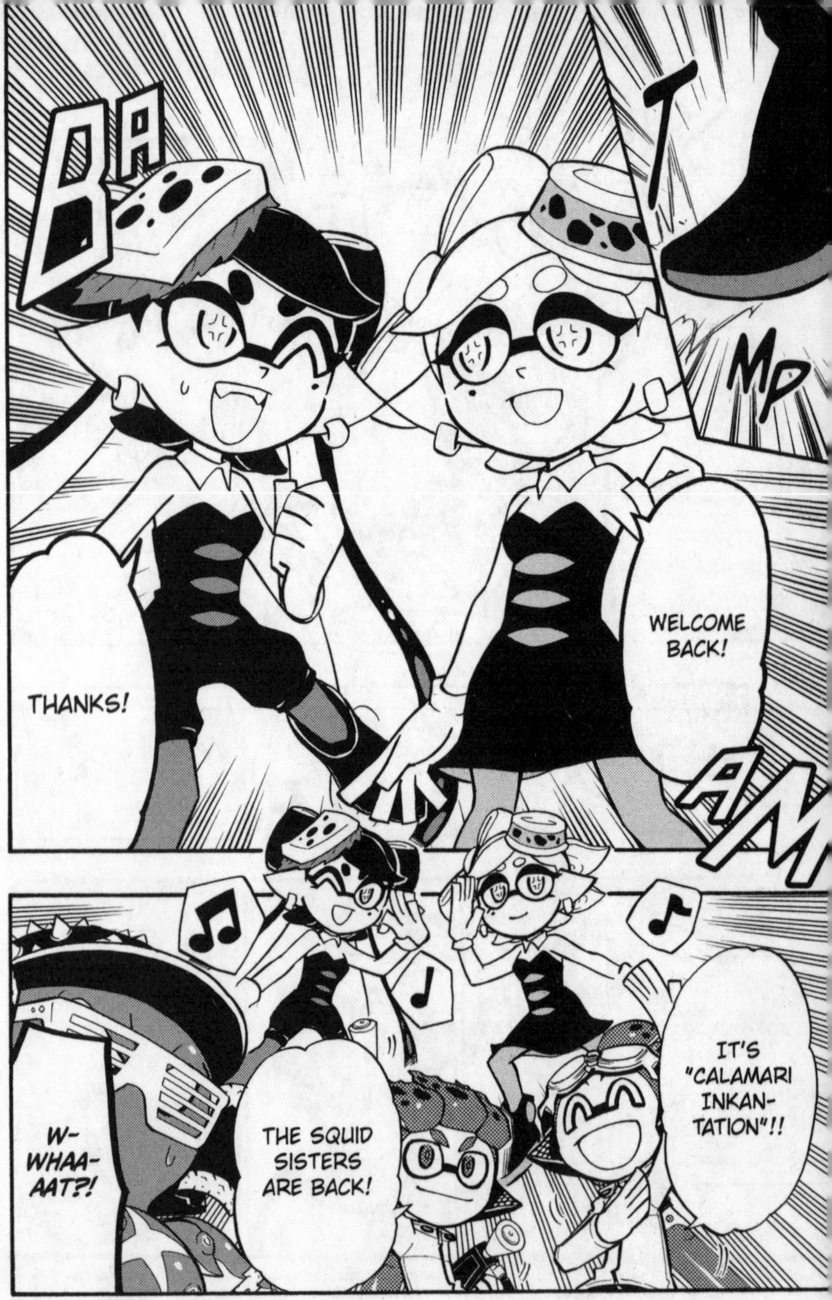
T
MP
WELCOME BACK!
THANKS!
BA
AM
IT'S "CALAMARI INKAN-TATION"!!
THE SQUID SISTERS ARE BACK!
W-WHAA-AAT?!

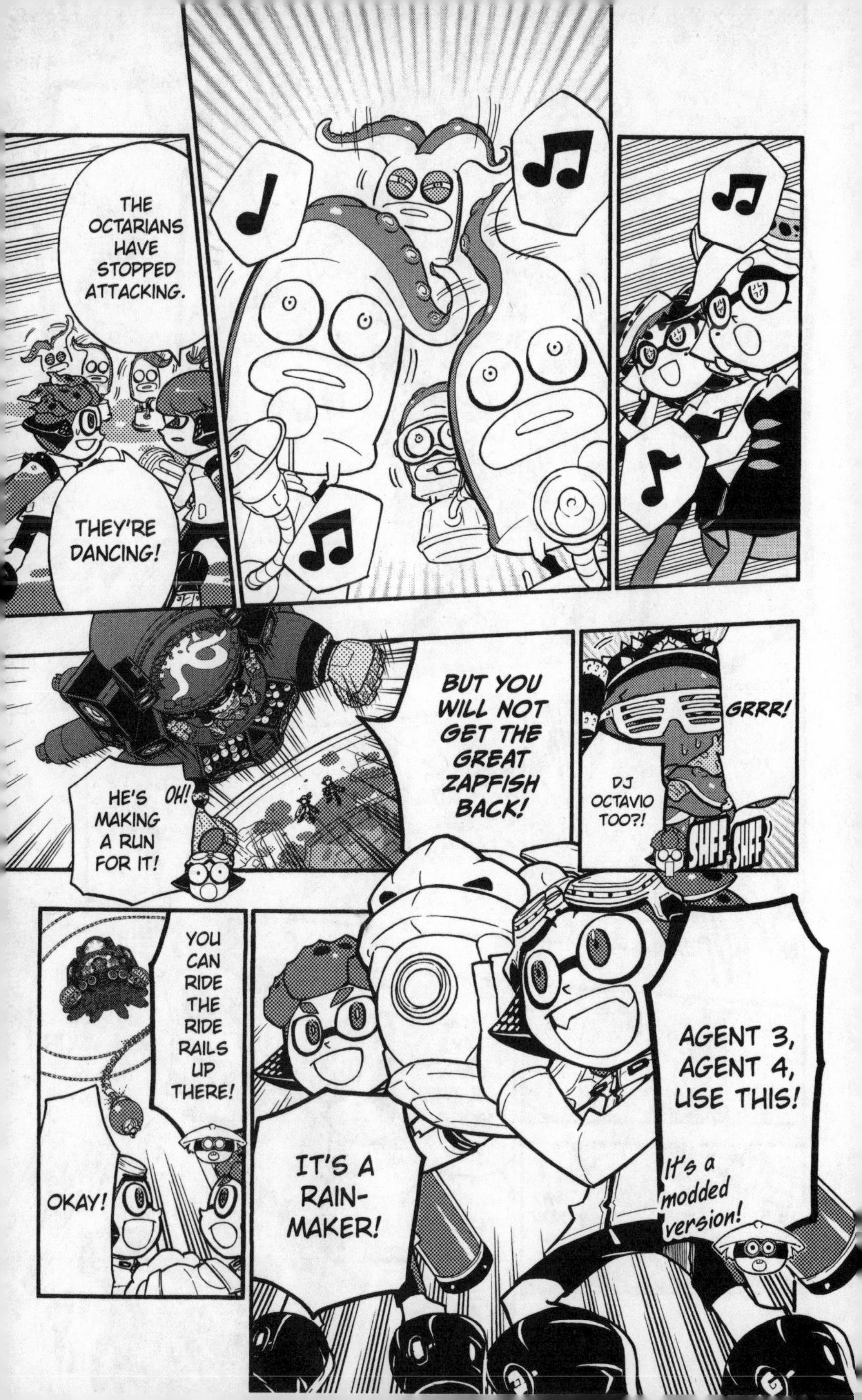
THE OCTARIANS HAVE STOPPED ATTACKING.
THEY'RE DANCING!
GRRR!
DJ OCTAVIO TOO?!
SHFF SHFF
BUT YOU WILL NOT GET THE GREAT ZAPFISH BACK!
OH!
HE'S MAKING A RUN FOR IT!
AGENT 3, AGENT 4, USE THIS!
IT'S A RAIN-MAKER!
It's a modded version!
YOU CAN RIDE THE RIDE RAILS UP THERE!
OKAY!

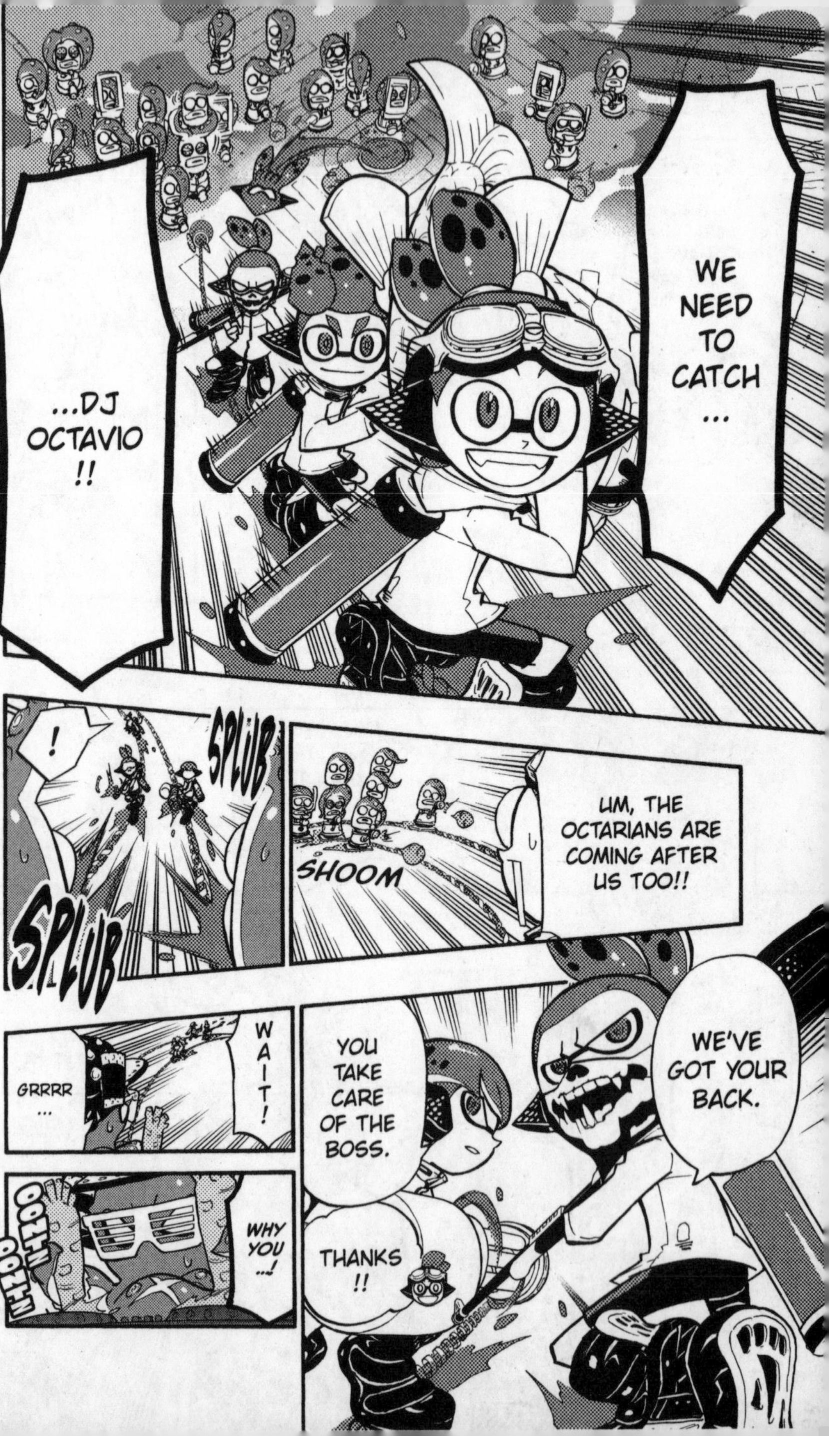
WE NEED TO CATCH ...
...DJ OCTAVIO !!
UM, THE OCTARIANS ARE COMING AFTER US TOO!!
SHOOM
!
SPLUB
SPLUB
WE'VE GOT YOUR BACK.
YOU TAKE CARE OF THE BOSS.
THANKS !!
WAIT!
GRRRR ...
WHY YOU ...!

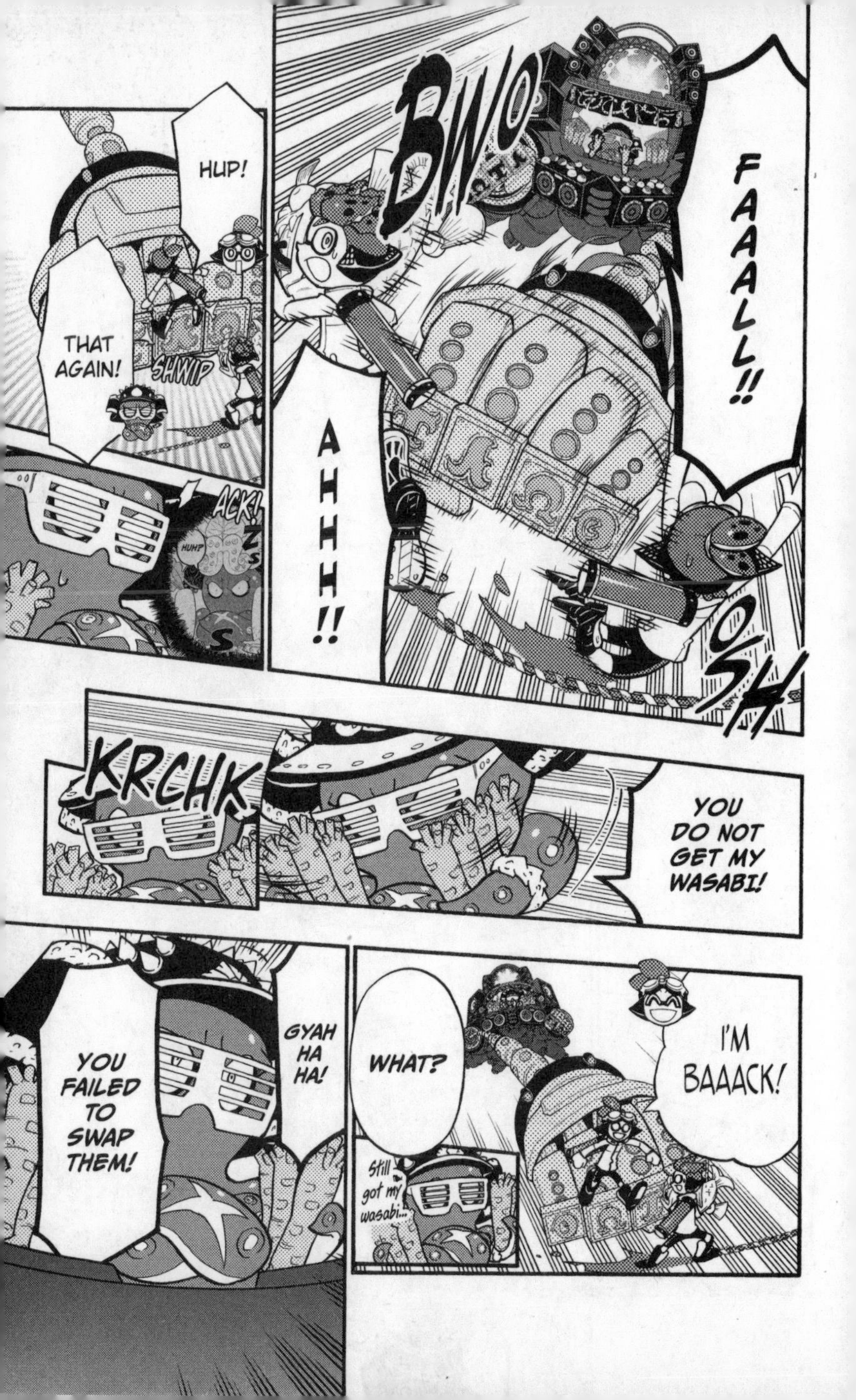
BWO
FAAAALL!!
AHHHH!!
OSH
HUP!
THAT AGAIN!
SHWIP
ACK!
HUMP?
YOU DO NOT GET MY WASABI!
KRCHK
I'M BAAACK!
WHAT?
Still got my wasabi...
GYAH HA HA!
YOU FAILED TO SWAP THEM!

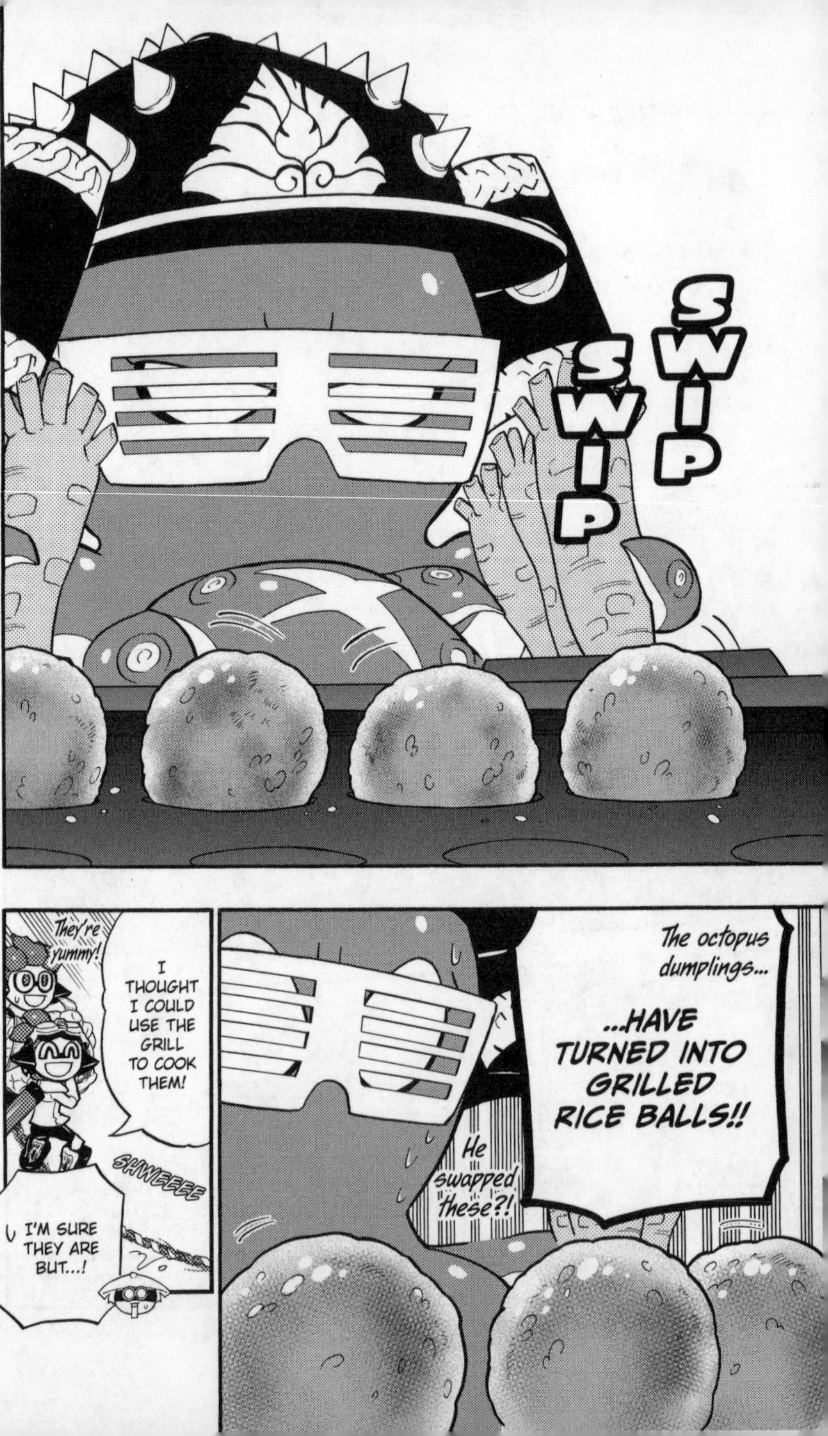
SWIP
SWIP
The octopus dumplings...
...HAVE TURNED INTO GRILLED RICE BALLS!!
He swapped these?!
They're yummy!
I THOUGHT I COULD USE THE GRILL TO COOK THEM!
SHWEEEE
I'M SURE THEY ARE BUT...!

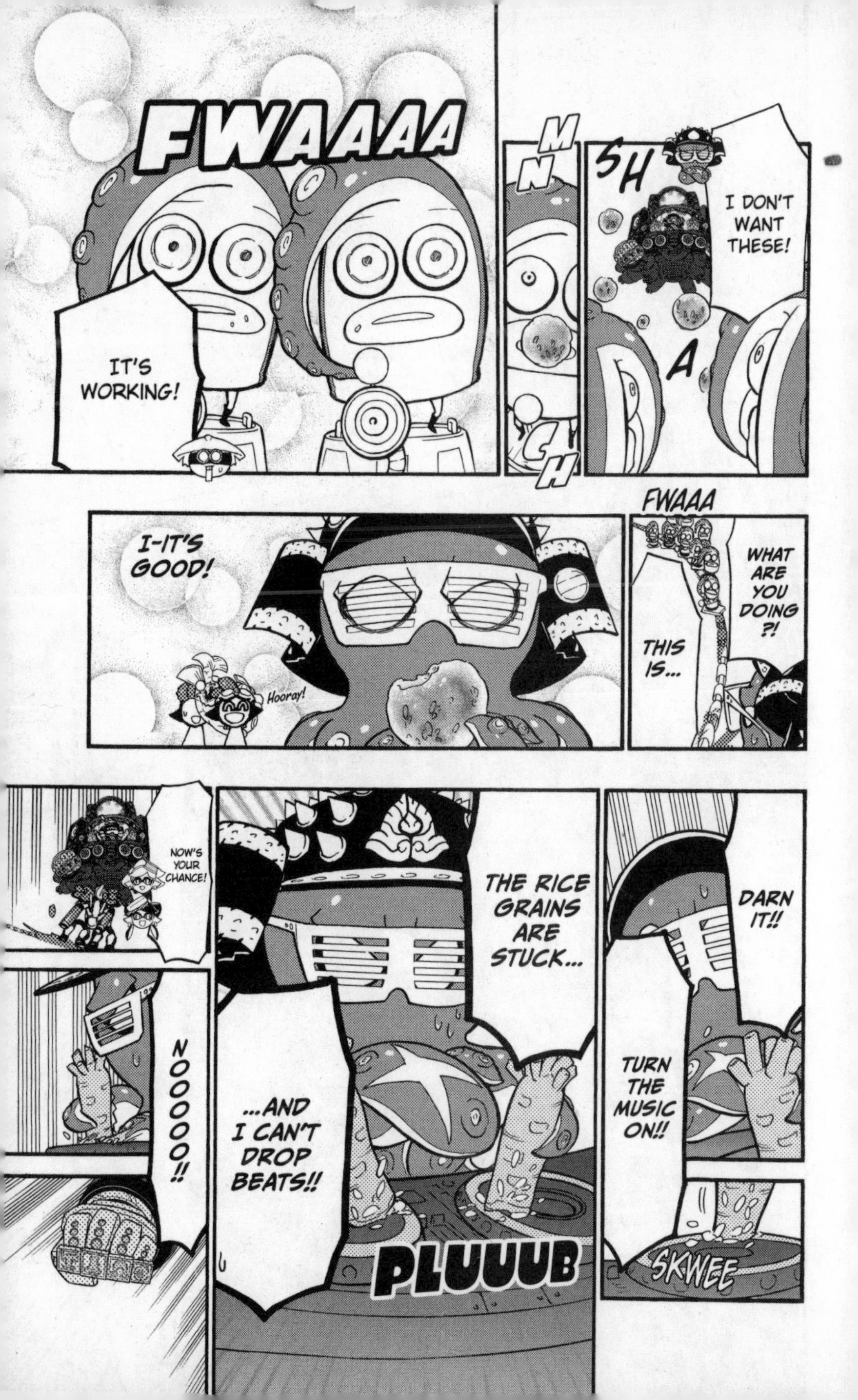

SH
I DON'T WANT THESE!
A
MNCH
FWAAAAA
IT'S WORKING!
FWAAA
WHAT ARE YOU DOING?!
THIS IS...
I-IT'S GOOD!
Hooray!
DARN IT!!
TURN THE MUSIC ON!!
SKWEE
THE RICE GRAINS ARE STUCK...
...AND I CAN'T DROP BEATS!!
PLUUUB
NOW'S YOUR CHANCE!
NOOOOOO!!

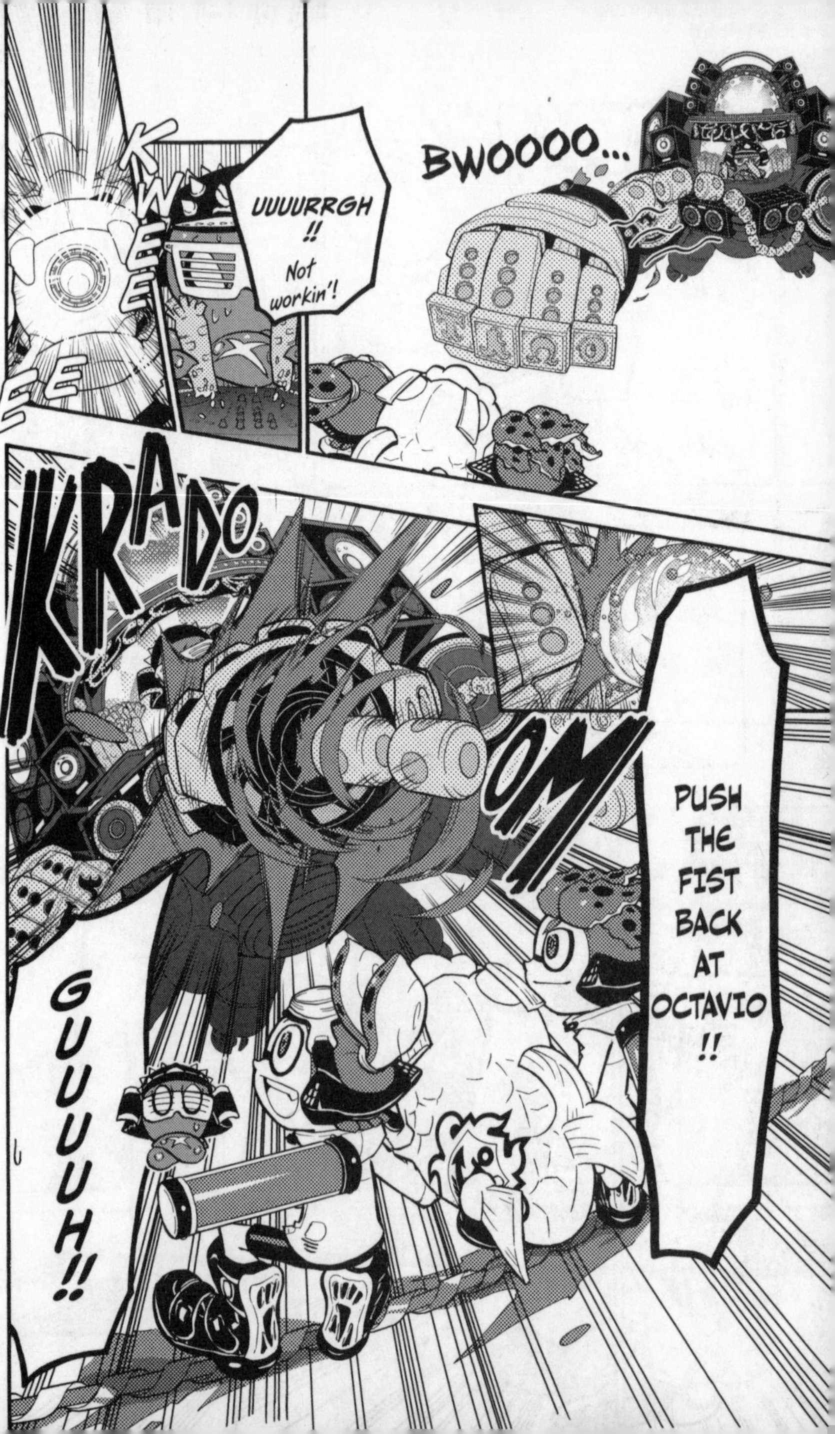

BWOOOO...
UUUURRGH!! Not workin'!
KWEEEE
KRADOOM
PUSH THE FIST BACK AT OCTAVIO!!
GUUUUUH!!

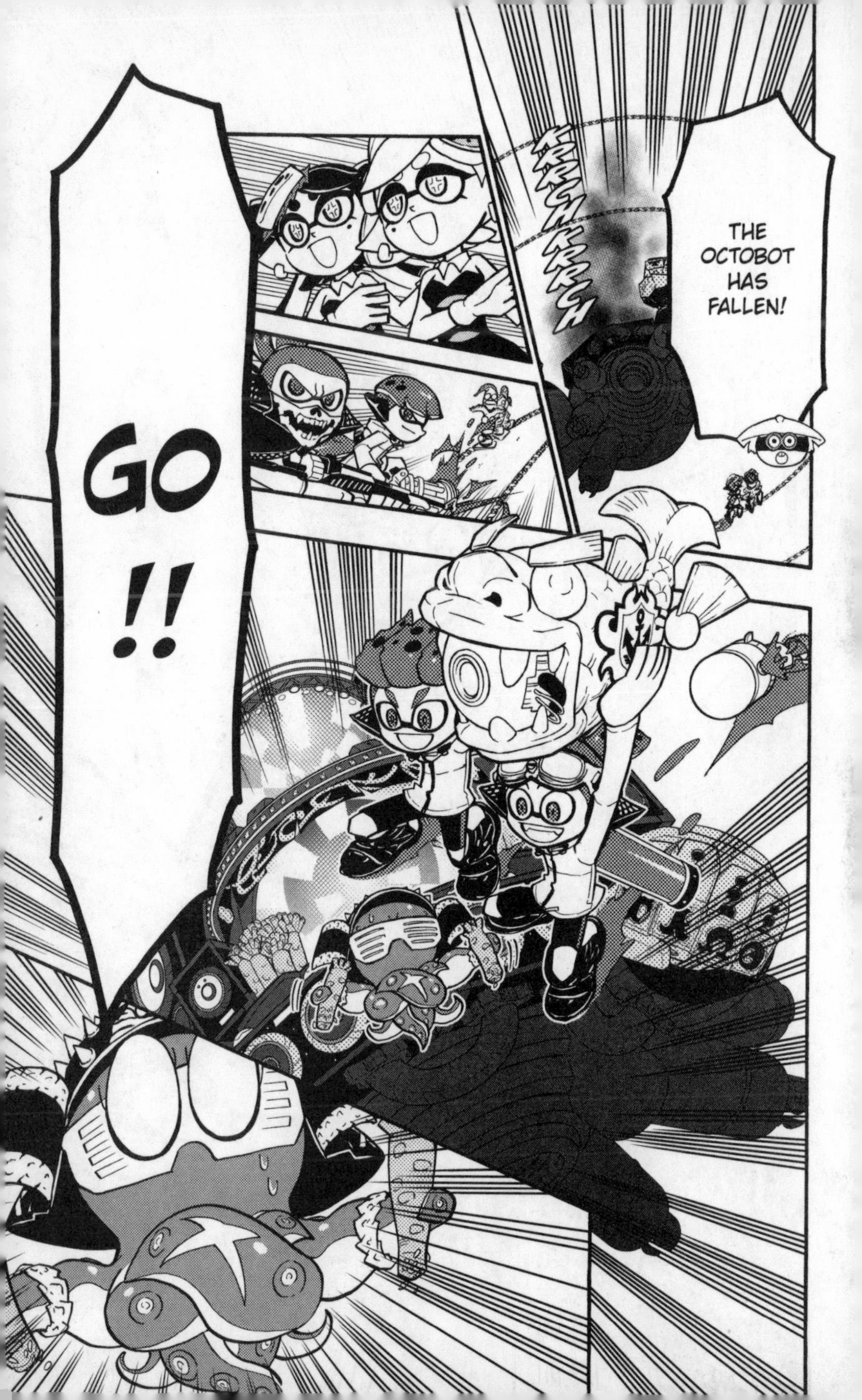
KRRCHKRRCH
THE OCTOBOT HAS FALLEN!
GO !!

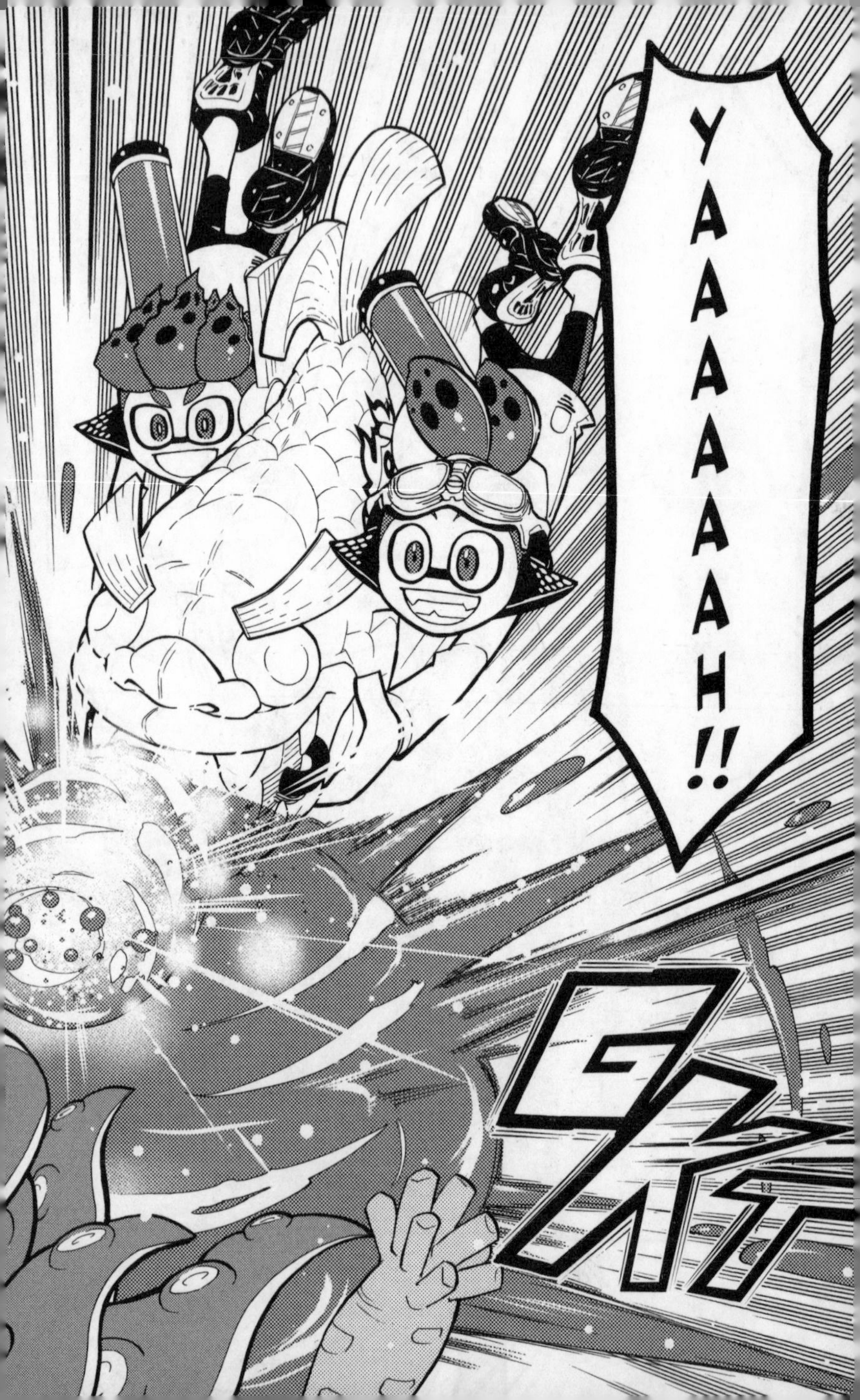
YAAAAAAH!!
GLAST

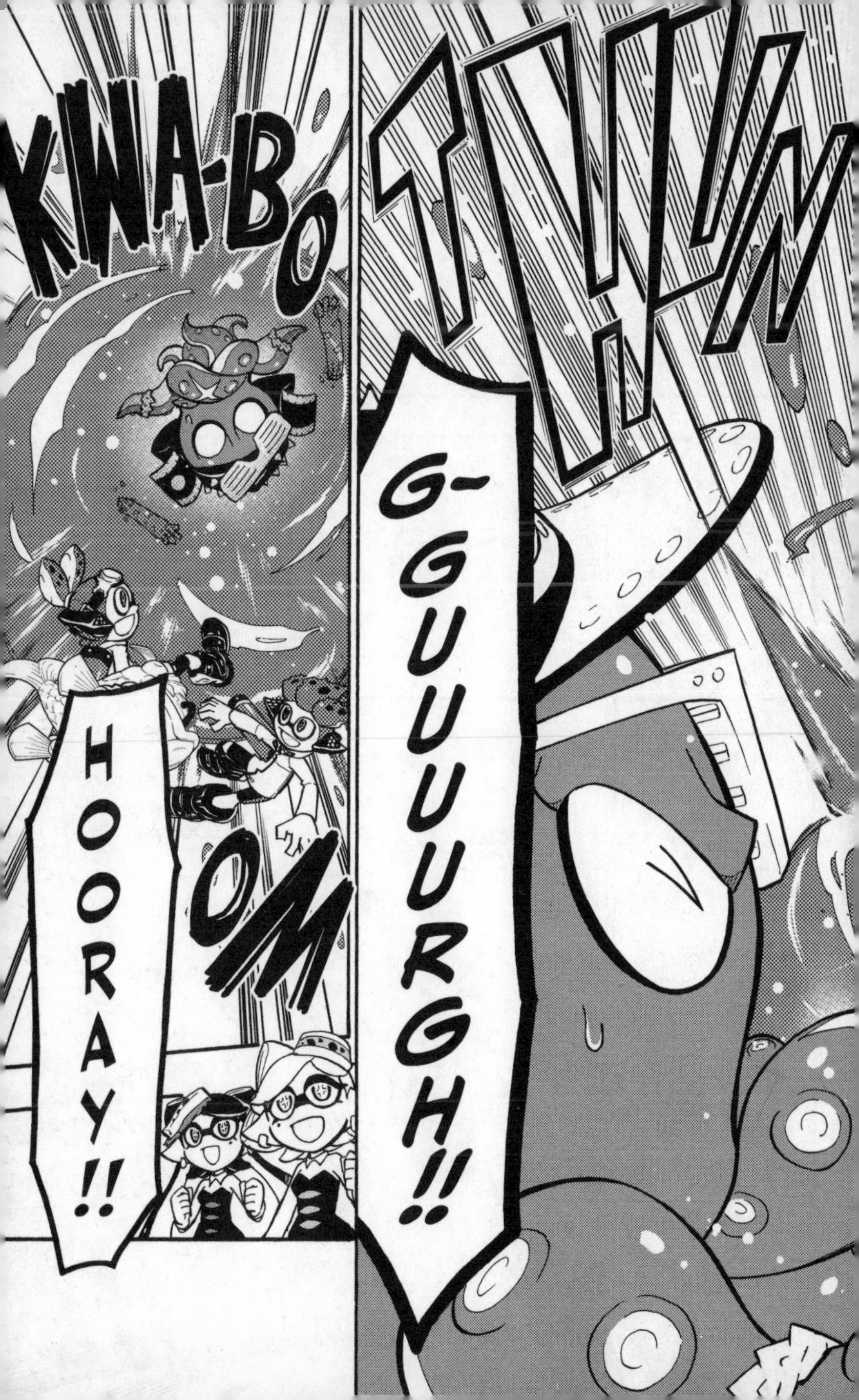
G-GUUURGH!!
KWA-BOOM
HOORAY!!

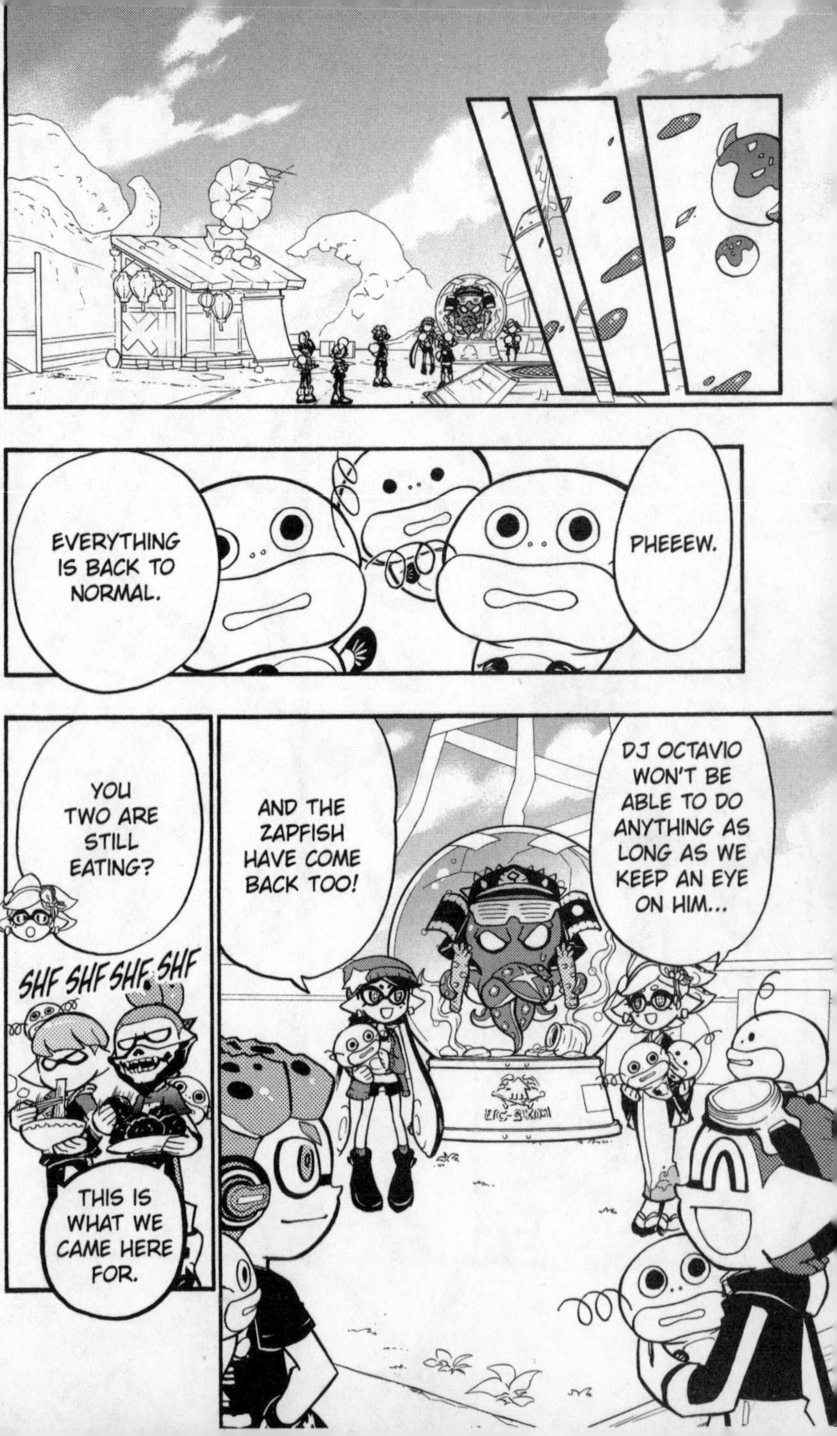
PHEEEW.
EVERYTHING IS BACK TO NORMAL.
DJ OCTAVIO WON'T BE ABLE TO DO ANYTHING AS LONG AS WE KEEP AN EYE ON HIM...
AND THE ZAPFISH HAVE COME BACK TOO!
YOU TWO ARE STILL EATING?
SHF SHF SHF SHF
THIS IS WHAT WE CAME HERE FOR.

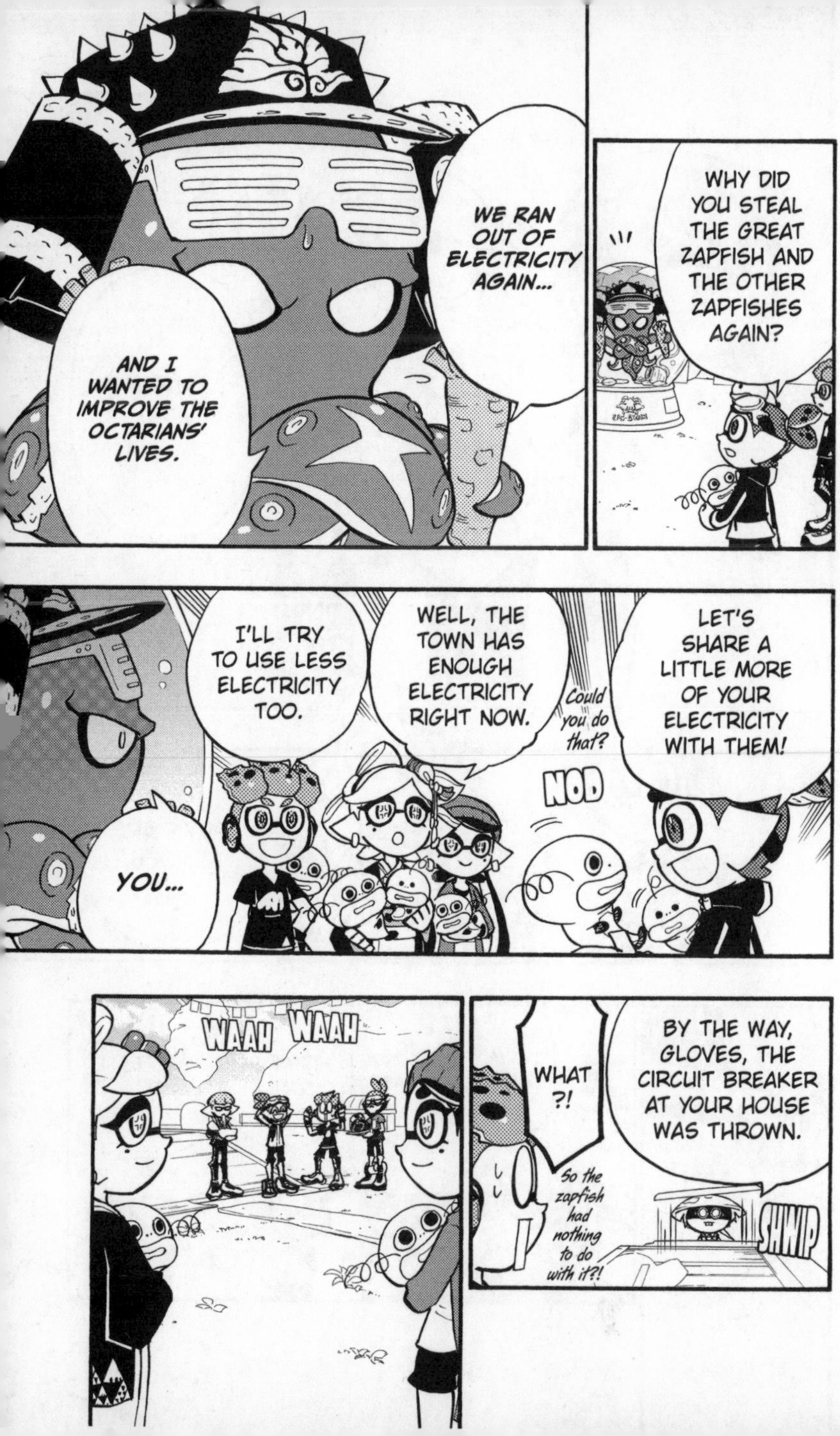
WHY DID YOU STEAL THE GREAT ZAPFISH AND THE OTHER ZAPFISHES AGAIN?
WE RAN OUT OF ELECTRICITY AGAIN...
AND I WANTED TO IMPROVE THE OCTARIANS' LIVES.
LET'S SHARE A LITTLE MORE OF YOUR ELECTRICITY WITH THEM!
NOD
Could you do that?
WELL, THE TOWN HAS ENOUGH ELECTRICITY RIGHT NOW.
I'LL TRY TO USE LESS ELECTRICITY TOO.
YOU...
BY THE WAY, GLOVES, THE CIRCUIT BREAKER AT YOUR HOUSE WAS THROWN.
WHAT?!
SHWIP
So the zapfish had nothing to do with it?!
WAAH WAAH

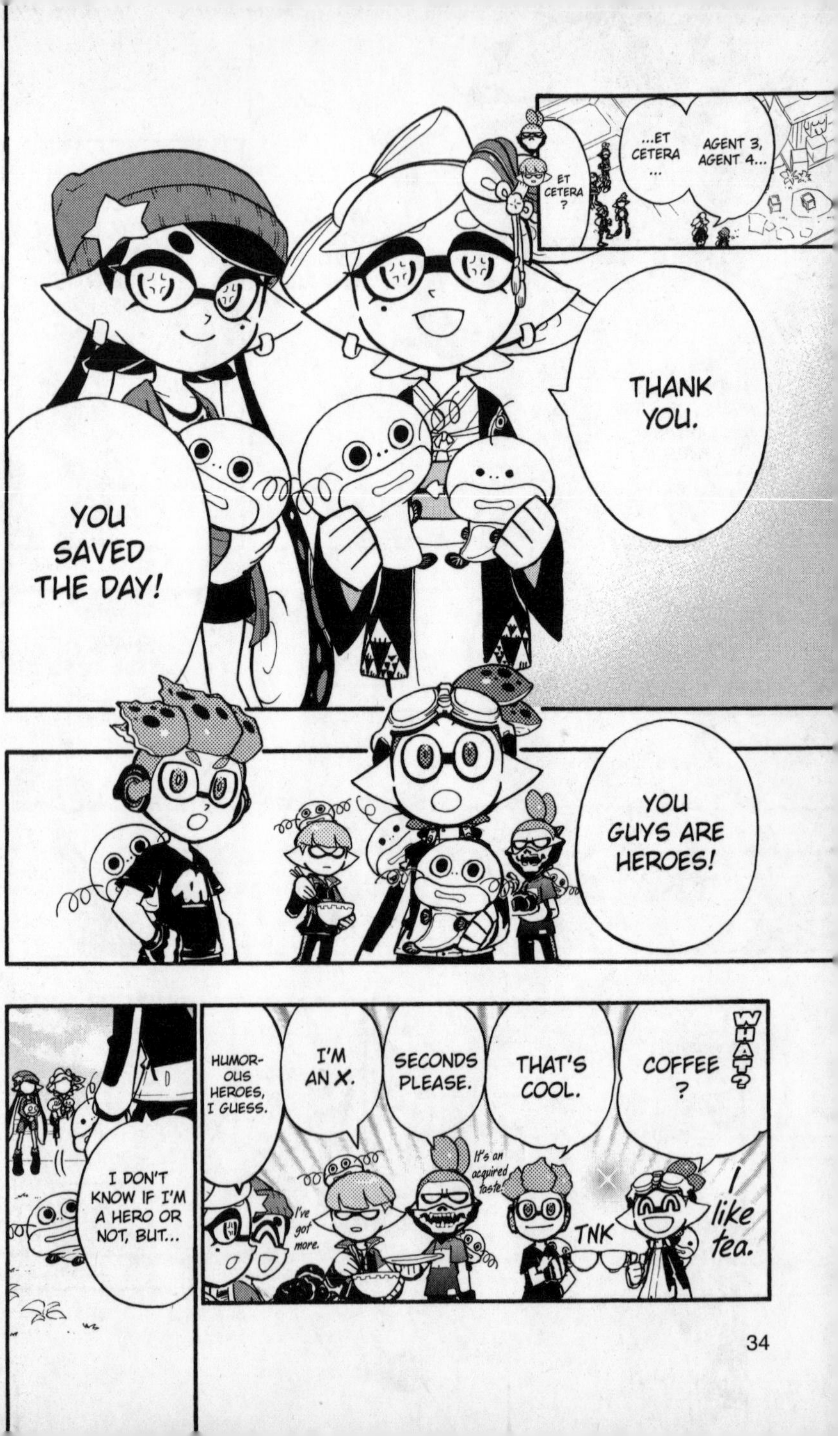
AGENT 3, AGENT 4...
...ET CETERA...
ET CETERA?
THANK YOU.
YOU SAVED THE DAY!
YOU GUYS ARE HEROES!
WHAT?
COFFEE?
I like tea.
TNK
THAT'S COOL.
It's an acquired taste.
SECONDS PLEASE.
I'M AN X.
I've got more.
HUMOR-OUS HEROES, I GUESS.
I DON'T KNOW IF I'M A HERO OR NOT, BUT...

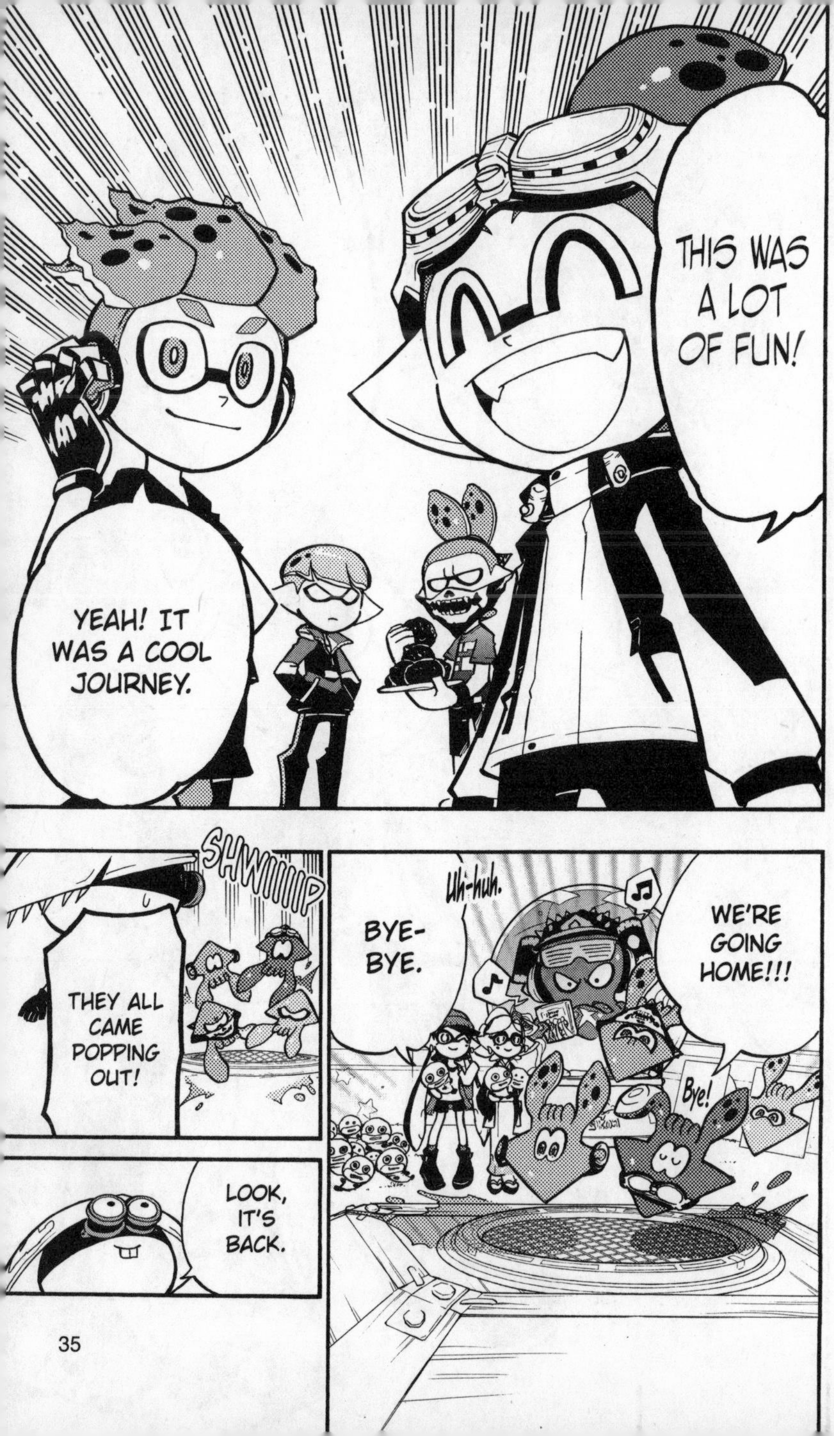
THIS WAS A LOT OF FUN!
YEAH! IT WAS A COOL JOURNEY.
WE'RE GOING HOME!!!
Uh-huh.
BYE-BYE.
Bye!
SHWIIIIIP
THEY ALL CAME POPPING OUT!
LOOK, IT'S BACK.

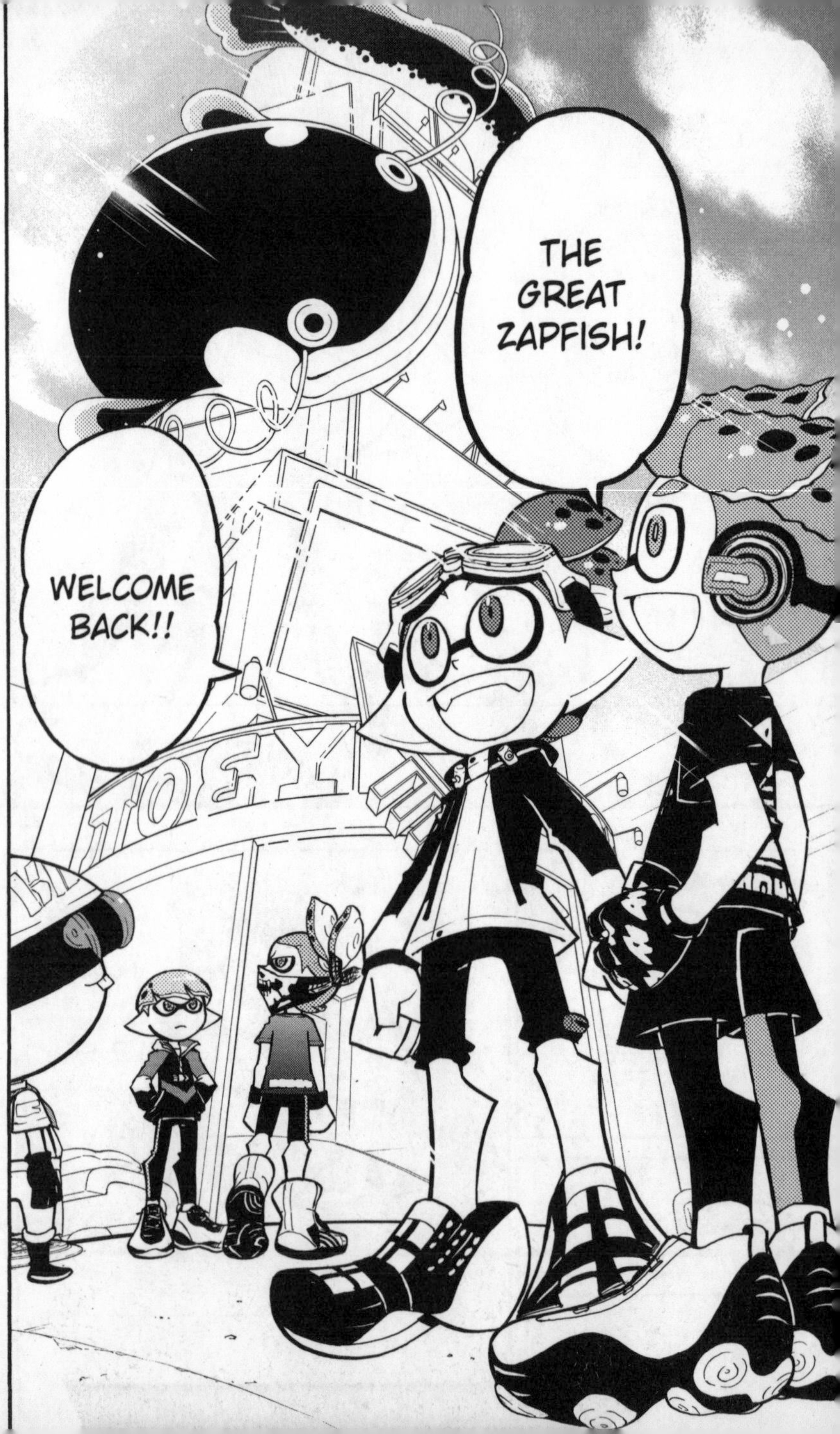
THE GREAT ZAPFISH!
WELCOME BACK!!

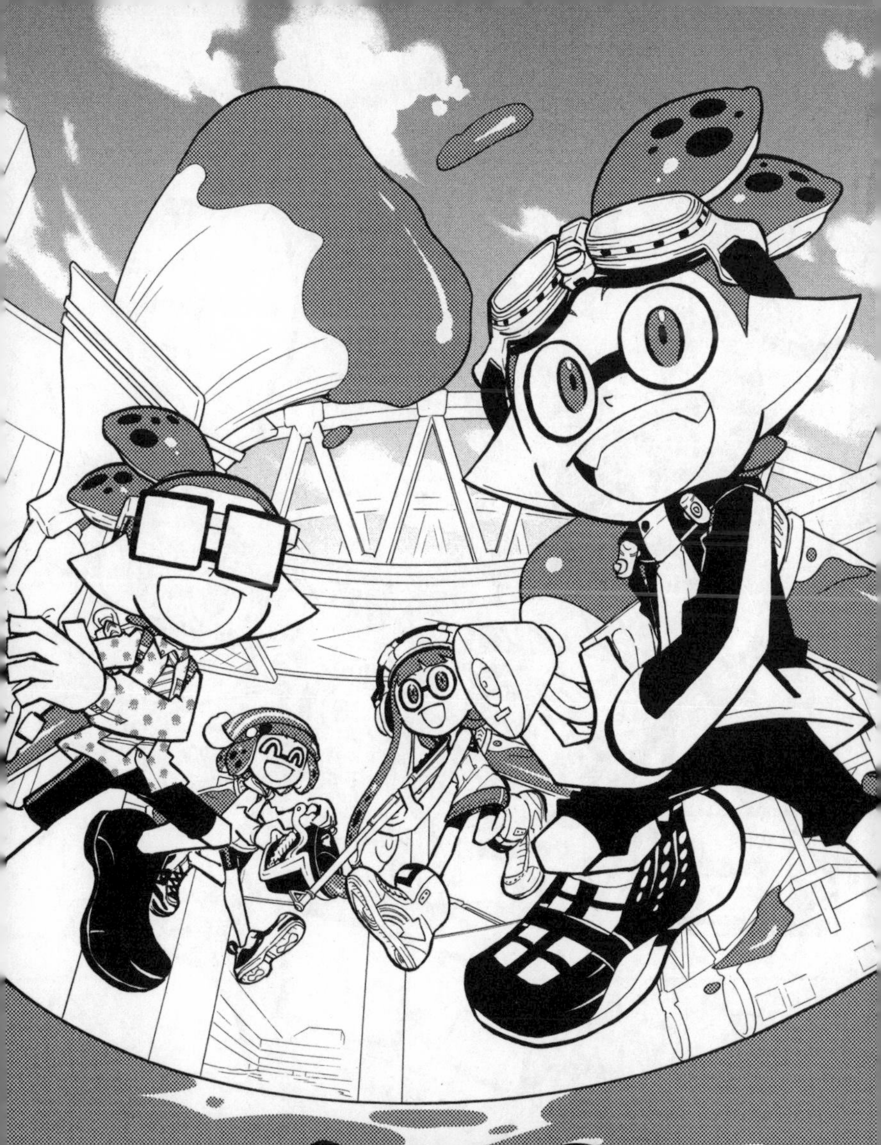

#46
SNAPPER CANAL

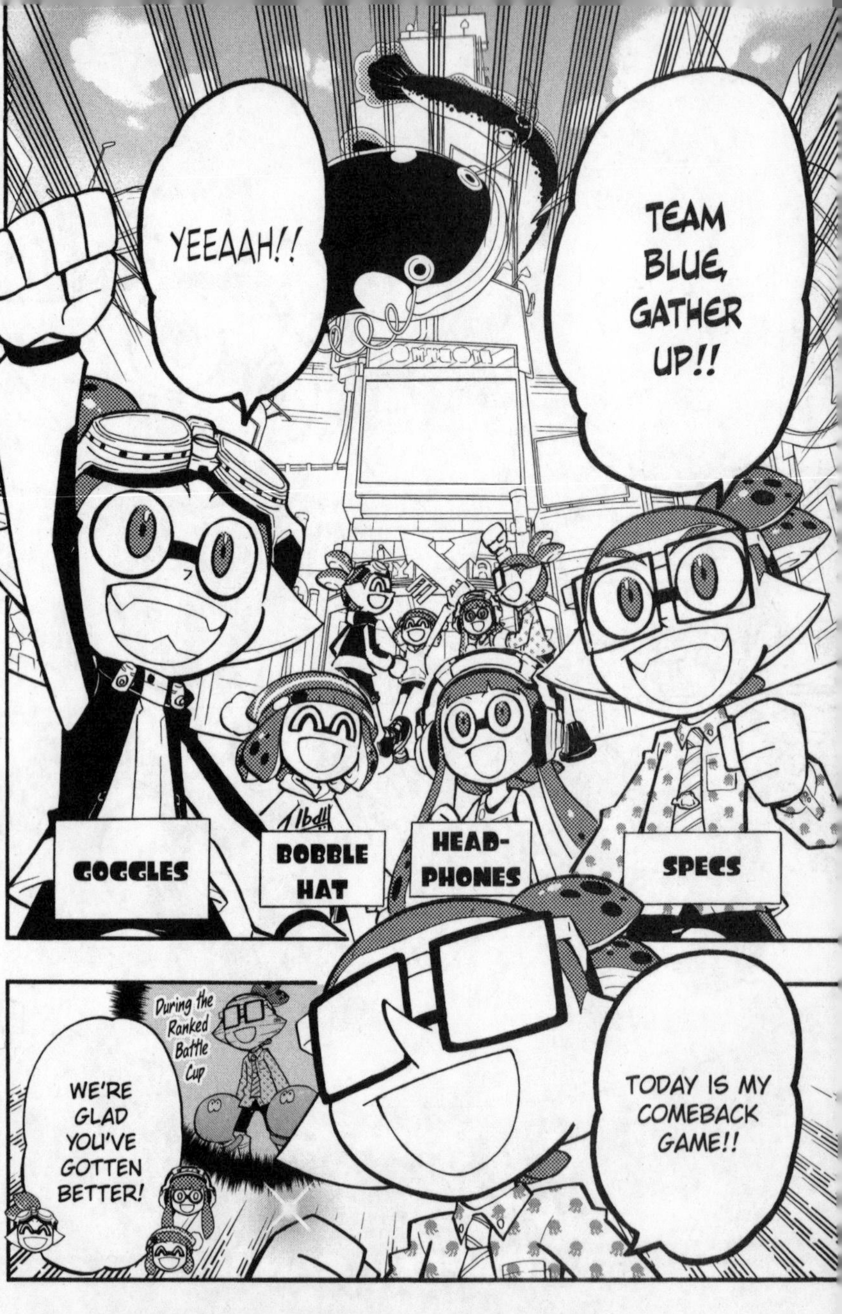
TEAM BLUE, GATHER UP!!
YEEAAH!!
SPECS
HEAD-PHONES
BOBBLE HAT
GOGGLES
TODAY IS MY COMEBACK GAME!!
During the Ranked Battle Cup
WE'RE GLAD YOU'VE GOTTEN BETTER!

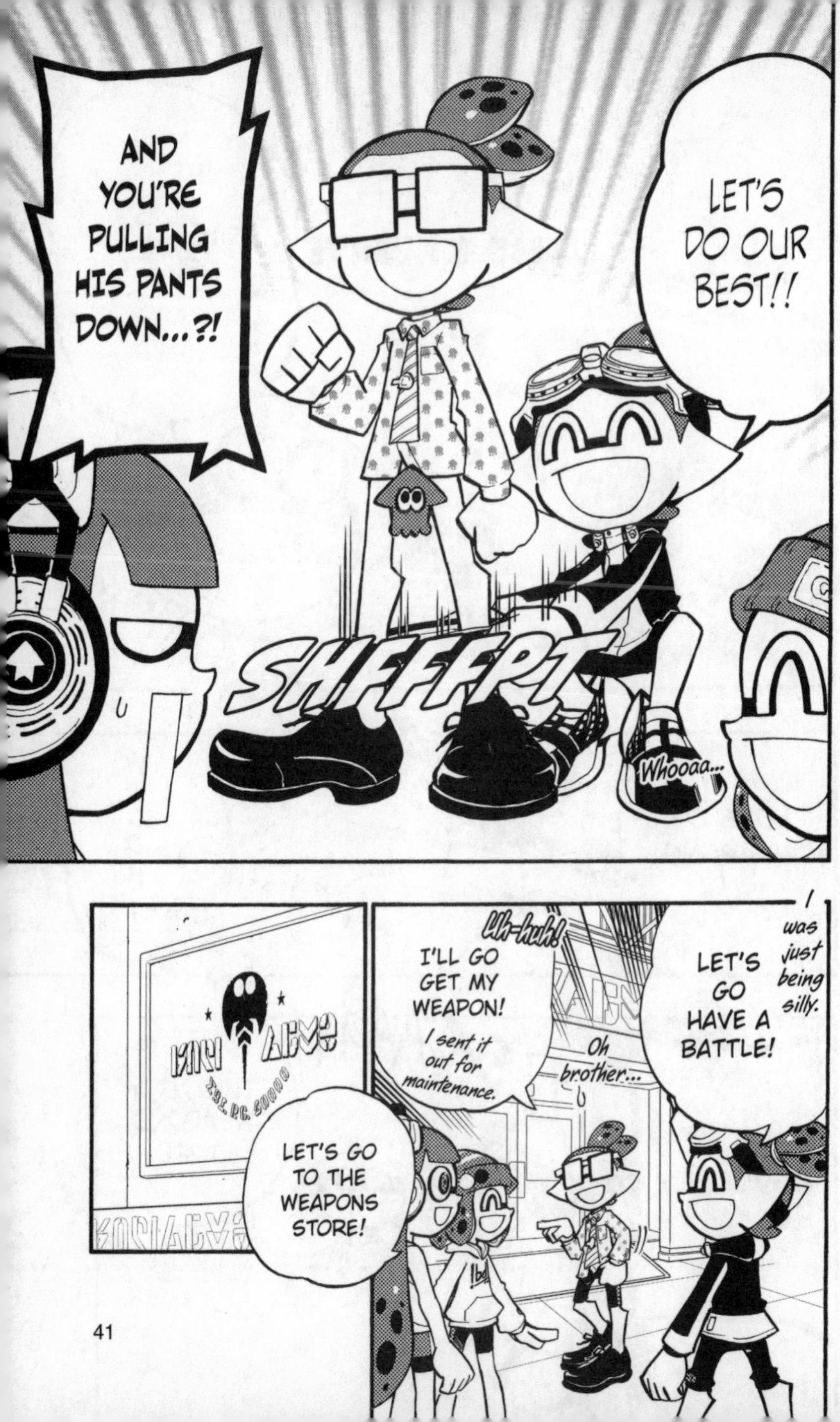
LET'S DO OUR BEST!!
AND YOU'RE PULLING HIS PANTS DOWN...?!
SHFFFPT
Whooaa...
I was just being silly.
LET'S GO HAVE A BATTLE!
Oh brother...
Uh-huh!
I'LL GO GET MY WEAPON!
I sent it out for maintenance.
LET'S GO TO THE WEAPONS STORE!

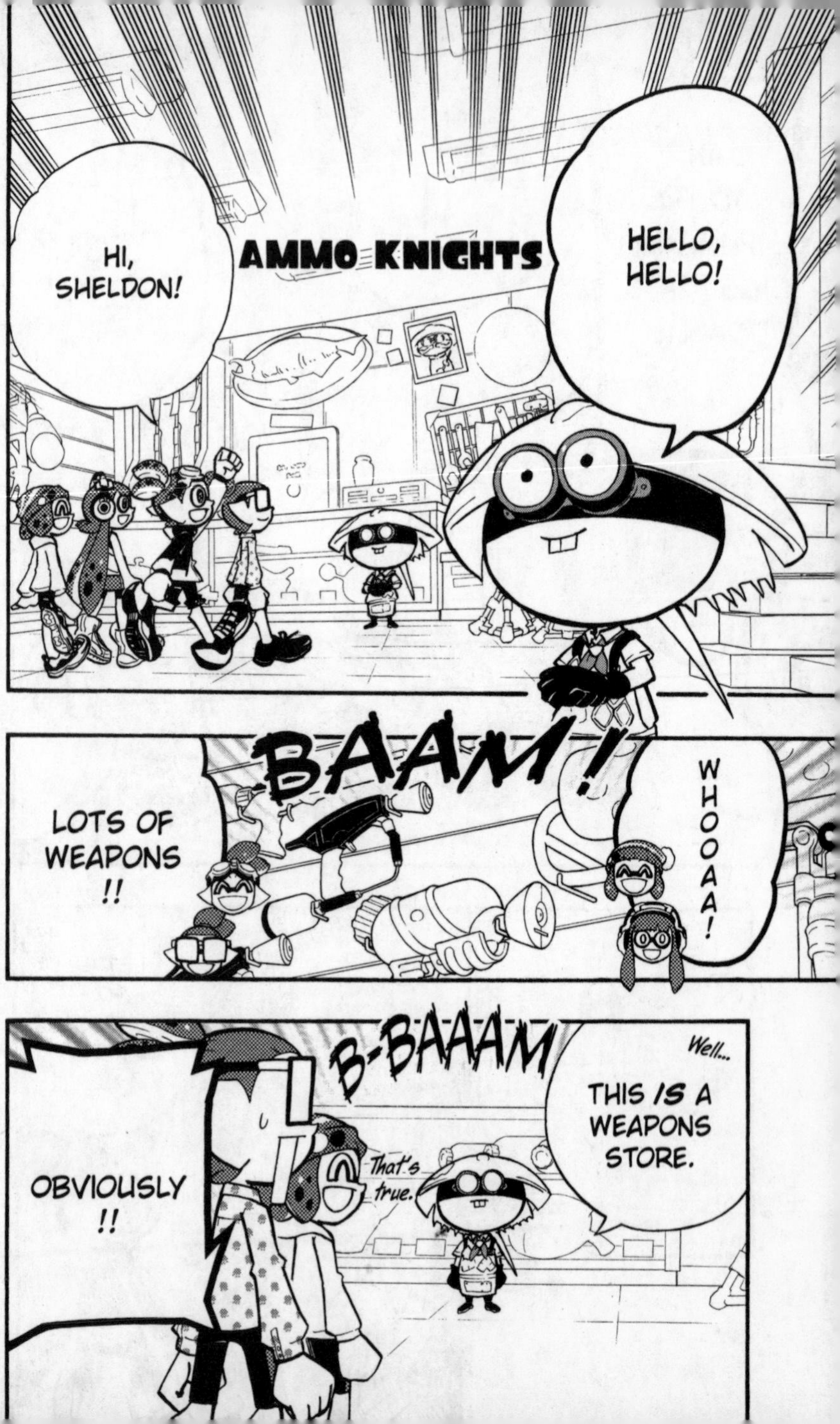
HELLO, HELLO!
AMMO KNIGHTS
HI, SHELDON!
BAAM!
WHOOAAA!
LOTS OF WEAPONS !!
Well...
THIS *IS* A WEAPONS STORE.
B-BAAAM
That's true.
OBVIOUSLY !!

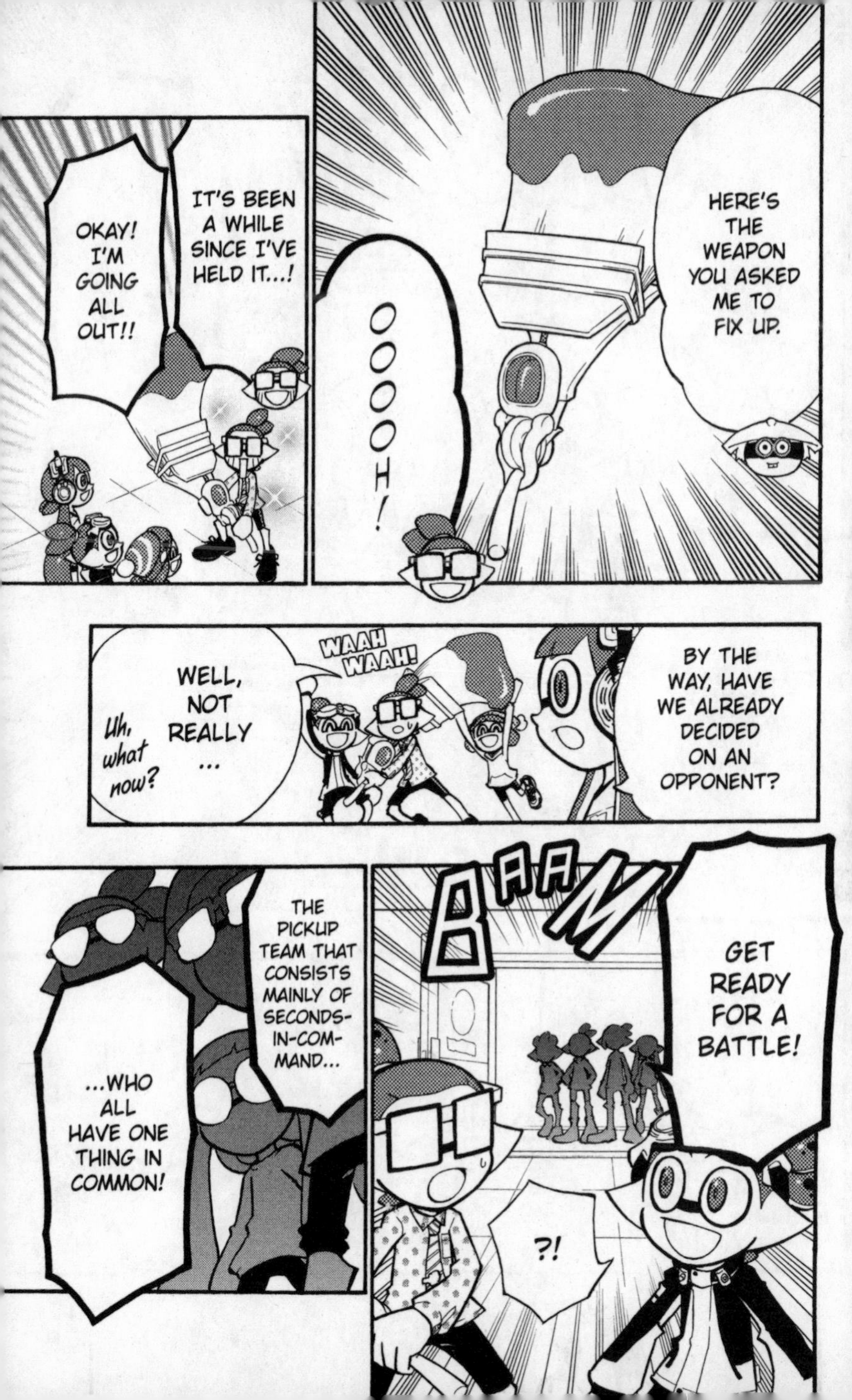
HERE'S THE WEAPON YOU ASKED ME TO FIX UP.
OOOOOH!
IT'S BEEN A WHILE SINCE I'VE HELD IT...!
OKAY! I'M GOING ALL OUT!!
BY THE WAY, HAVE WE ALREADY DECIDED ON AN OPPONENT?
WAAH WAAH!
WELL, NOT REALLY...
Uh, what now?
BAAAM
GET READY FOR A BATTLE!
?!
THE PICKUP TEAM THAT CONSISTS MAINLY OF SECONDS-IN-COMMAND...
...WHO ALL HAVE ONE THING IN COMMON!

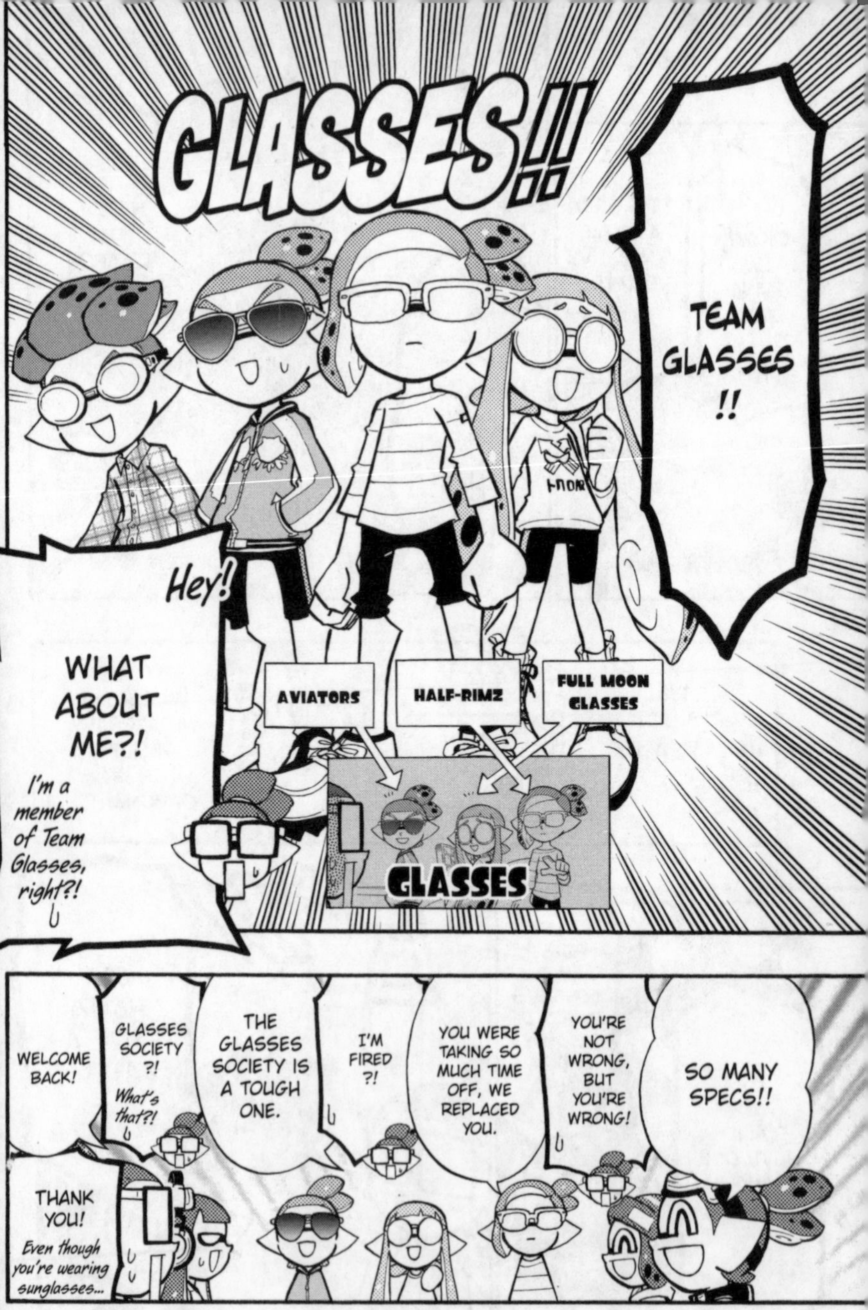
TEAM GLASSES !!
GLASSES!!
FULL MOON GLASSES
HALF-RIMZ
AVIATORS
GLASSES
Hey!
WHAT ABOUT ME?!
I'm a member of Team Glasses, right?!
SO MANY SPECS!!
YOU'RE NOT WRONG, BUT YOU'RE WRONG!
YOU WERE TAKING SO MUCH TIME OFF, WE REPLACED YOU.
I'M FIRED ?!
THE GLASSES SOCIETY IS A TOUGH ONE.
GLASSES SOCIETY ?!
What's that?!
WELCOME BACK!
THANK YOU!
Even though you're wearing sunglasses...

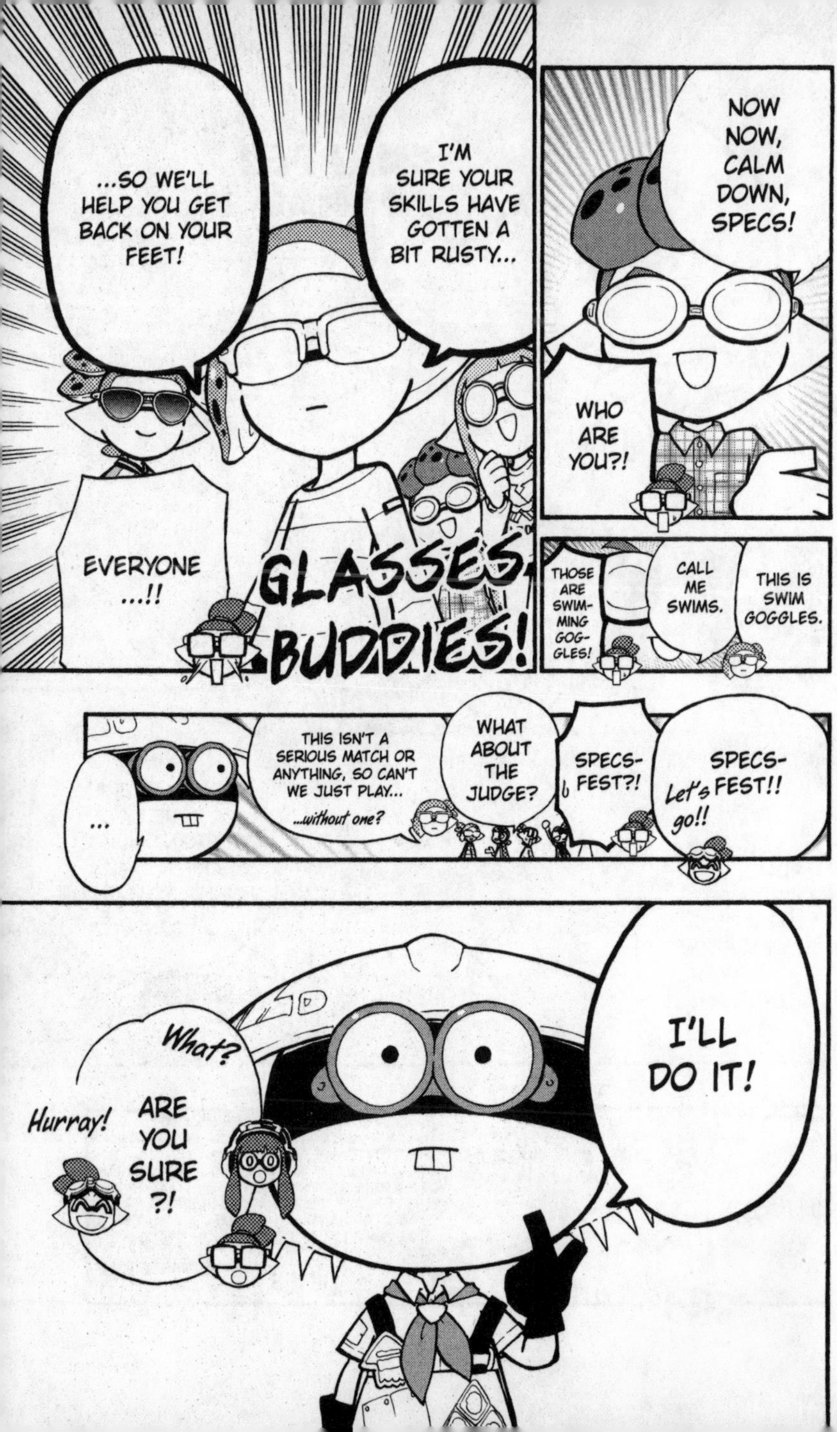
NOW NOW, CALM DOWN, SPECS!
WHO ARE YOU?!
THIS IS SWIM GOGGLES.
CALL ME SWIMS.
THOSE ARE SWIMMING GOGGLES!
I'M SURE YOUR SKILLS HAVE GOTTEN A BIT RUSTY...
...SO WE'LL HELP YOU GET BACK ON YOUR FEET!
EVERYONE ...!!
GLASSES BUDDIES!
SPECS-FEST!!
Let's go!!
SPECS-FEST?!
WHAT ABOUT THE JUDGE?
THIS ISN'T A SERIOUS MATCH OR ANYTHING, SO CAN'T WE JUST PLAY...
...without one?
...
I'LL DO IT!
What?
ARE YOU SURE?!
Hurray!

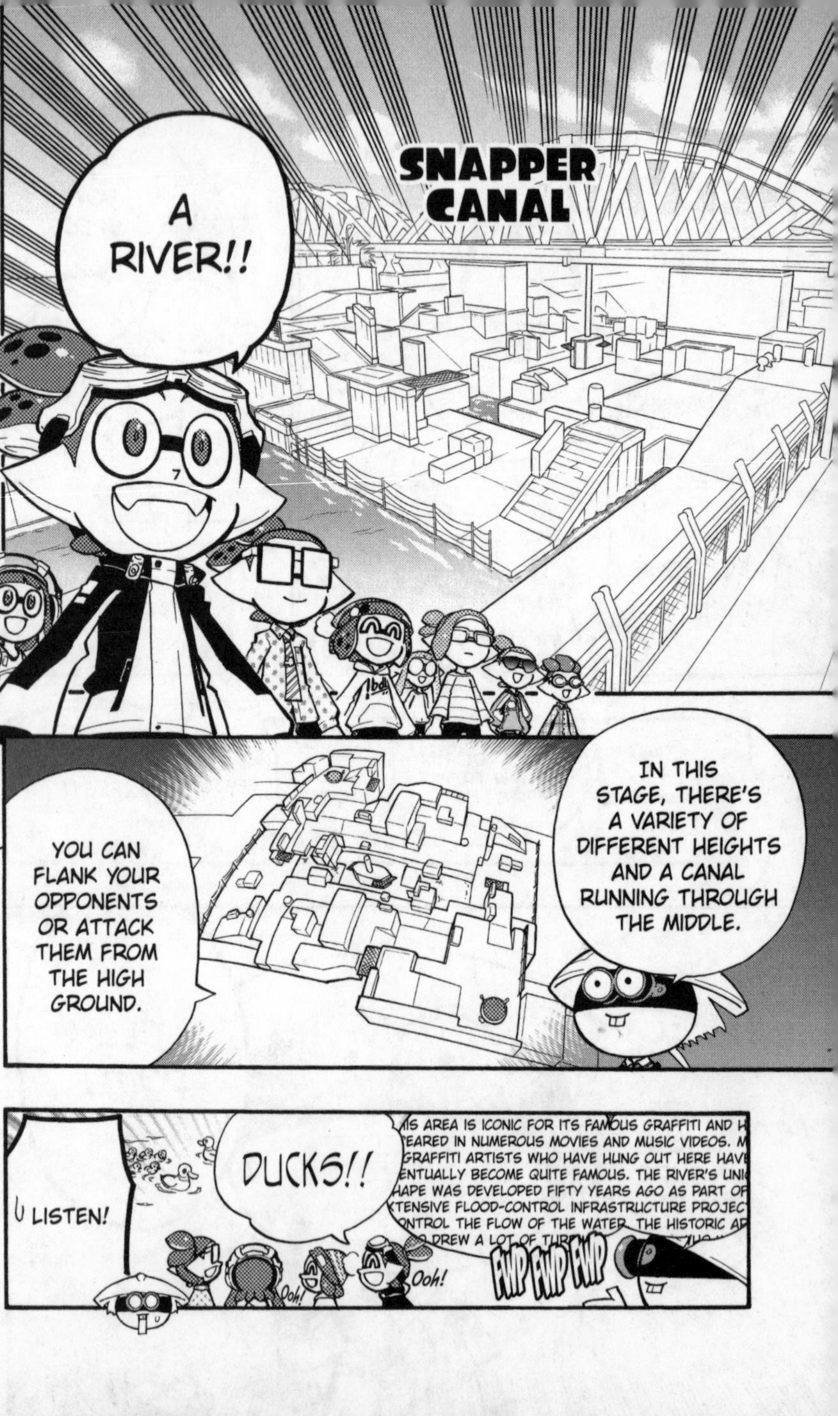
SNAPPER CANAL
A RIVER!!
IN THIS STAGE, THERE'S A VARIETY OF DIFFERENT HEIGHTS AND A CANAL RUNNING THROUGH THE MIDDLE.
YOU CAN FLANK YOUR OPPONENTS OR ATTACK THEM FROM THE HIGH GROUND.
IS AREA IS ICONIC FOR ITS FAMOUS GRAFFITI AND H
PEARED IN NUMEROUS MOVIES AND MUSIC VIDEOS. M
GRAFFITI ARTISTS WHO HAVE HUNG OUT HERE HAVE
ENTUALLY BECOME QUITE FAMOUS. THE RIVER'S UNIQ
HAPE WAS DEVELOPED FIFTY YEARS AGO AS PART OF
XTENSIVE FLOOD-CONTROL INFRASTRUCTURE PROJECT
ONTROL THE FLOW OF THE WATER. THE HISTORIC AR
DREW A LOT OF
FWP FWP FWP
DUCKS!!
Ooh!
Ooh!
LISTEN!

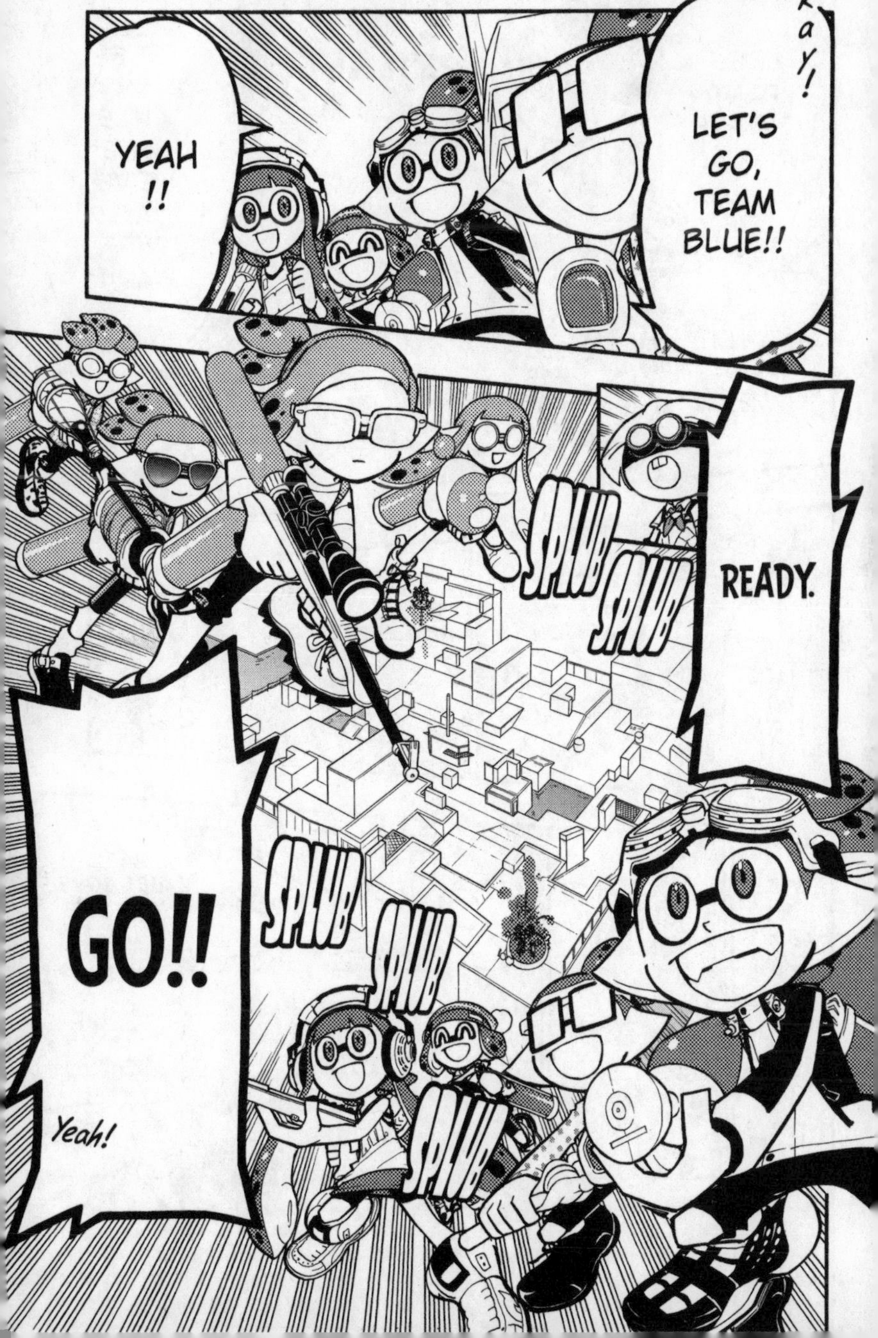
Okay!
LET'S GO, TEAM BLUE!!
YEAH!!
READY.
SPLUB
SPLUB
SPLUB
SPLUB
SPLUB
GO!!
Yeah!

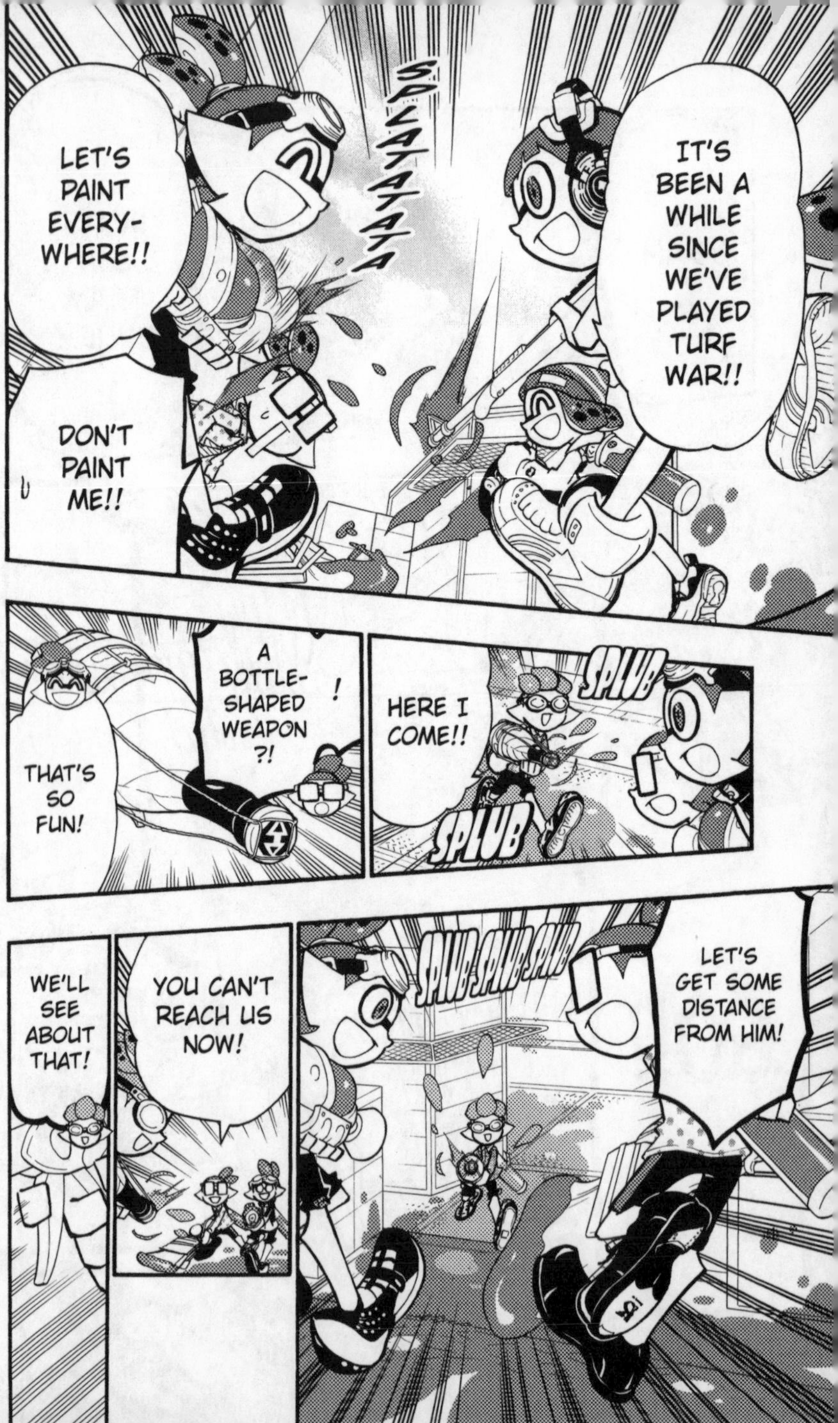
IT'S BEEN A WHILE SINCE WE'VE PLAYED TURF WAR!!
SPLATATATATA
LET'S PAINT EVERY-WHERE!!
DON'T PAINT ME!!
SPLUB
HERE I COME!!
SPLUB
!
A BOTTLE-SHAPED WEAPON?!
THAT'S SO FUN!
LET'S GET SOME DISTANCE FROM HIM!
SPLUB SPLUB SPLUB
YOU CAN'T REACH US NOW!
WE'LL SEE ABOUT THAT!

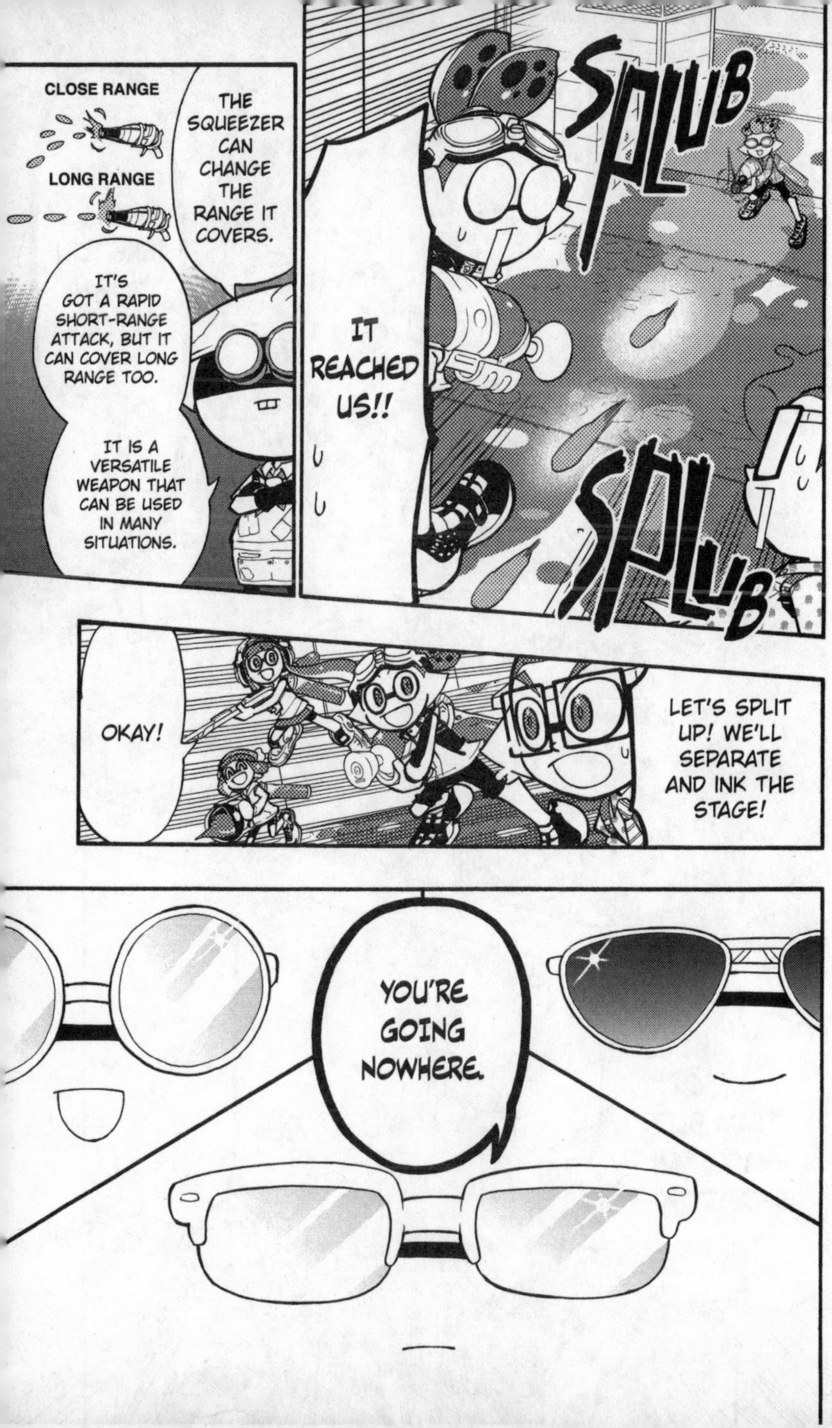
SPLUB
IT REACHED US!!
SPLUB
CLOSE RANGE
LONG RANGE
THE SQUEEZER CAN CHANGE THE RANGE IT COVERS.
IT'S GOT A RAPID SHORT-RANGE ATTACK, BUT IT CAN COVER LONG RANGE TOO.
IT IS A VERSATILE WEAPON THAT CAN BE USED IN MANY SITUATIONS.
LET'S SPLIT UP! WE'LL SEPARATE AND INK THE STAGE!
OKAY!
YOU'RE GOING NOWHERE.

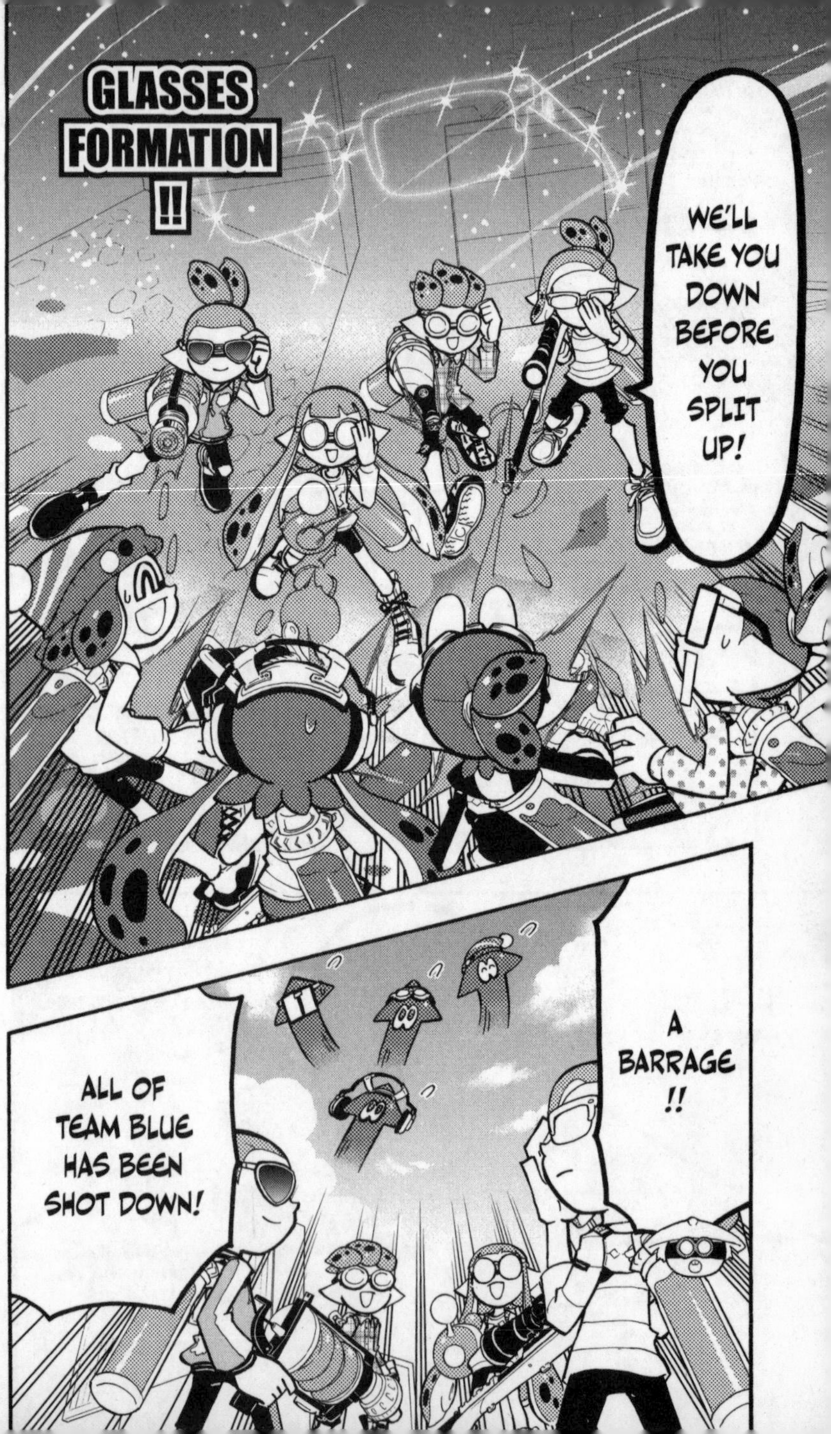
WE'LL TAKE YOU DOWN BEFORE YOU SPLIT UP!
GLASSES FORMATION !!
A BARRAGE !!
ALL OF TEAM BLUE HAS BEEN SHOT DOWN!

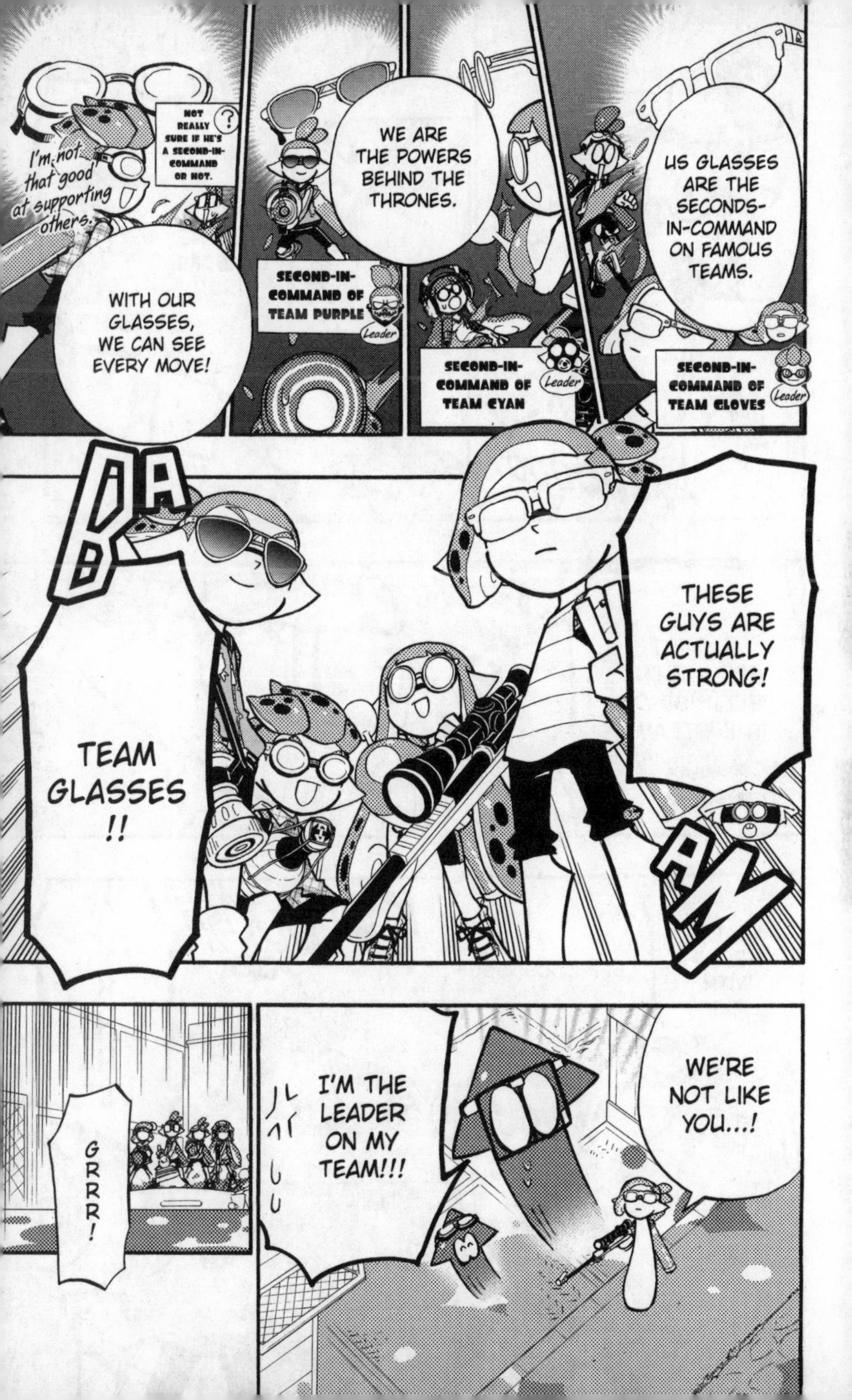
US GLASSES ARE THE SECONDS-IN-COMMAND ON FAMOUS TEAMS.
SECOND-IN-COMMAND OF TEAM CLOVES
Leader
SECOND-IN-COMMAND OF TEAM CYAN
Leader
WE ARE THE POWERS BEHIND THE THRONES.
SECOND-IN-COMMAND OF TEAM PURPLE
Leader
NOT REALLY SURE IF HE'S A SECOND-IN-COMMAND OR NOT.
I'm not that good at supporting others.
WITH OUR GLASSES, WE CAN SEE EVERY MOVE!
THESE GUYS ARE ACTUALLY STRONG!
TEAM GLASSES!!
WE'RE NOT LIKE YOU...!
I'M THE LEADER ON MY TEAM!!!
GRRR!

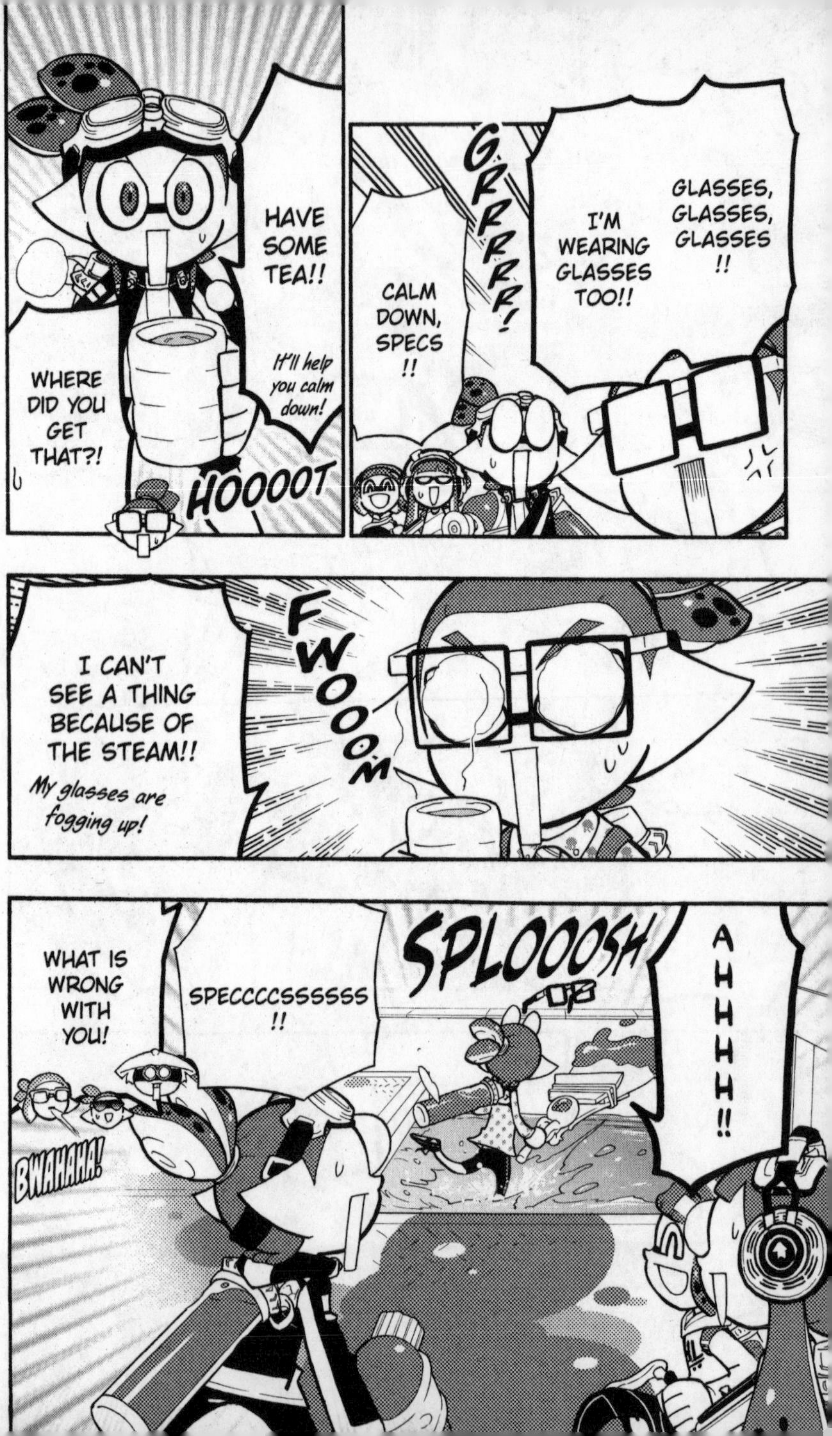
GLASSES, GLASSES, GLASSES!!
I'M WEARING GLASSES TOO!!
GRRRRR!
CALM DOWN, SPECS!!
HAVE SOME TEA!!
It'll help you calm down!
HOOOOT
WHERE DID YOU GET THAT?!
FWOOOOM
I CAN'T SEE A THING BECAUSE OF THE STEAM!!
My glasses are fogging up!
AHHHH!!
SPLOOOSH
SPECCCCSSSSSS!!
WHAT IS WRONG WITH YOU!
BWAHAHA!

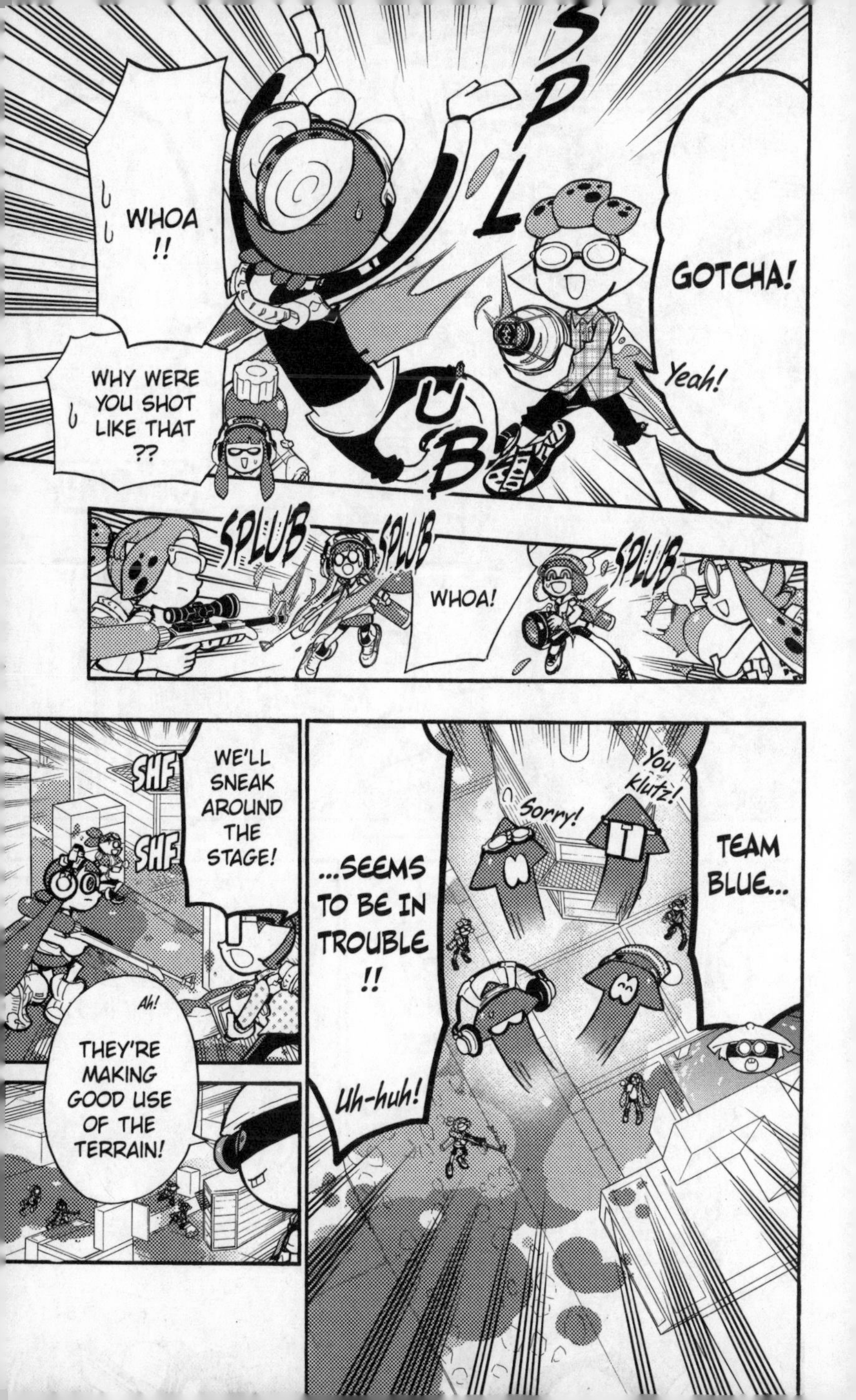
GOTCHA!
Yeah!
SPLUB
WHOA !!
WHY WERE YOU SHOT LIKE THAT ??
SPLUB
WHOA!
SPLUB
SPLUB
TEAM BLUE...
You klutz!
Sorry!
...SEEMS TO BE IN TROUBLE !!
Uh-huh!
WE'LL SNEAK AROUND THE STAGE!
SHF
SHF
Ah!
THEY'RE MAKING GOOD USE OF THE TERRAIN!

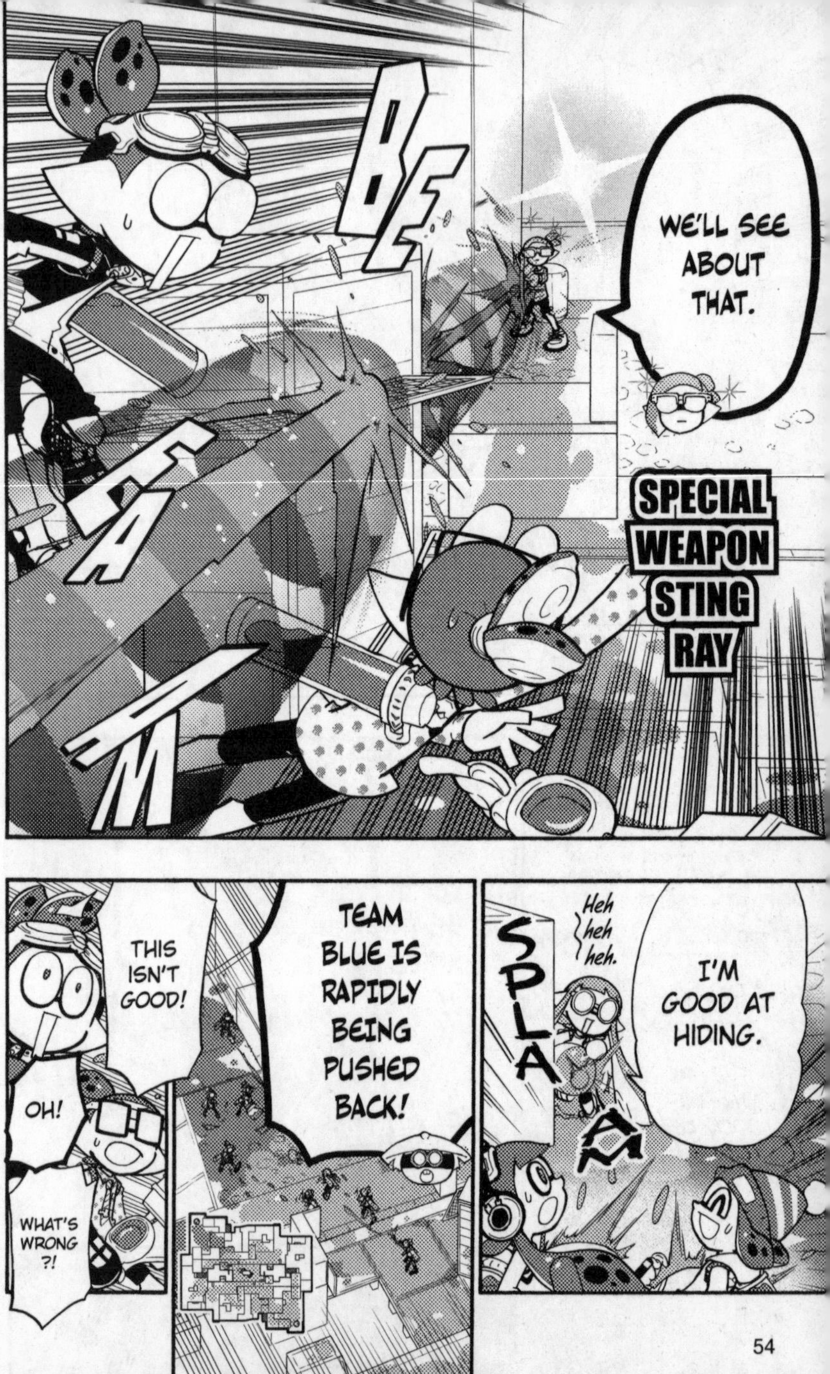
WE'LL SEE ABOUT THAT.
SPECIAL WEAPON STING RAY
Heh heh heh.
I'M GOOD AT HIDING.
TEAM BLUE IS RAPIDLY BEING PUSHED BACK!
THIS ISN'T GOOD!
OH!
WHAT'S WRONG ?!

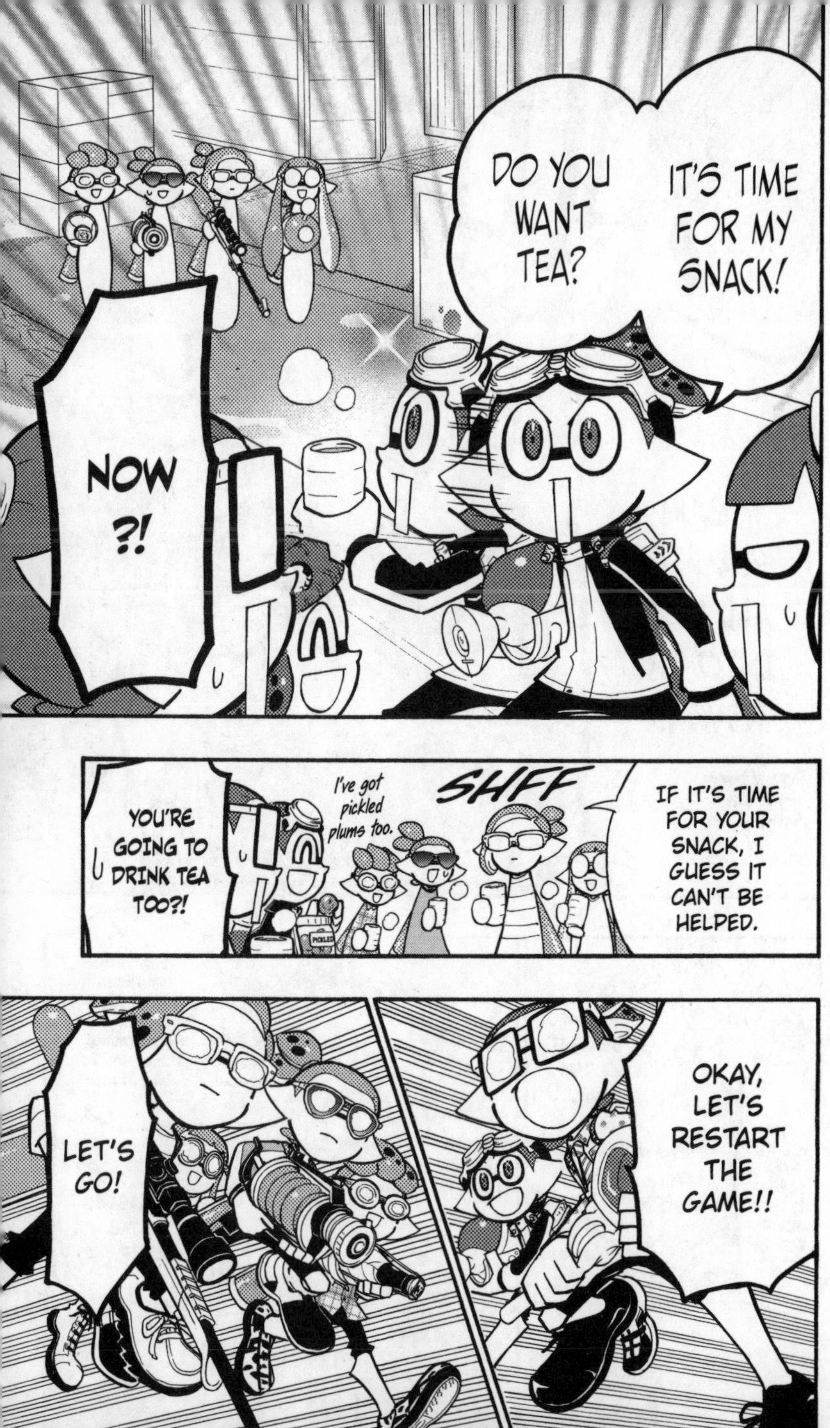
IT'S TIME FOR MY SNACK!
DO YOU WANT TEA?
NOW?!
IF IT'S TIME FOR YOUR SNACK, I GUESS IT CAN'T BE HELPED.
SHFF
I've got pickled plums too.
YOU'RE GOING TO DRINK TEA TOO?!
OKAY, LET'S RESTART THE GAME!!
LET'S GO!

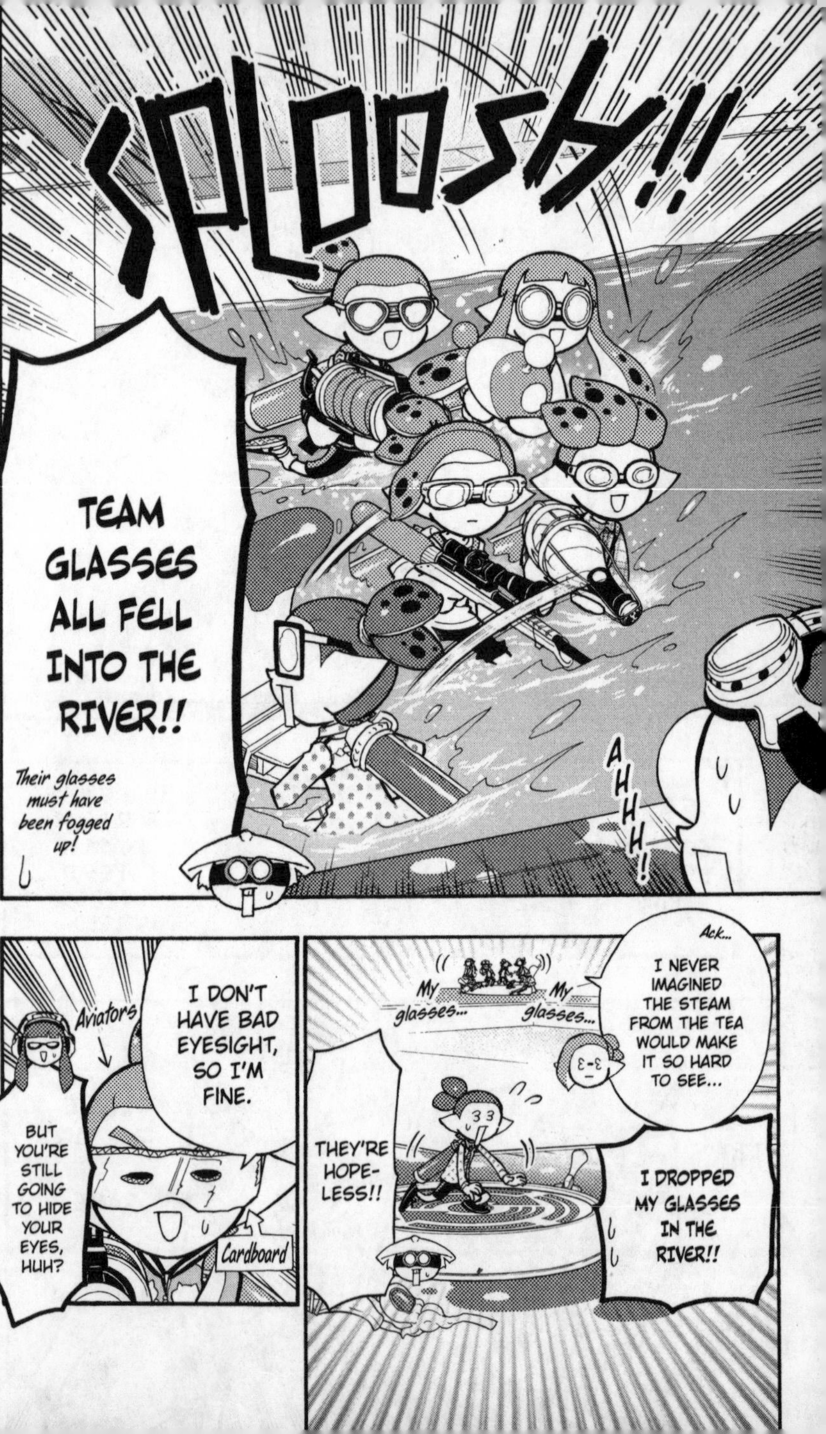
SPLOOSH!!
AHHHH!
TEAM GLASSES ALL FELL INTO THE RIVER!!
Their glasses must have been fogged up!
Ack...
I NEVER IMAGINED THE STEAM FROM THE TEA WOULD MAKE IT SO HARD TO SEE...
My glasses...
My glasses...
I DROPPED MY GLASSES IN THE RIVER!!
THEY'RE HOPE-LESS!!
I DON'T HAVE BAD EYESIGHT, SO I'M FINE.
Aviators
BUT YOU'RE STILL GOING TO HIDE YOUR EYES, HUH?
Cardboard

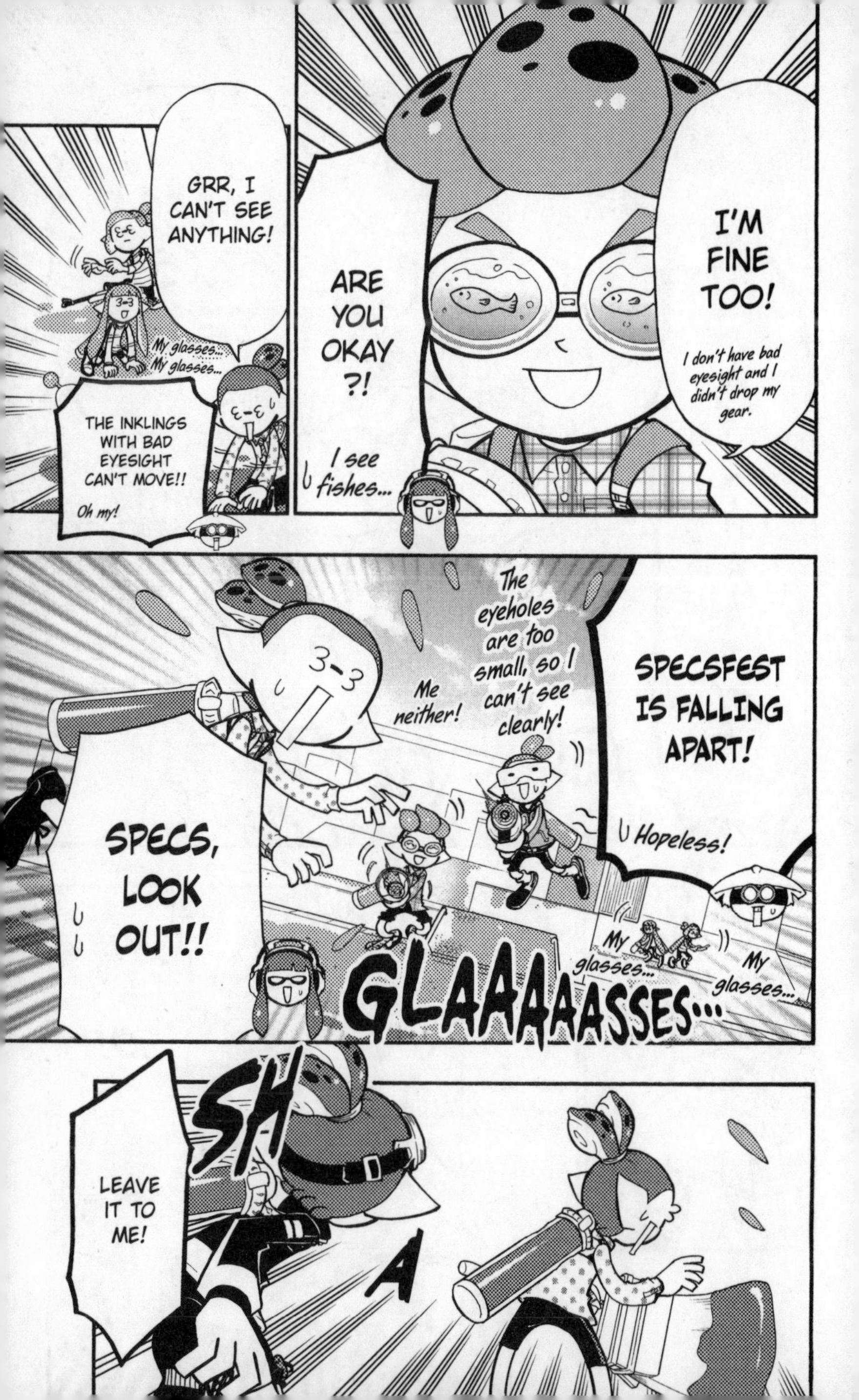
I'M FINE TOO!
I don't have bad eyesight and I didn't drop my gear.
ARE YOU OKAY ?!
I see fishes...
GRR, I CAN'T SEE ANYTHING!
My glasses... My glasses...
THE INKLINGS WITH BAD EYESIGHT CAN'T MOVE!!
Oh my!
SPECSFEST IS FALLING APART!
The eyeholes are too small, so I can't see clearly!
Me neither!
Hopeless!
SPECS, LOOK OUT!!
My glasses...
My glasses...
GLAAAAAASSES...
SH
LEAVE IT TO ME!
A

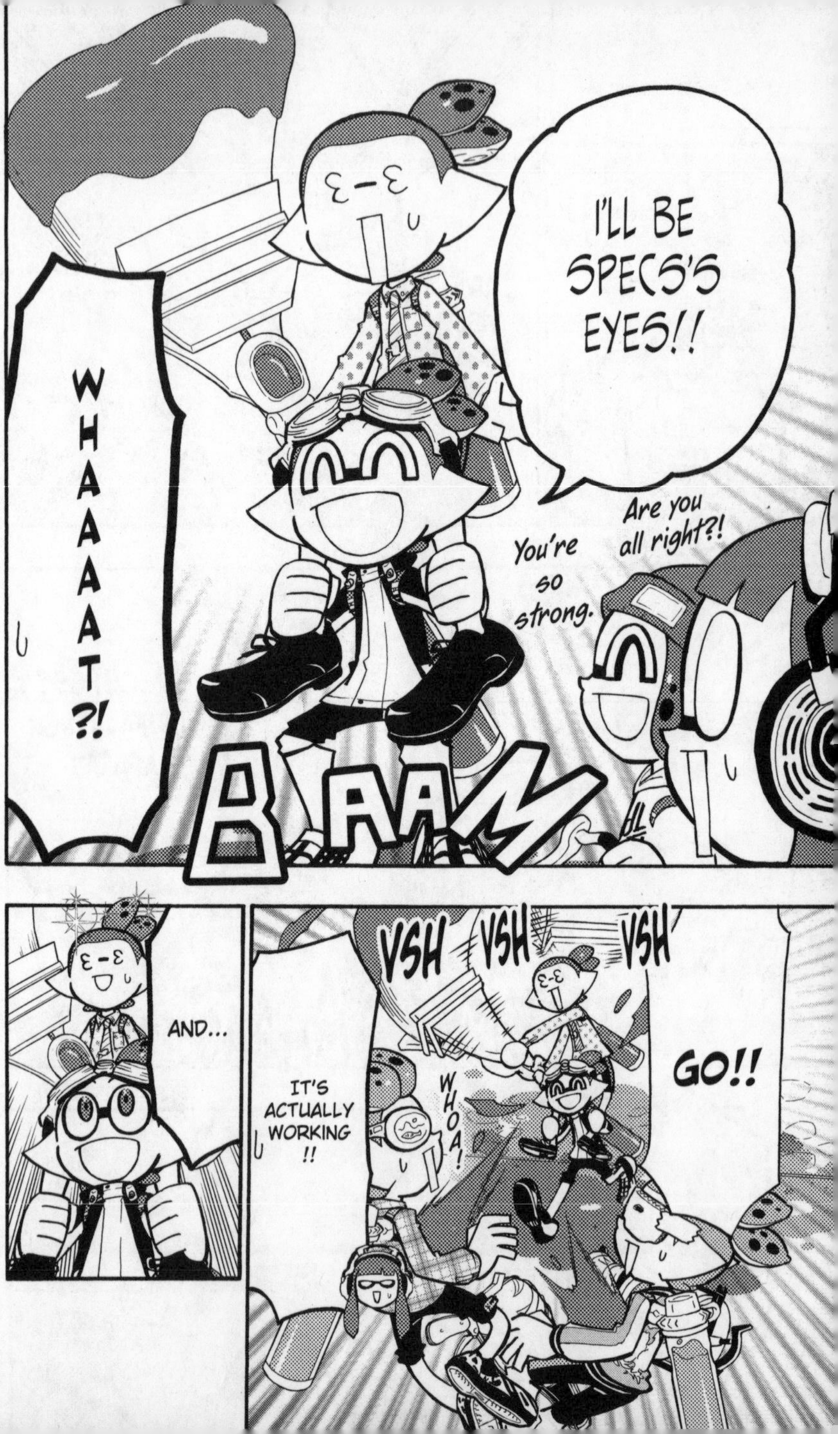
I'LL BE SPECS'S EYES!!
Are you all right?!
You're so strong.
BAAM
WHAAAAAT?!
AND...
VSH VSH VSH
GO!!
WHOA!
IT'S ACTUALLY WORKING !!

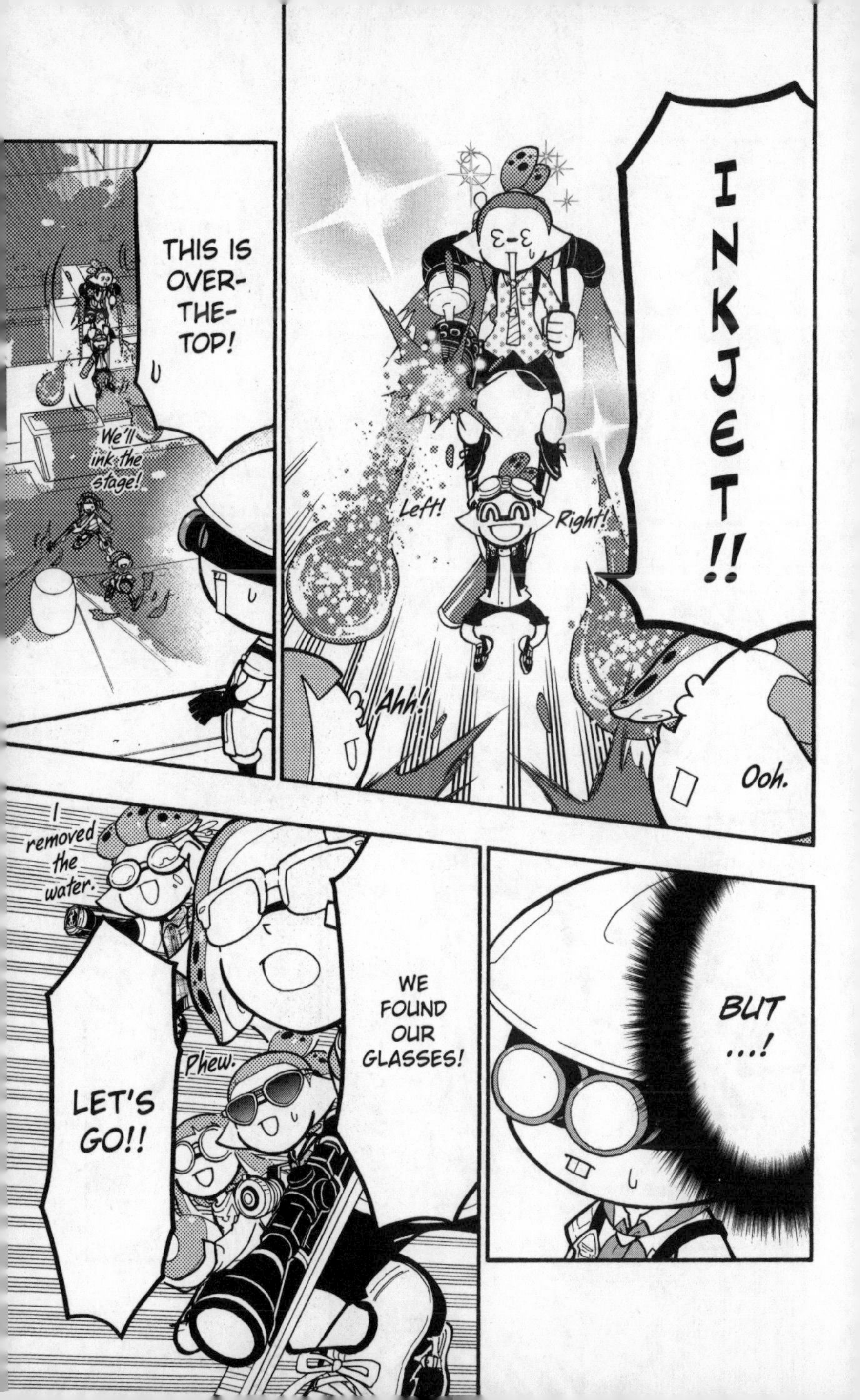

INKJET!!
Right!
Left!
Ahh!
Ooh.
THIS IS OVER-THE-TOP!
We'll ink the stage!
BUT...!
I removed the water.
WE FOUND OUR GLASSES!
Phew.
LET'S GO!!

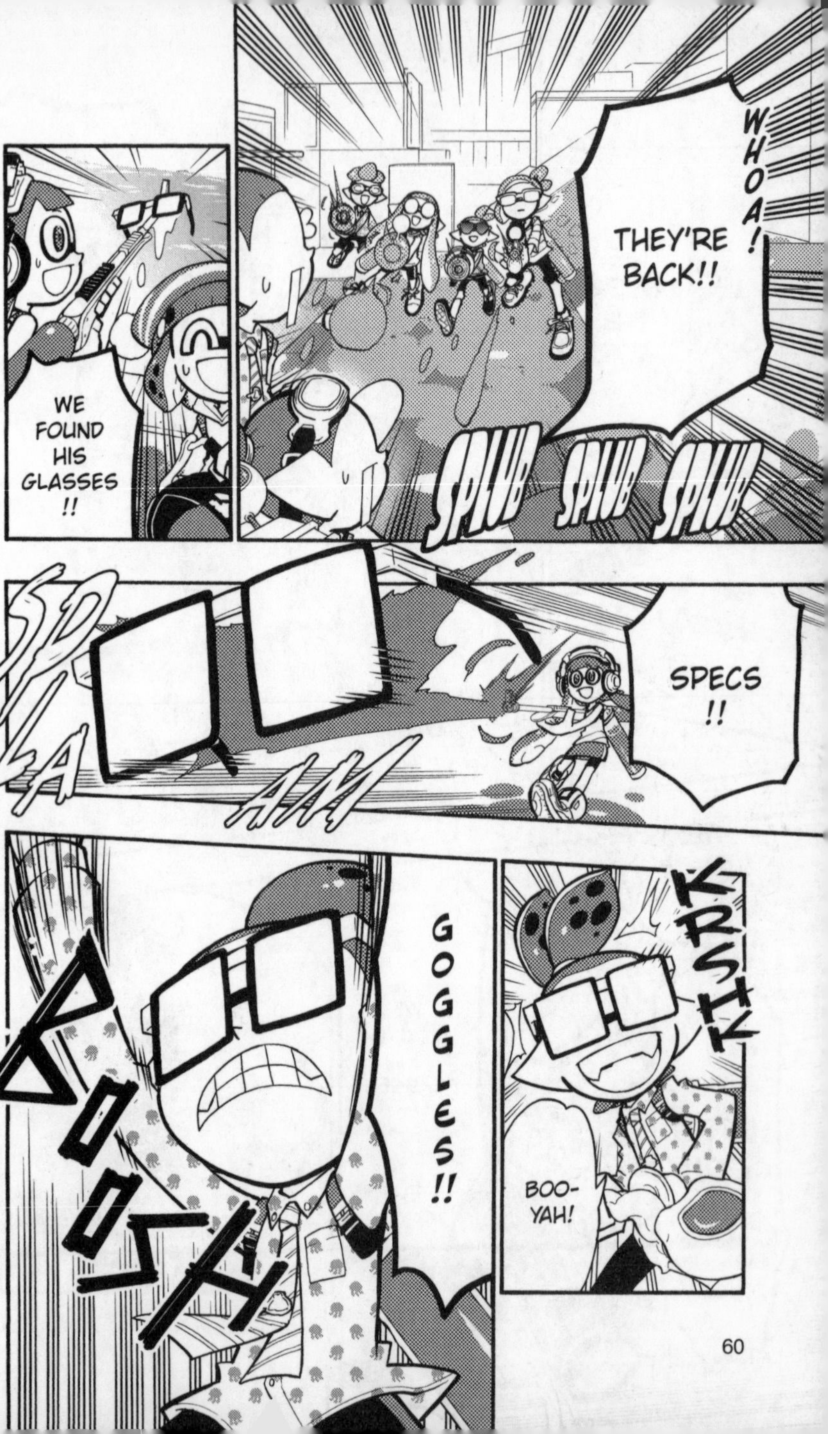
WHOA!
THEY'RE BACK!!
SPLUB SPLUB SPLUB
WE FOUND HIS GLASSES!!
SPECS!!
SPLAAAM
KRSHK
BOO-YAH!
GOGGLES!!
BOOSH

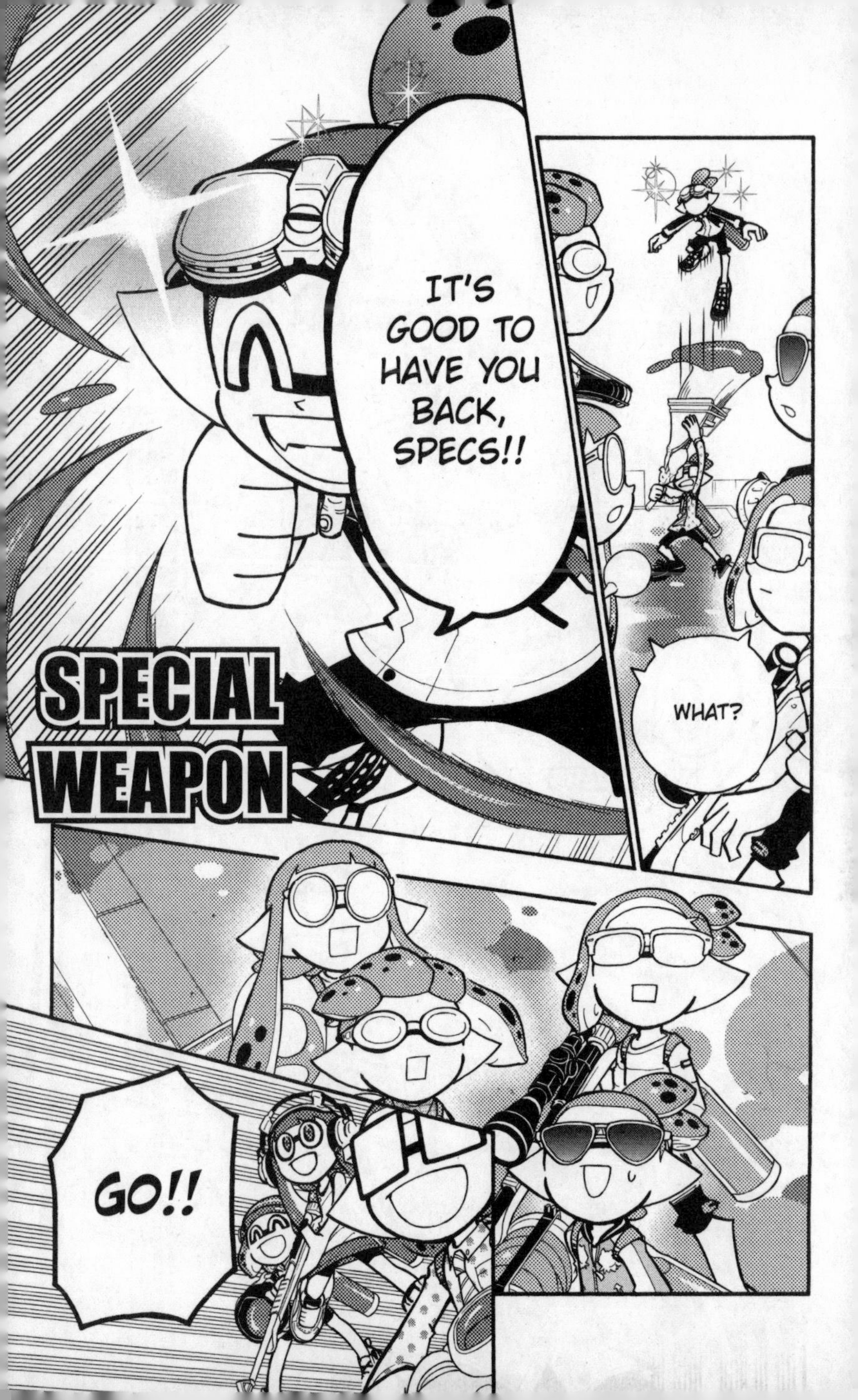
WHAT?
IT'S GOOD TO HAVE YOU BACK, SPECS!!
SPECIAL WEAPON
GO!!

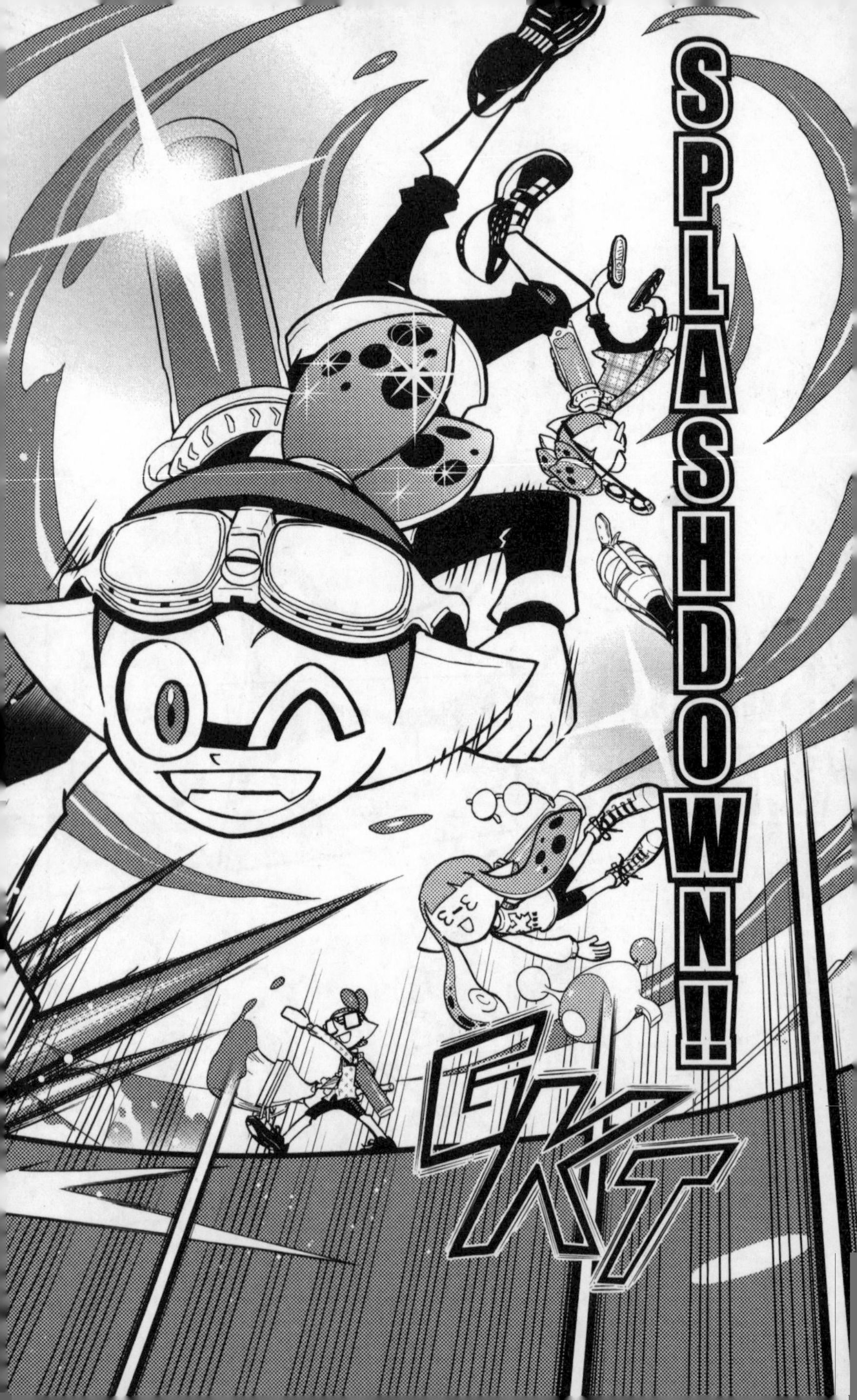
SPLASHDOWN!!

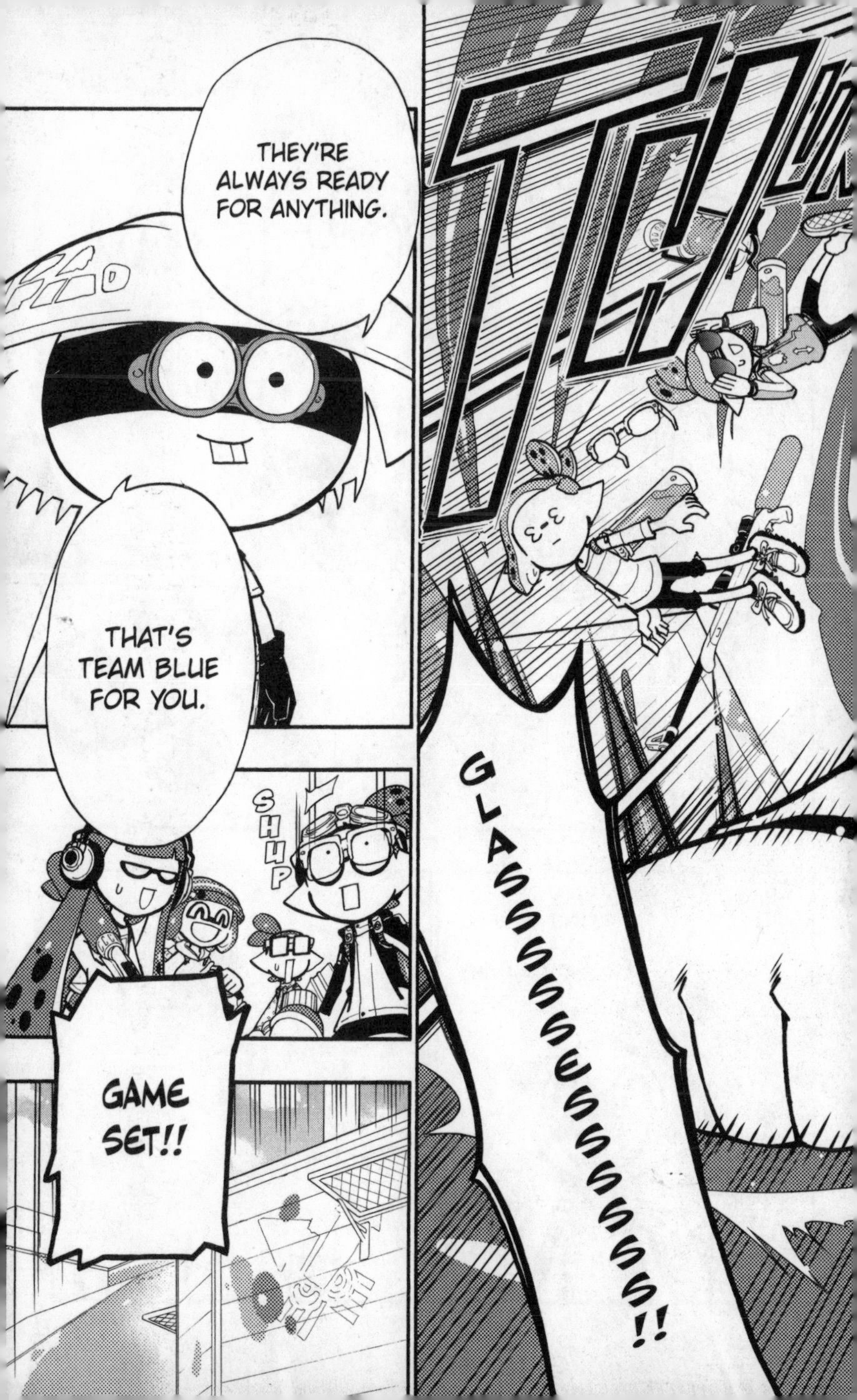
GLASSSSSSSSSSSS!!
THEY'RE ALWAYS READY FOR ANYTHING.
THAT'S TEAM BLUE FOR YOU.
SHUP
GAME SET!!

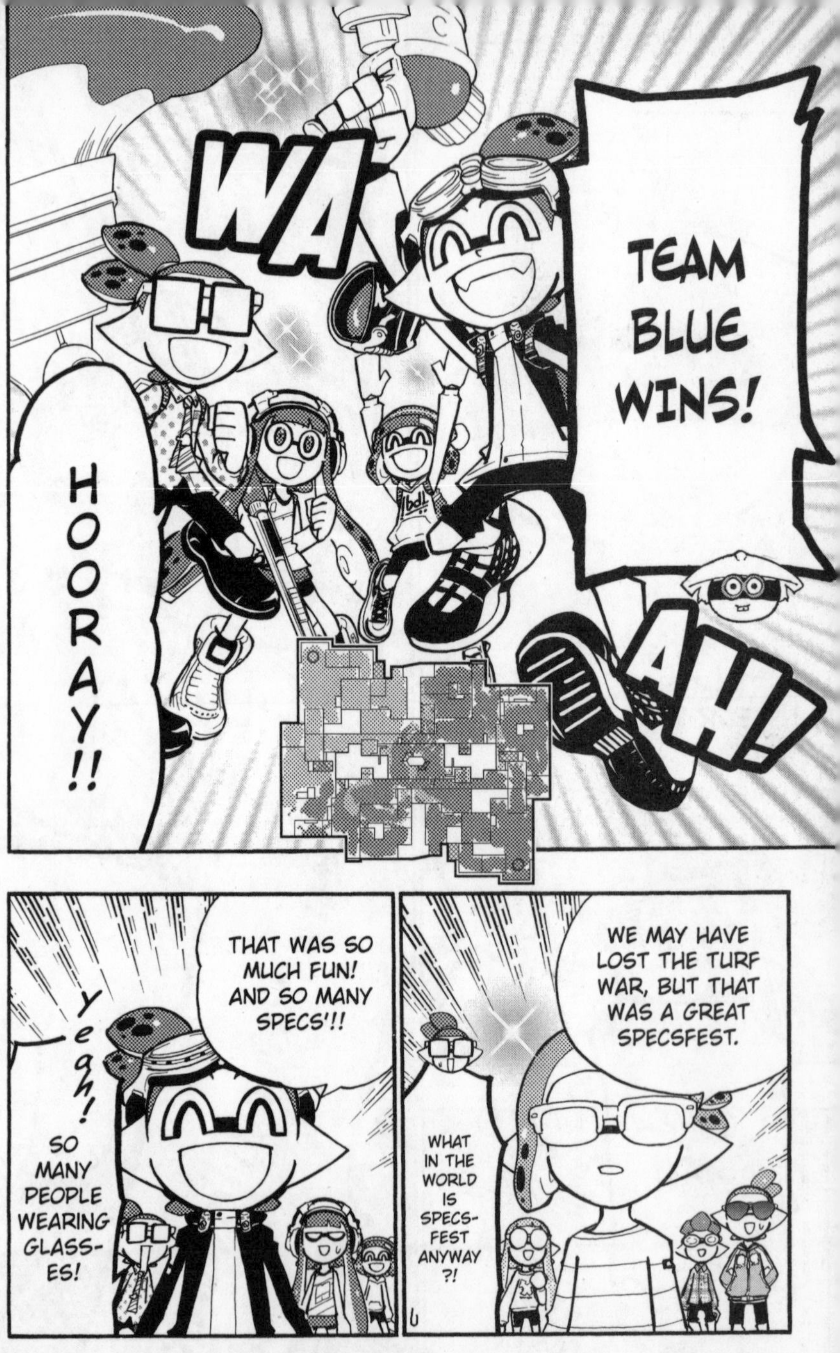
TEAM BLUE WINS!
WA
AH!
HOORAY!!
WE MAY HAVE LOST THE TURF WAR, BUT THAT WAS A GREAT SPECSFEST.
WHAT IN THE WORLD IS SPECS-FEST ANYWAY?!
THAT WAS SO MUCH FUN! AND SO MANY SPECS'!!
Yeah!
SO MANY PEOPLE WEARING GLASS-ES!

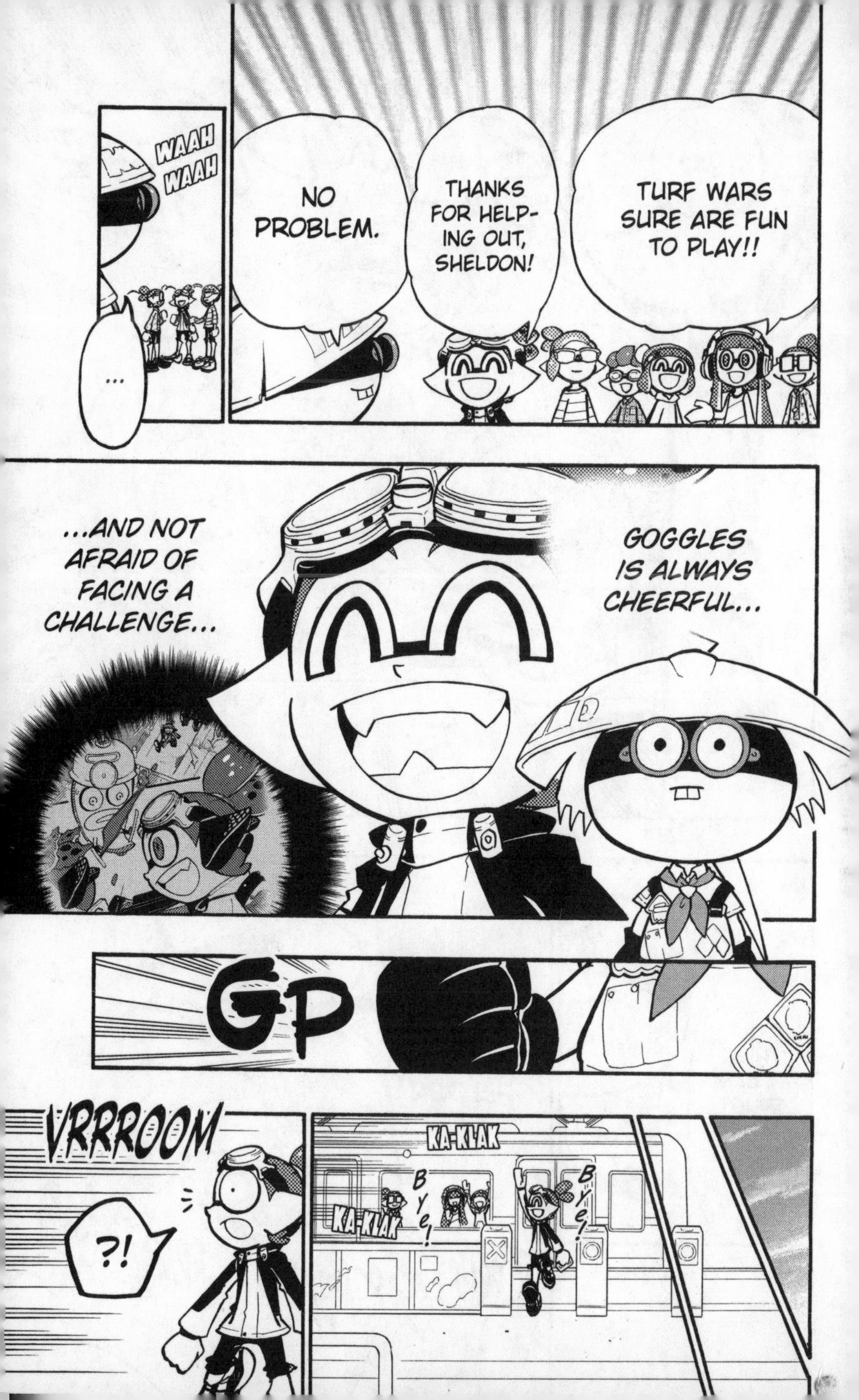
TURF WARS SURE ARE FUN TO PLAY!!
THANKS FOR HELP-ING OUT, SHELDON!
NO PROBLEM.
WAAH WAAH
...
GOGGLES IS ALWAYS CHEERFUL...
...AND NOT AFRAID OF FACING A CHALLENGE...
GP
KA-KLAK
Bye!
Bye!
KA-KLAK
VRRROOM
?!

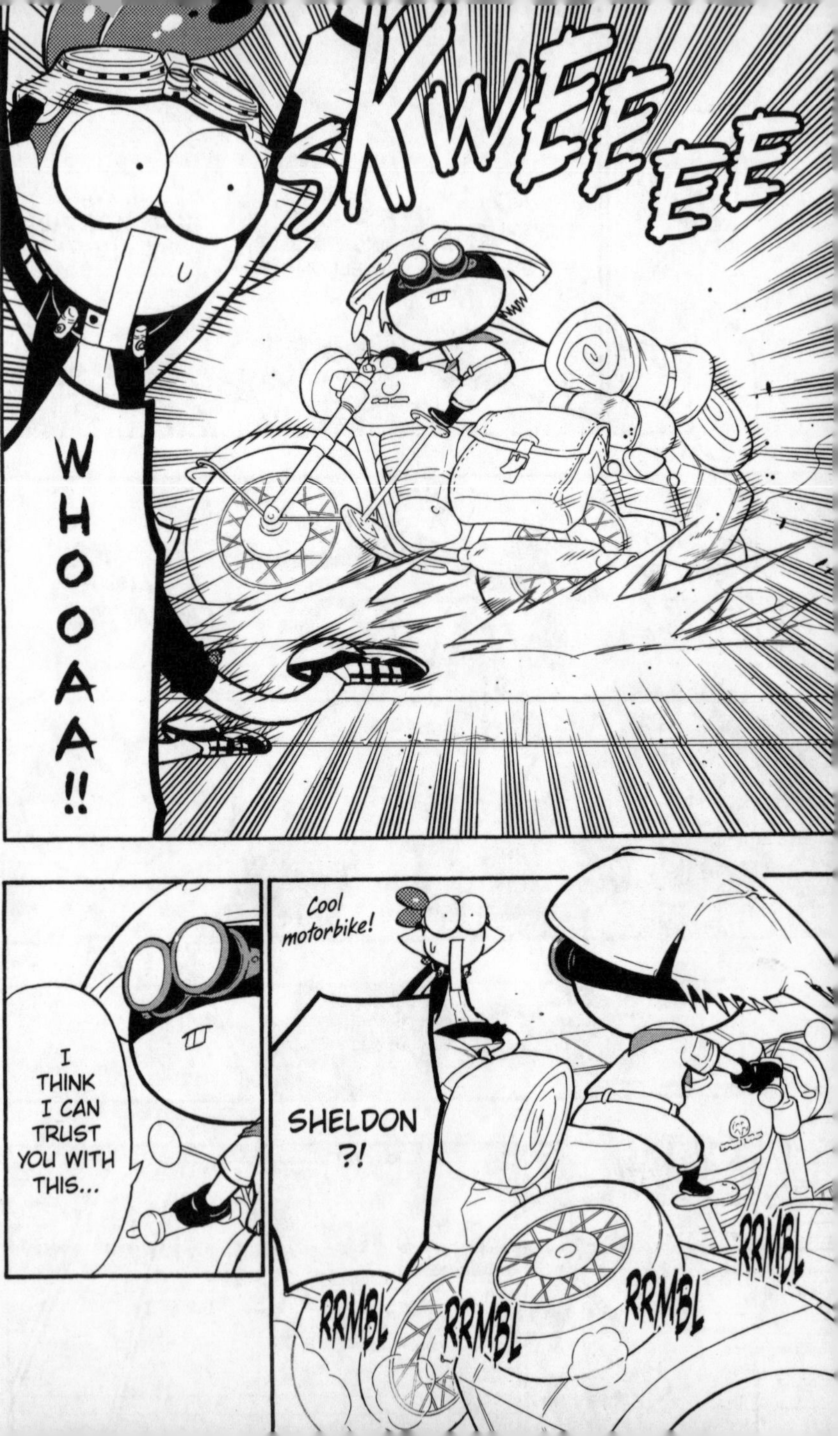
SKWEEEEE
WHOOAA!!
Cool motorbike!
SHELDON ?!
RRMBL
RRMBL
RRMBL
RRMBL
I THINK I CAN TRUST YOU WITH THIS...

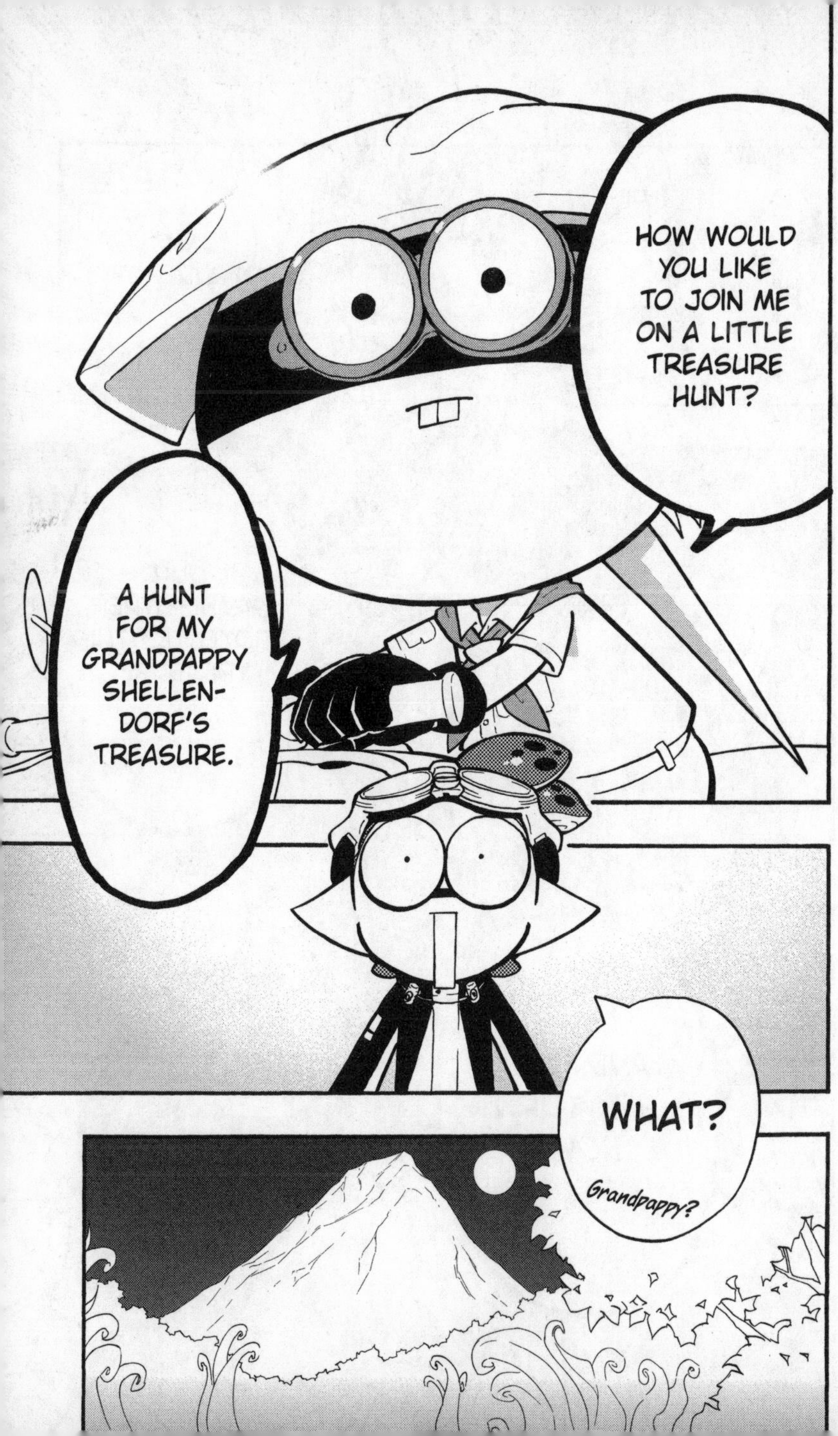
HOW WOULD YOU LIKE TO JOIN ME ON A LITTLE TREASURE HUNT?
A HUNT FOR MY GRANDPAPPY SHELLEN-DORF'S TREASURE.
WHAT?
Grandpappy?

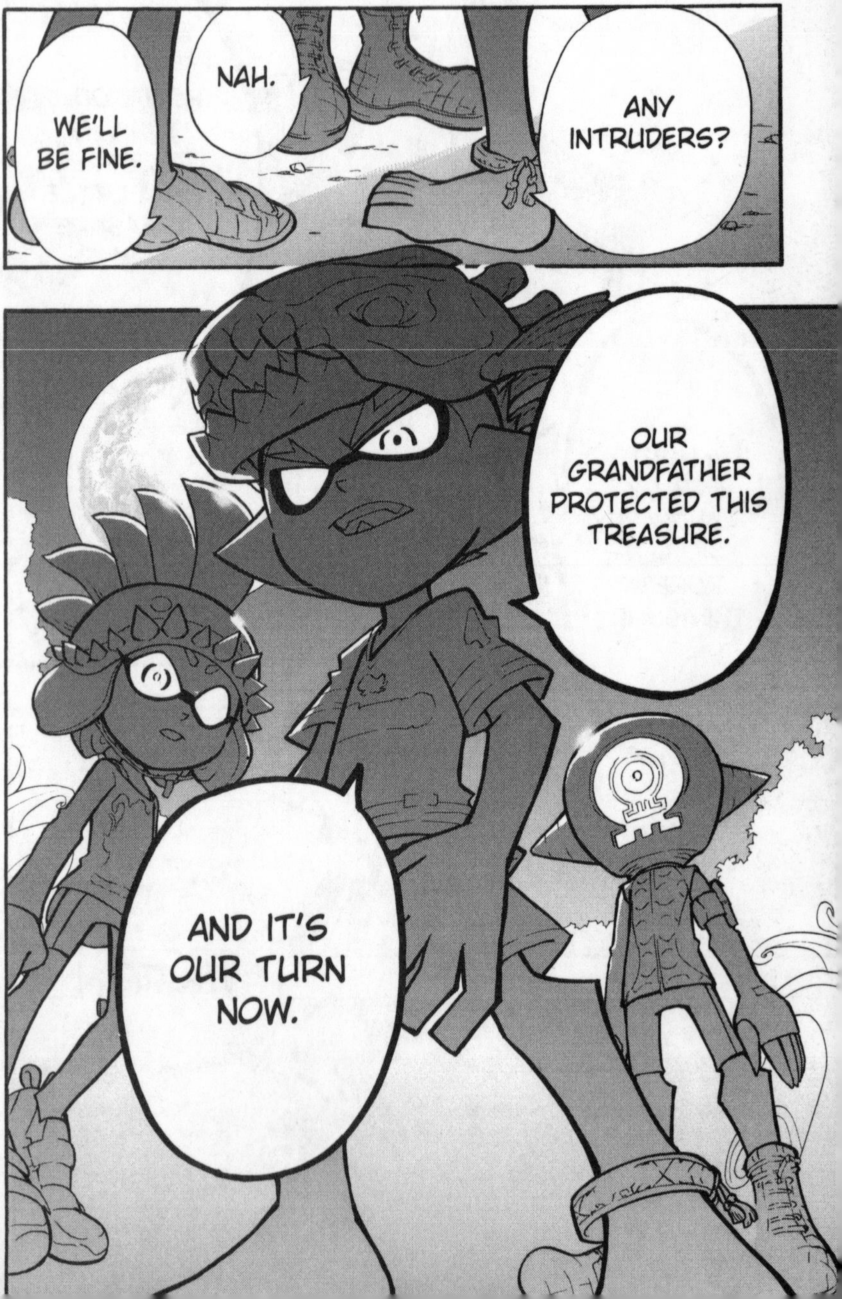
ANY INTRUDERS?
NAH.
WE'LL BE FINE.
OUR GRANDFATHER PROTECTED THIS TREASURE.
AND IT'S OUR TURN NOW.

THEY TOOK A GROUP PHOTO.

SAY "GLASSES"!!

Glasses
?!

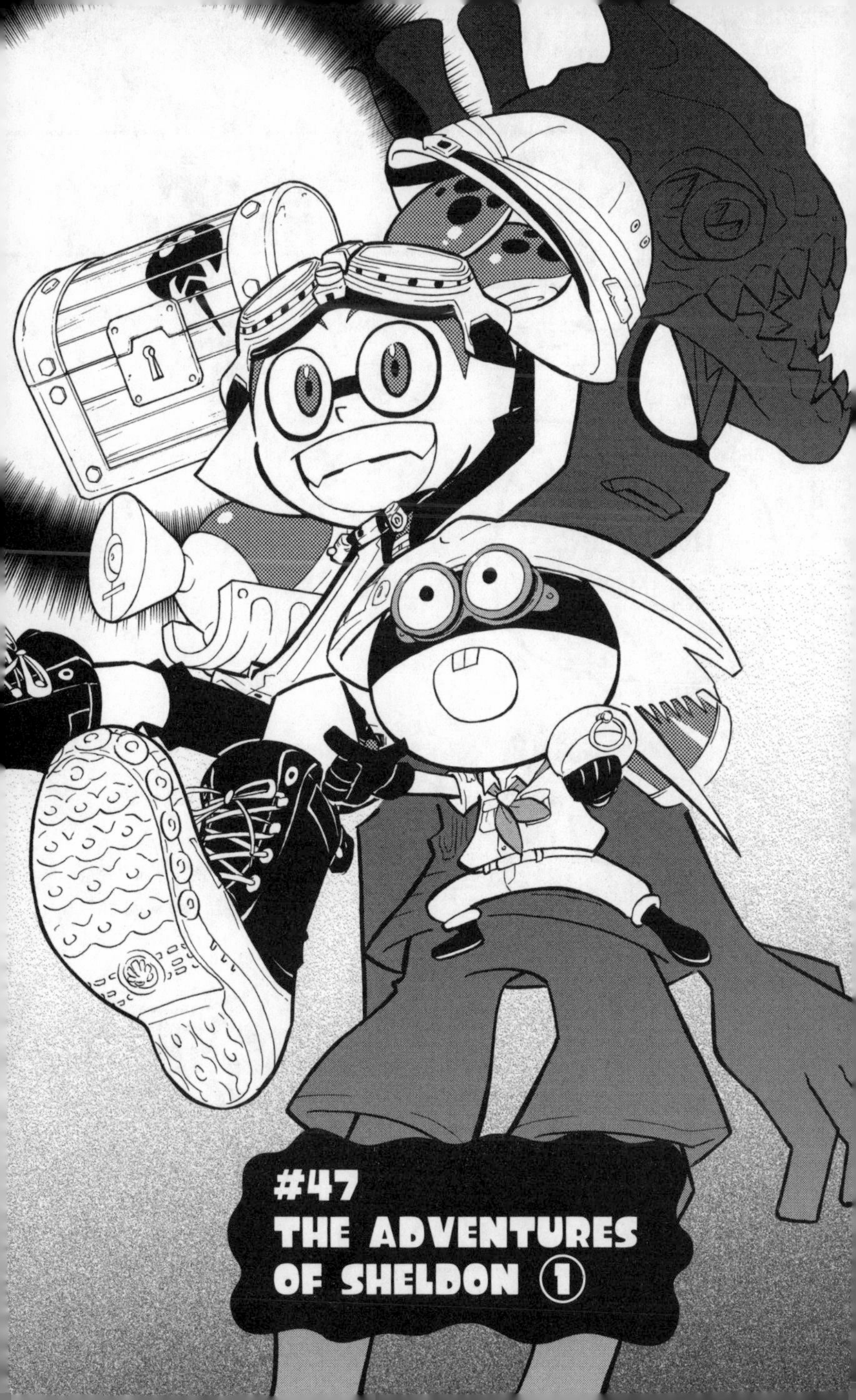
#47
THE ADVENTURES OF SHELDON ①

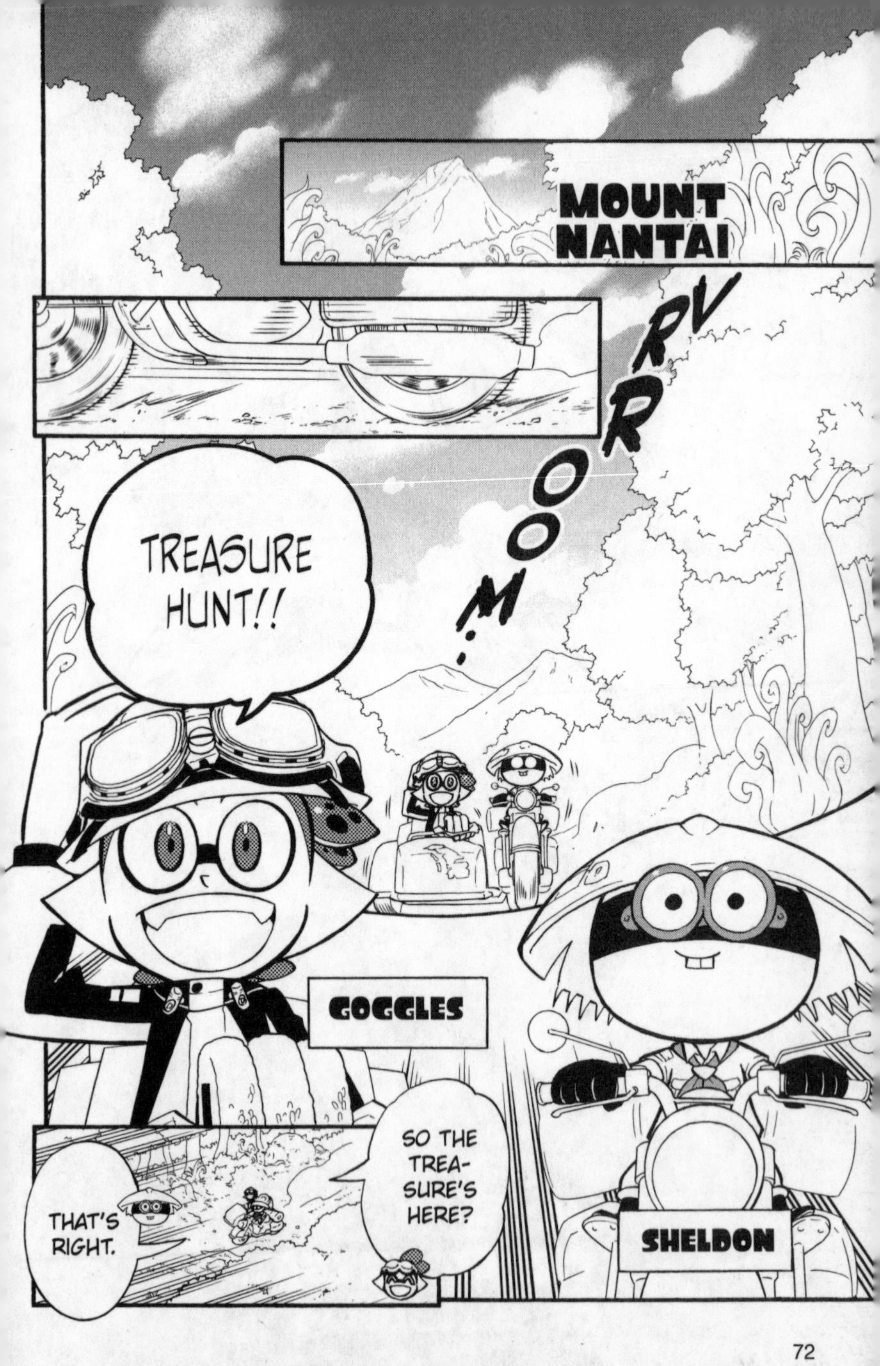
MOUNT NANTAI
RVROOOM...
TREASURE HUNT!!
SHELDON
GOGGLES
SO THE TREASURE'S HERE?
THAT'S RIGHT.

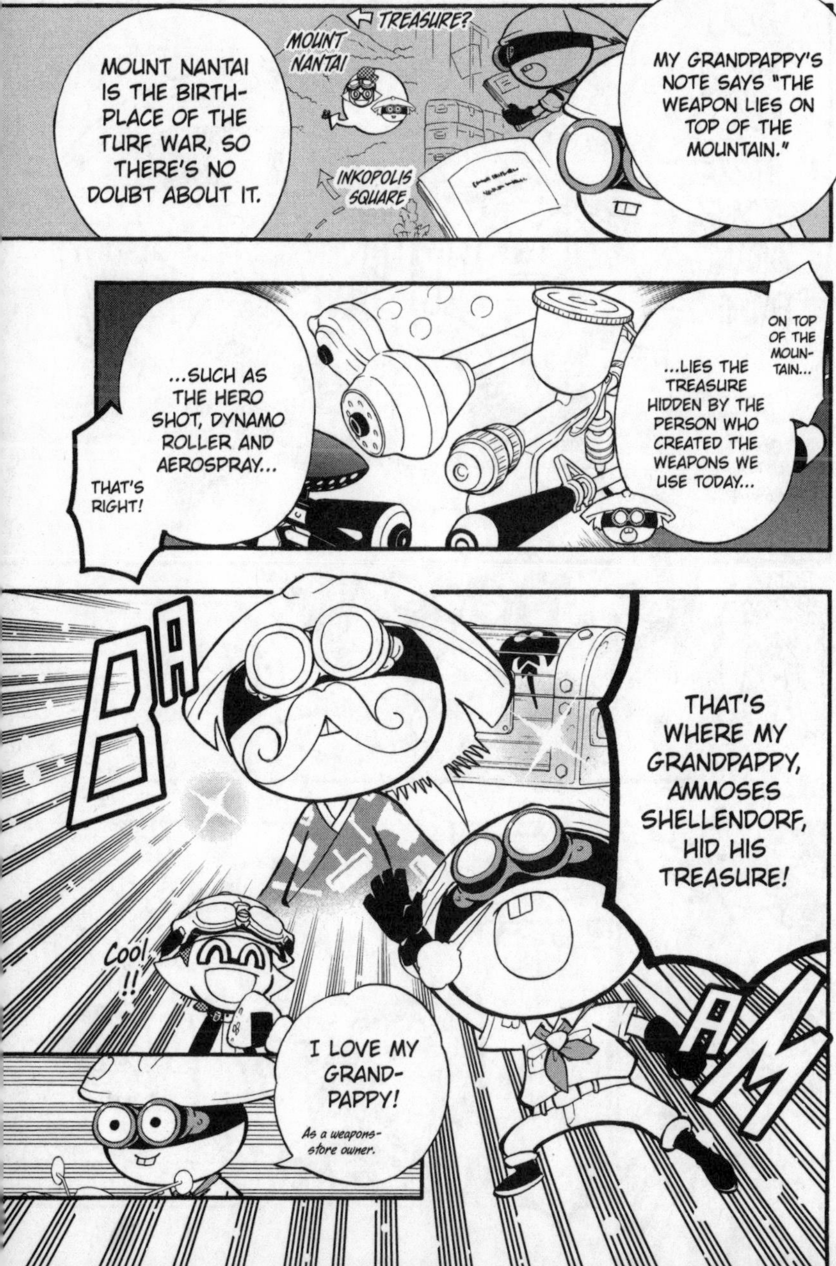

MY GRANDPAPPY'S NOTE SAYS "THE WEAPON LIES ON TOP OF THE MOUNTAIN."
TREASURE?
MOUNT NANTAI
INKOPOLIS SQUARE
MOUNT NANTAI IS THE BIRTH-PLACE OF THE TURF WAR, SO THERE'S NO DOUBT ABOUT IT.
ON TOP OF THE MOUN-TAIN...
...LIES THE TREASURE HIDDEN BY THE PERSON WHO CREATED THE WEAPONS WE USE TODAY...
...SUCH AS THE HERO SHOT, DYNAMO ROLLER AND AEROSPRAY...
THAT'S RIGHT!
BA
AM
THAT'S WHERE MY GRANDPAPPY, AMMOSES SHELLENDORF, HID HIS TREASURE!
Cool!!
I LOVE MY GRAND-PAPPY!
As a weapons-store owner.

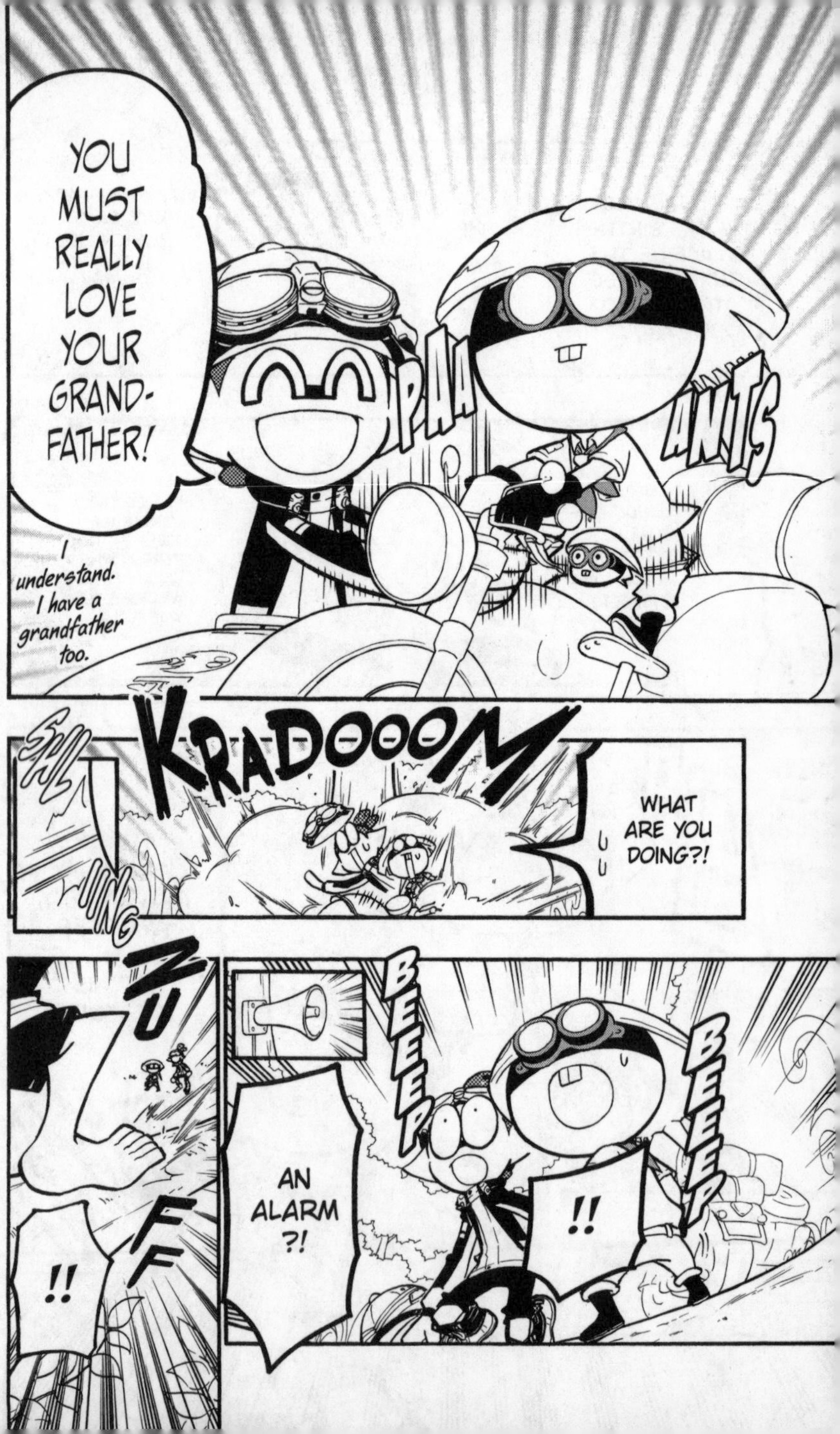
PAANTS
YOU MUST REALLY LOVE YOUR GRAND-FATHER!
I understand. I have a grandfather too.
KRADOOOM
WHAT ARE YOU DOING?!
BEEEP
BEEEP
!!
AN ALARM ?!
ZUFF
!!

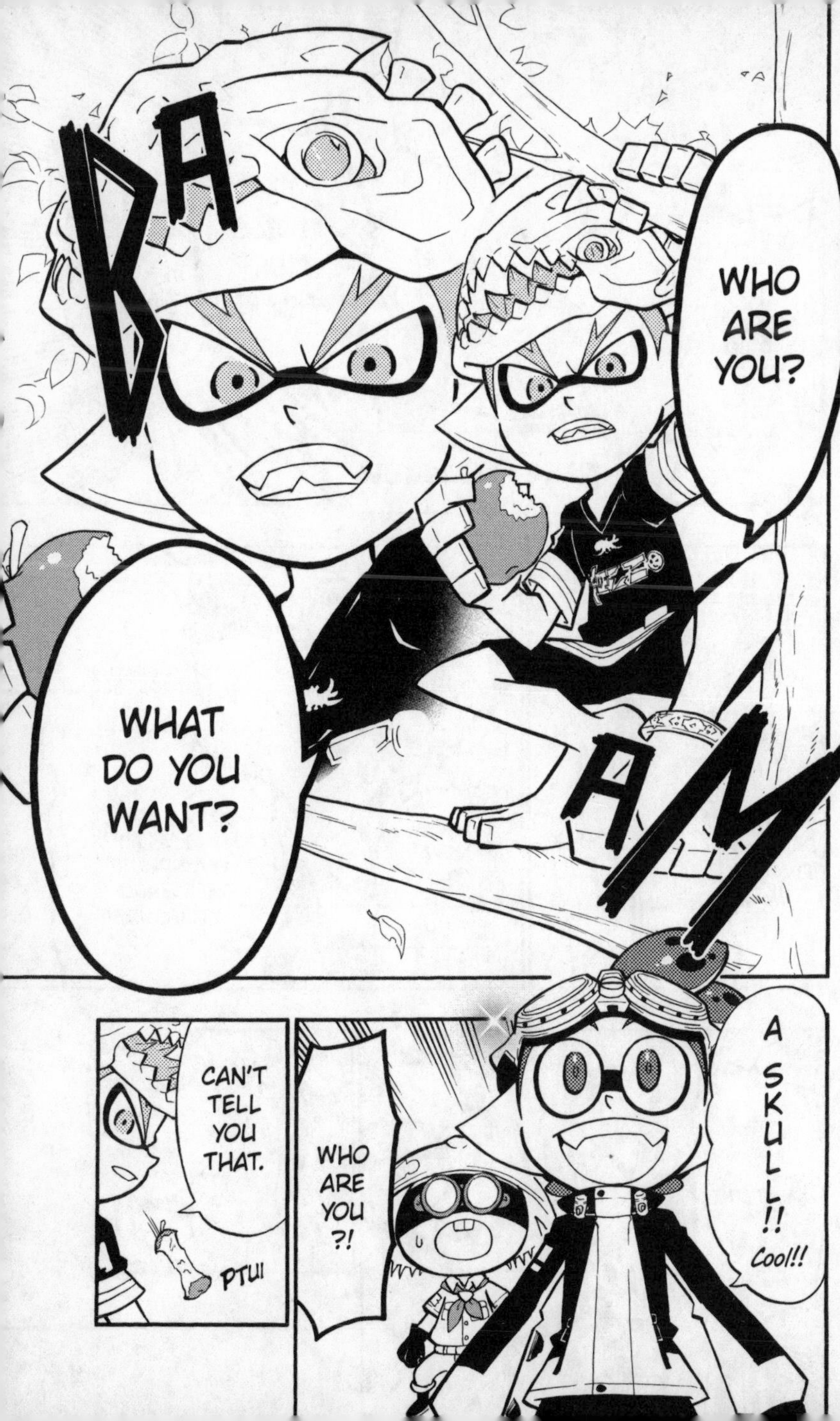
WHO ARE YOU?
BAM
WHAT DO YOU WANT?
A SKULL!!
Cool!!
WHO ARE YOU?!
CAN'T TELL YOU THAT.
PTUI

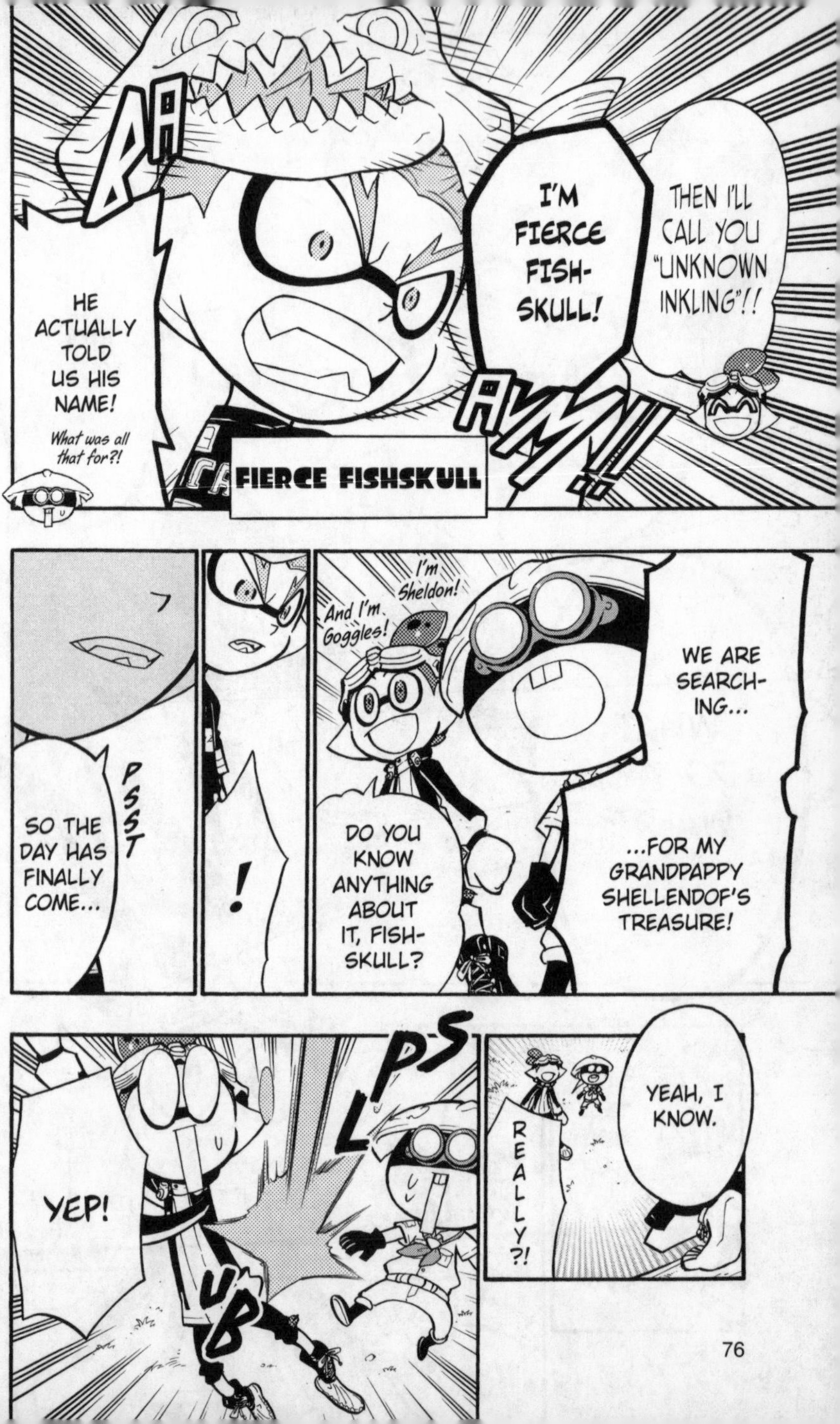
THEN I'LL CALL YOU "UNKNOWN INKLING"!!
BA
AM!!
I'M FIERCE FISH-SKULL!
FIERCE FISHSKULL
HE ACTUALLY TOLD US HIS NAME!
What was all that for?!
WE ARE SEARCH-ING...
I'm Sheldon!
And I'm Goggles!
...FOR MY GRANDPAPPY SHELLENDOF'S TREASURE!
DO YOU KNOW ANYTHING ABOUT IT, FISH-SKULL?
!
PSST
SO THE DAY HAS FINALLY COME...
YEAH, I KNOW.
REALLY?!
PS
L
UB
YEP!

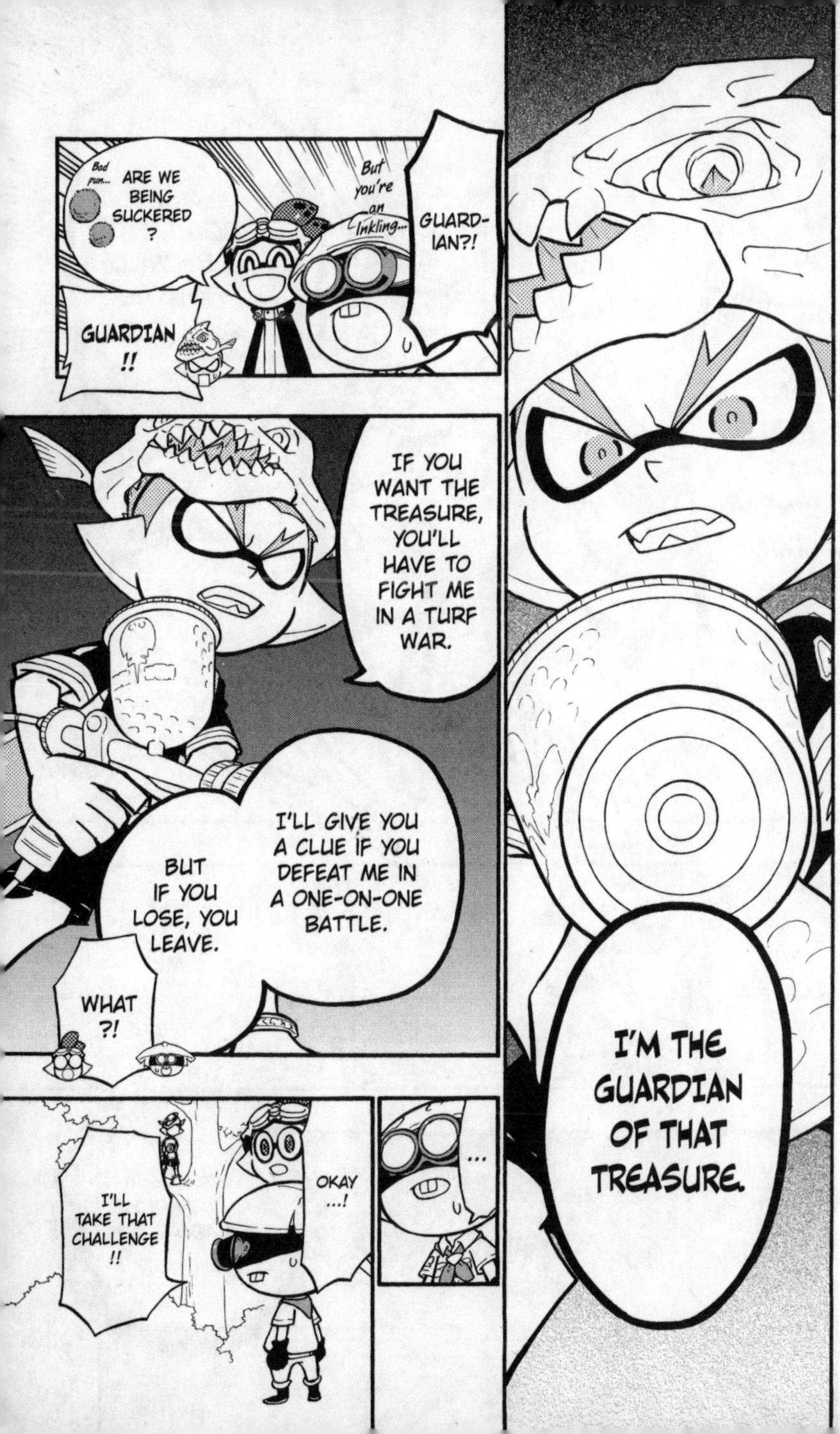
I'M THE GUARDIAN OF THAT TREASURE.
GUARD-IAN?!
But you're an Inkling...
ARE WE BEING SUCKERED?
Bad pun...
GUARDIAN!!
IF YOU WANT THE TREASURE, YOU'LL HAVE TO FIGHT ME IN A TURF WAR.
I'LL GIVE YOU A CLUE IF YOU DEFEAT ME IN A ONE-ON-ONE BATTLE.
BUT IF YOU LOSE, YOU LEAVE.
WHAT?!
...
OKAY ...!
I'LL TAKE THAT CHALLENGE!!

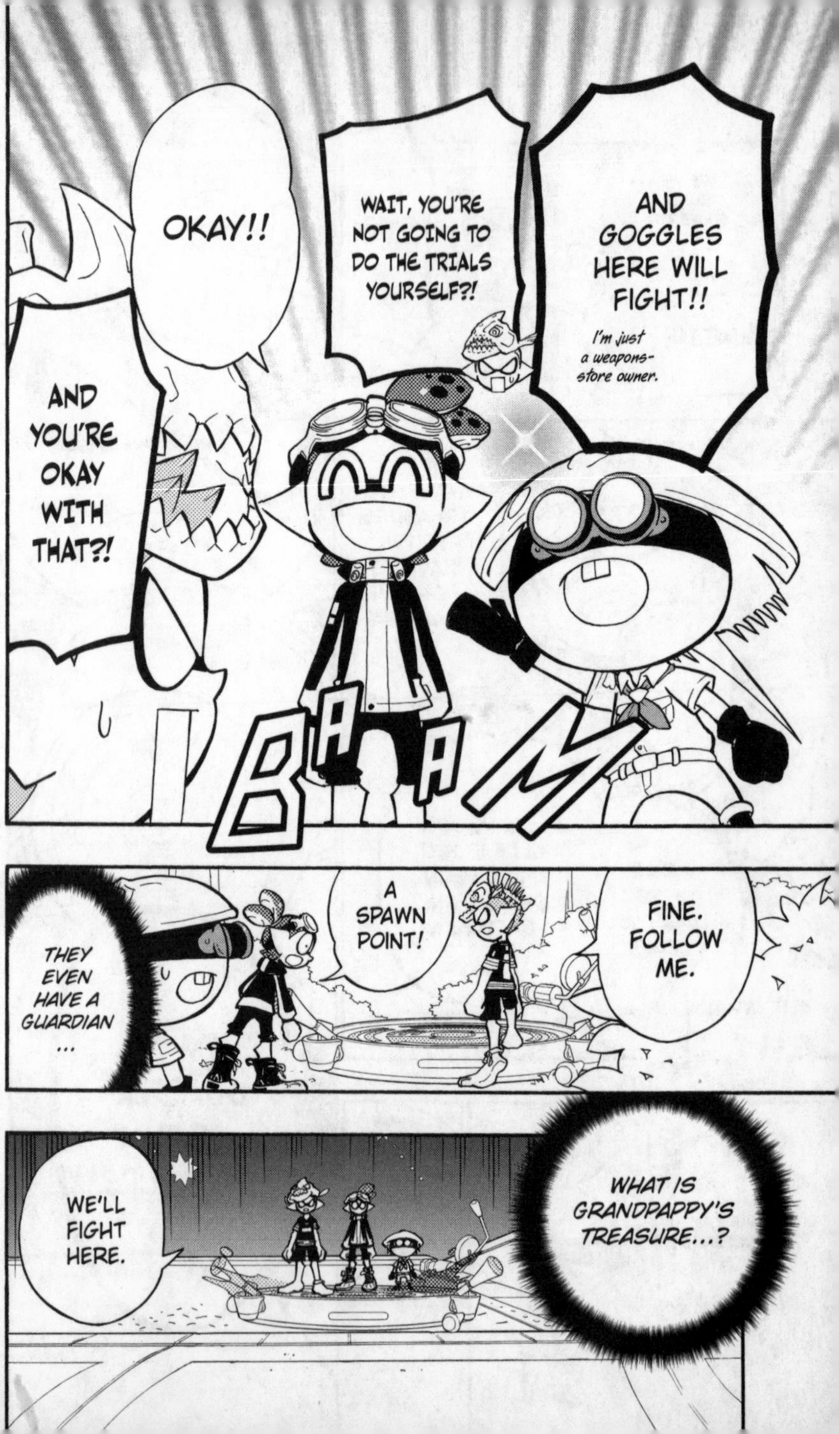
AND GOGGLES HERE WILL FIGHT!!
I'm just a weapons-store owner.
WAIT, YOU'RE NOT GOING TO DO THE TRIALS YOURSELF?!
OKAY!!
AND YOU'RE OKAY WITH THAT?!
BAAM
FINE. FOLLOW ME.
A SPAWN POINT!
THEY EVEN HAVE A GUARDIAN...
WHAT IS GRANDPAPPY'S TREASURE...?
WE'LL FIGHT HERE.

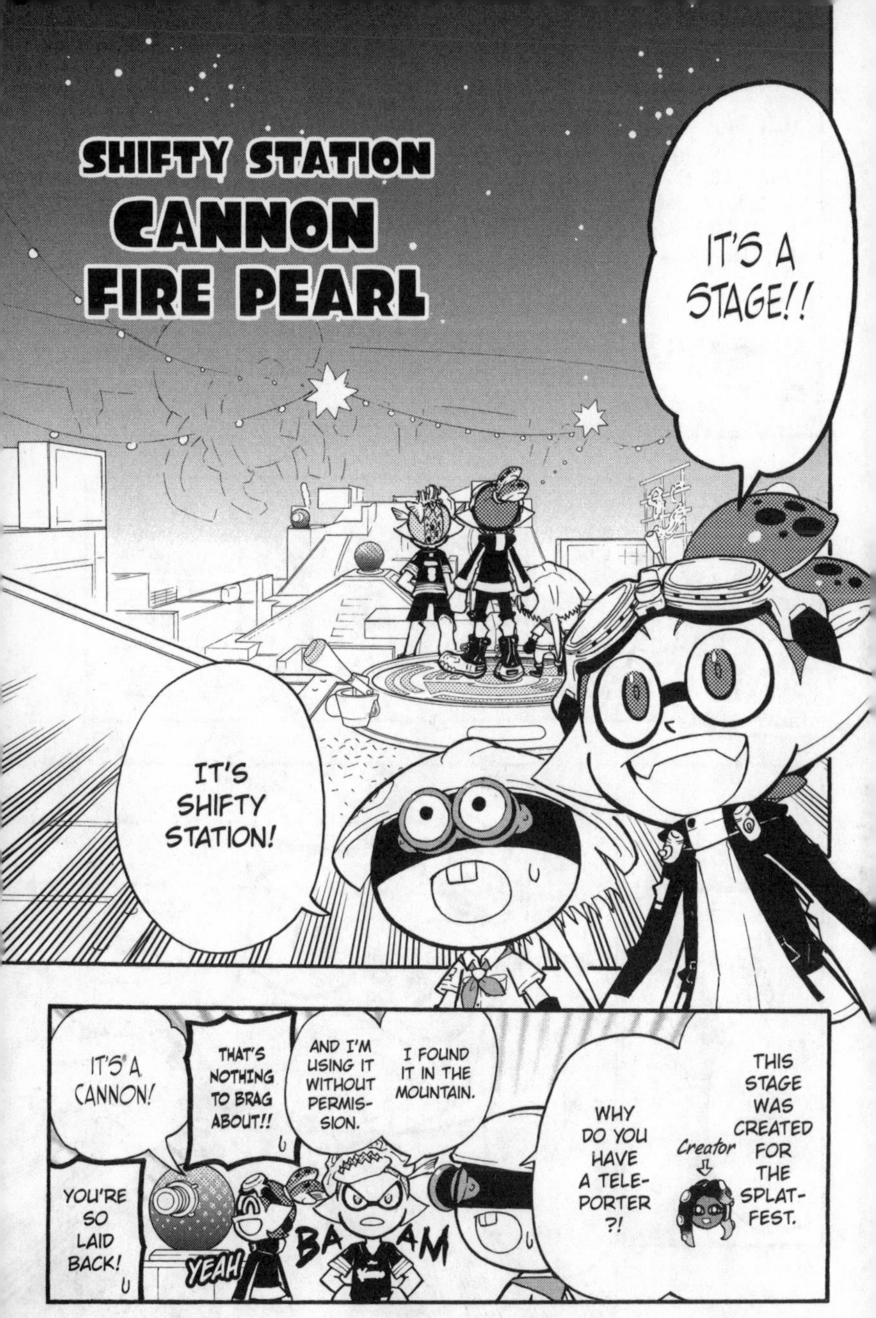
SHIFTY STATION
CANNON FIRE PEARL
IT'S A STAGE!!
IT'S SHIFTY STATION!
THIS STAGE WAS CREATED FOR THE SPLAT-FEST.
Creator
WHY DO YOU HAVE A TELE-PORTER?!
I FOUND IT IN THE MOUNTAIN.
AND I'M USING IT WITHOUT PERMIS-SION.
BAAM
THAT'S NOTHING TO BRAG ABOUT!!
IT'S A CANNON!
YEAH
YOU'RE SO LAID BACK!

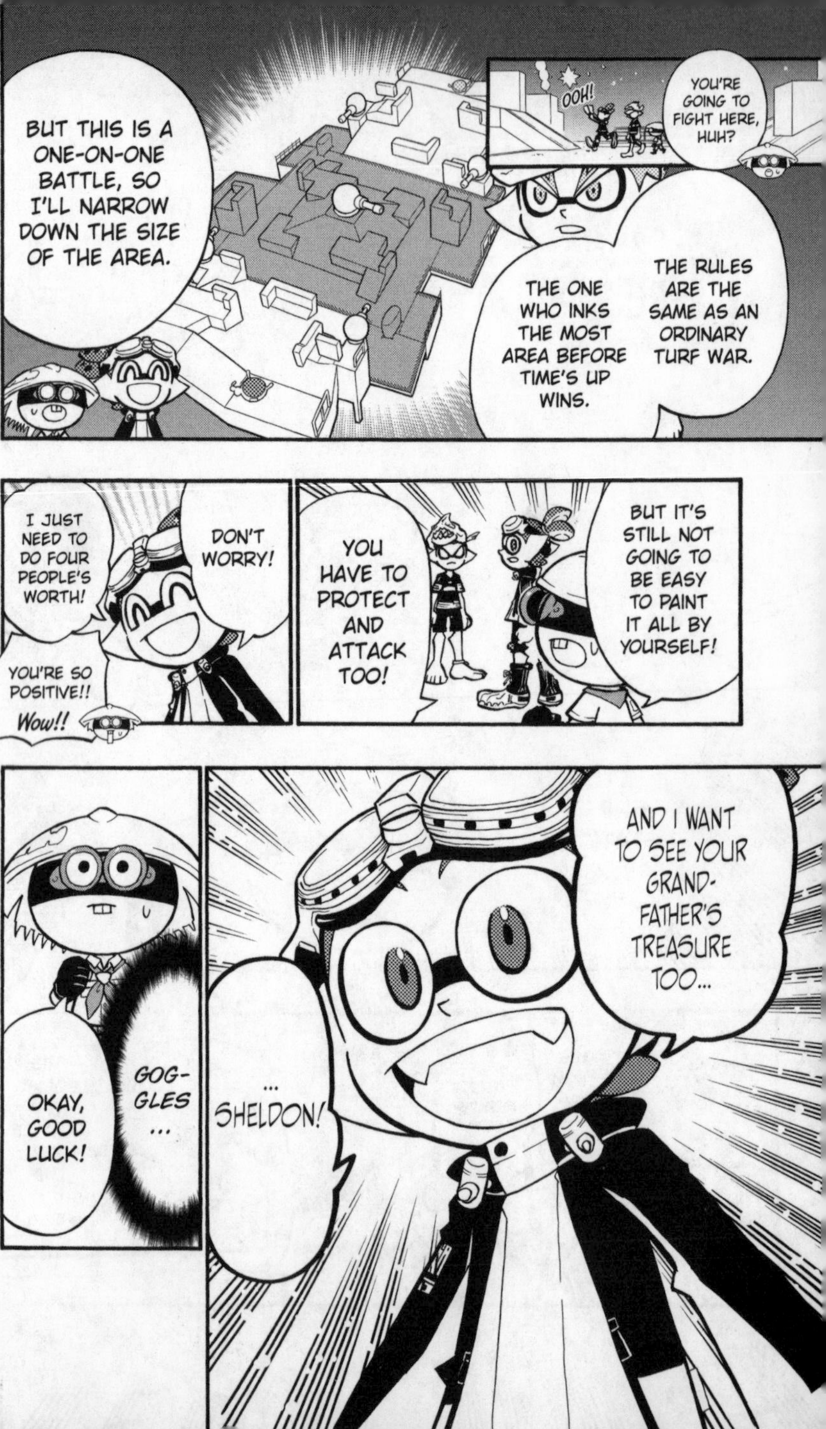
OOH!
YOU'RE GOING TO FIGHT HERE, HUH?
THE RULES ARE THE SAME AS AN ORDINARY TURF WAR.
THE ONE WHO INKS THE MOST AREA BEFORE TIME'S UP WINS.
BUT THIS IS A ONE-ON-ONE BATTLE, SO I'LL NARROW DOWN THE SIZE OF THE AREA.
BUT IT'S STILL NOT GOING TO BE EASY TO PAINT IT ALL BY YOURSELF!
YOU HAVE TO PROTECT AND ATTACK TOO!
DON'T WORRY!
I JUST NEED TO DO FOUR PEOPLE'S WORTH!
YOU'RE SO POSITIVE!!
Wow!!
AND I WANT TO SEE YOUR GRAND-FATHER'S TREASURE TOO...
...SHELDON!
GOG-GLES...
OKAY, GOOD LUCK!

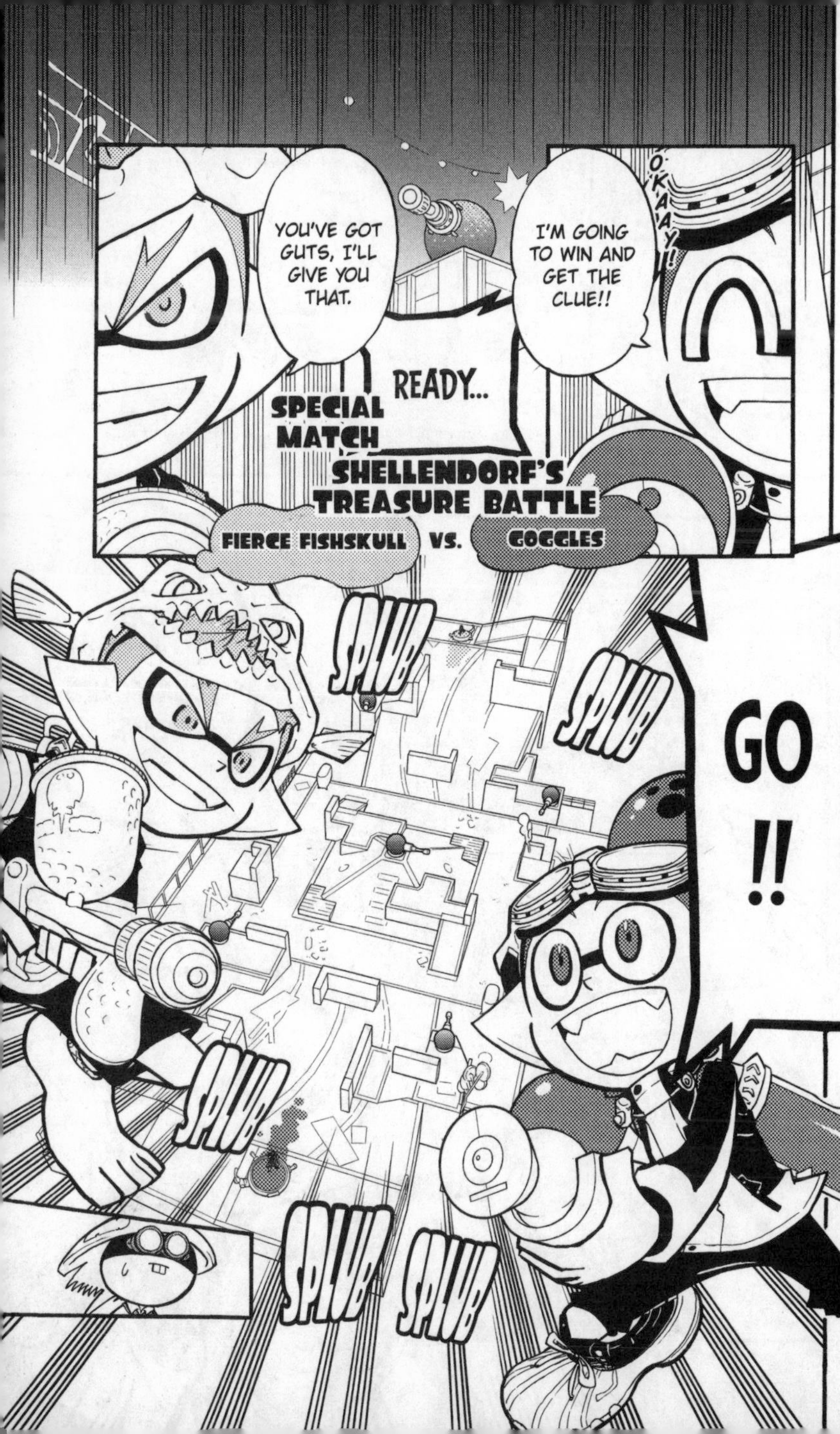
OKAAY!!
I'M GOING TO WIN AND GET THE CLUE!!
YOU'VE GOT GUTS, I'LL GIVE YOU THAT.
READY...
SPECIAL MATCH
SHELLENDORF'S TREASURE BATTLE
FIERCE FISHSKULL VS. GOGGLES
GO!!
SPLUB
SPLUB
SPLUB
SPLUB
SPLUB

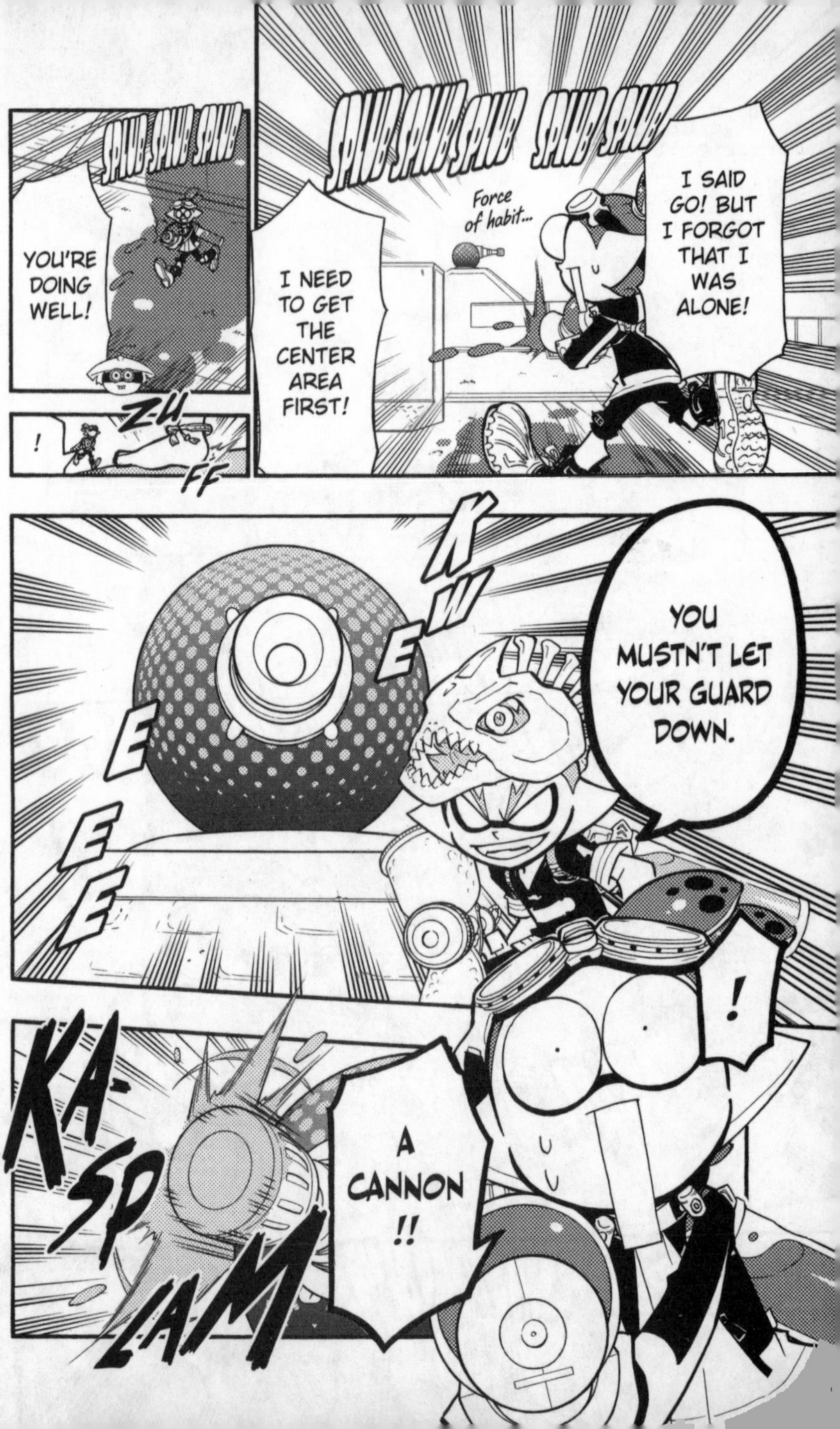
SPLUD SPLUD SPLUD SPLUD SPLUD
I SAID GO! BUT I FORGOT THAT I WAS ALONE!
Force of habit...
I NEED TO GET THE CENTER AREA FIRST!
SPLUD SPLUD SPLUD
YOU'RE DOING WELL!
Z-U
!
FF
KWEEEE
YOU MUSTN'T LET YOUR GUARD DOWN.
!
KA-SPLAM
A CANNON!!

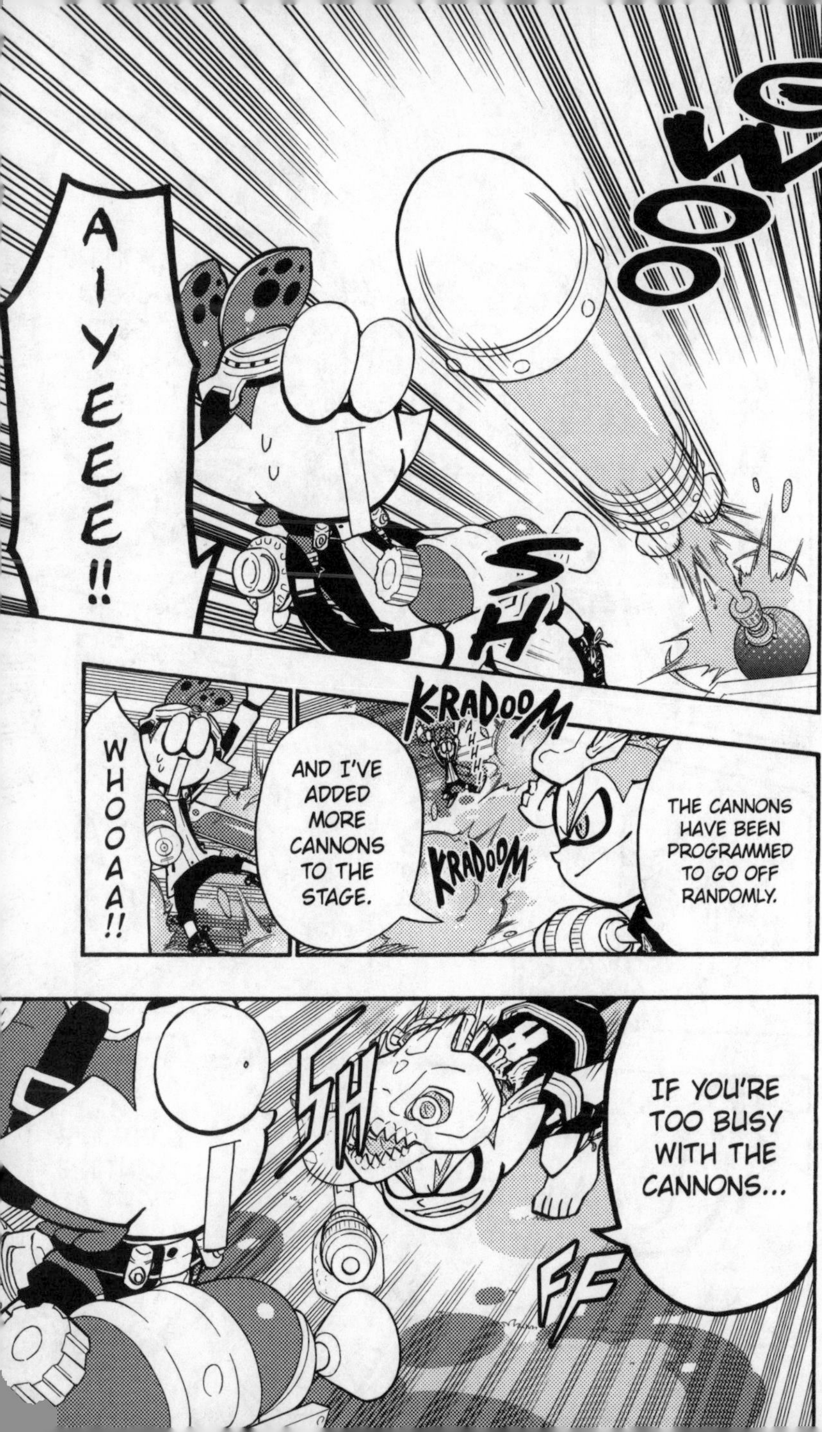
SH
AIYEEE!!
KRADOOM
AHHH!
THE CANNONS HAVE BEEN PROGRAMMED TO GO OFF RANDOMLY.
KRADOOM
AND I'VE ADDED MORE CANNONS TO THE STAGE.
WHOOOAA!!
IF YOU'RE TOO BUSY WITH THE CANNONS...
FF
SH

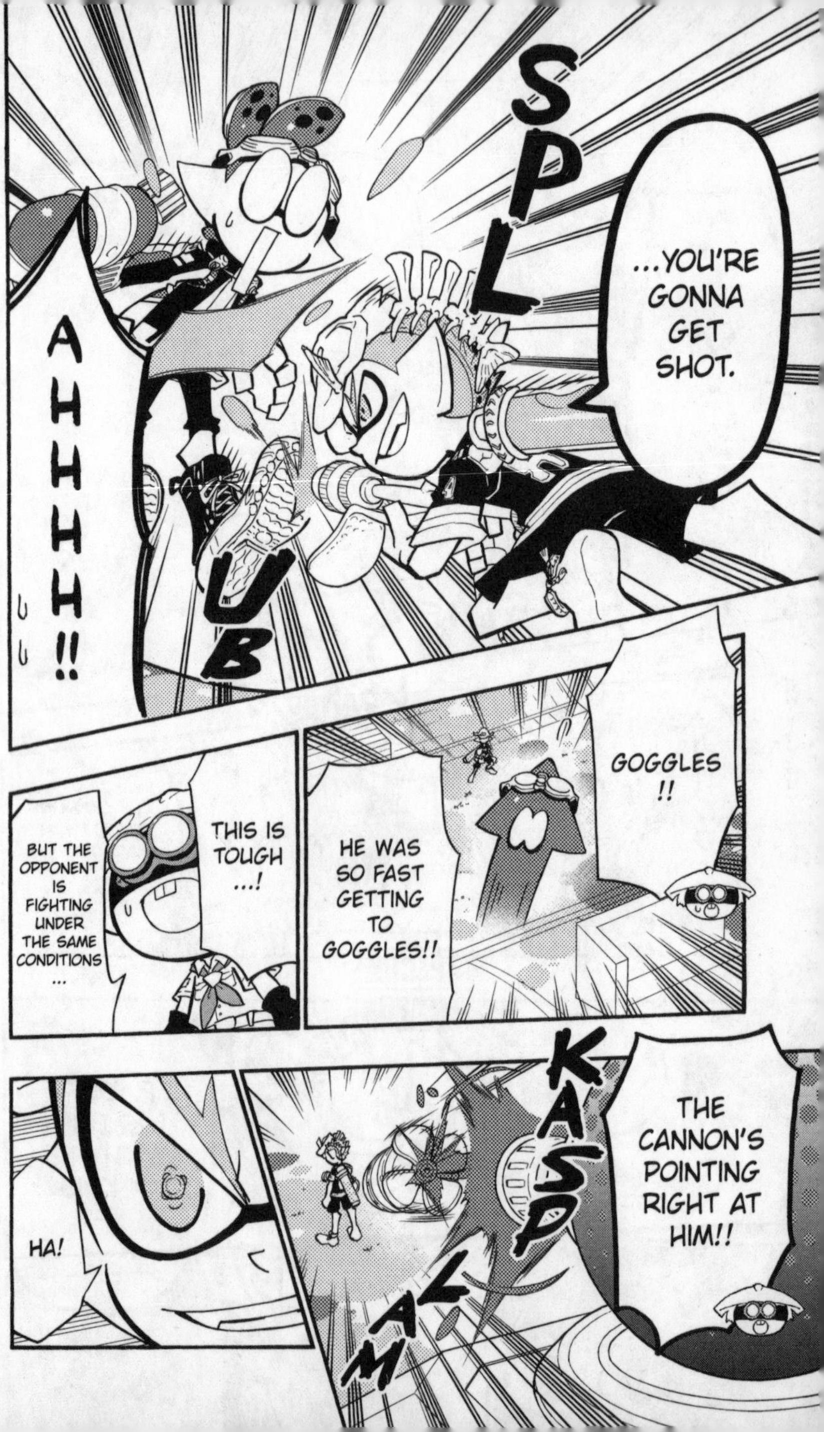
...YOU'RE GONNA GET SHOT.
SPLUB
AHHHH!!
GOGGLES!!
HE WAS SO FAST GETTING TO GOGGLES!!
THIS IS TOUGH...!
BUT THE OPPONENT IS FIGHTING UNDER THE SAME CONDITIONS...
THE CANNON'S POINTING RIGHT AT HIM!!
KASPLAM
HA!

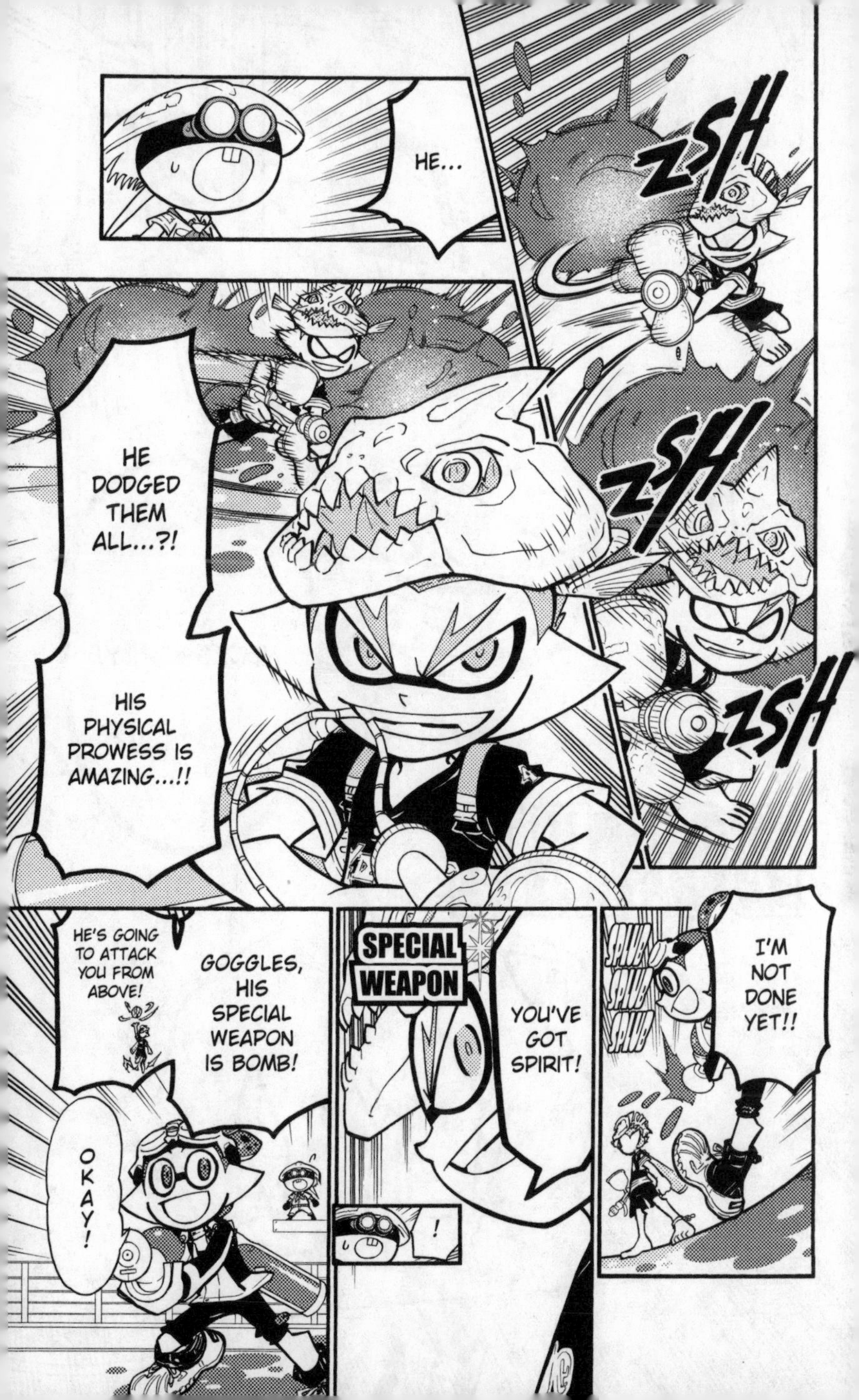
ZSH
ZSH
ZSH
HE...
HE DODGED THEM ALL...?!
HIS PHYSICAL PROWESS IS AMAZING...!!
I'M NOT DONE YET!!
SPECIAL WEAPON
YOU'VE GOT SPIRIT!
!
GOGGLES, HIS SPECIAL WEAPON IS BOMB!
HE'S GOING TO ATTACK YOU FROM ABOVE!
OKAY!

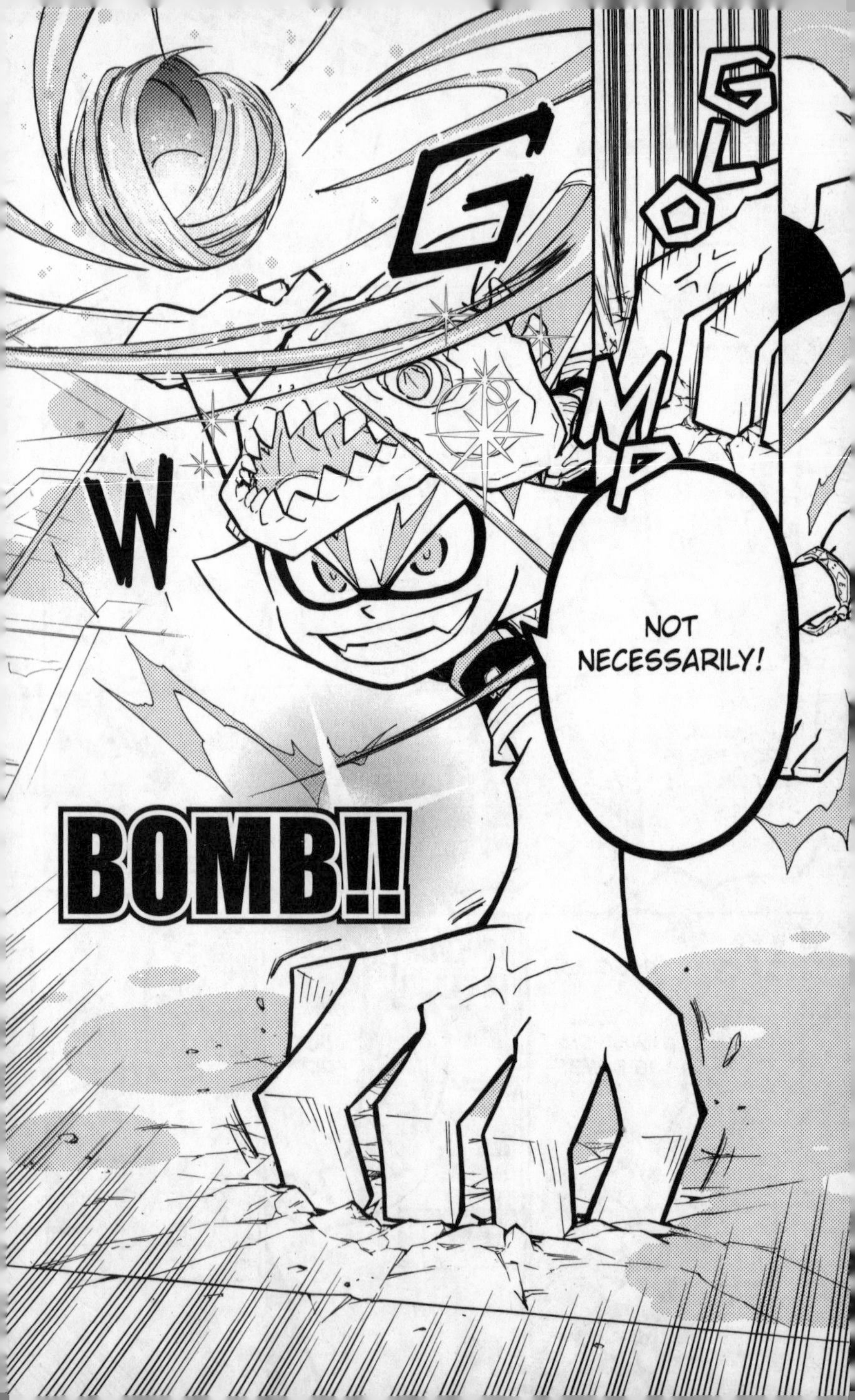
GLOMP
NOT NECESSARILY!
BOMB!!

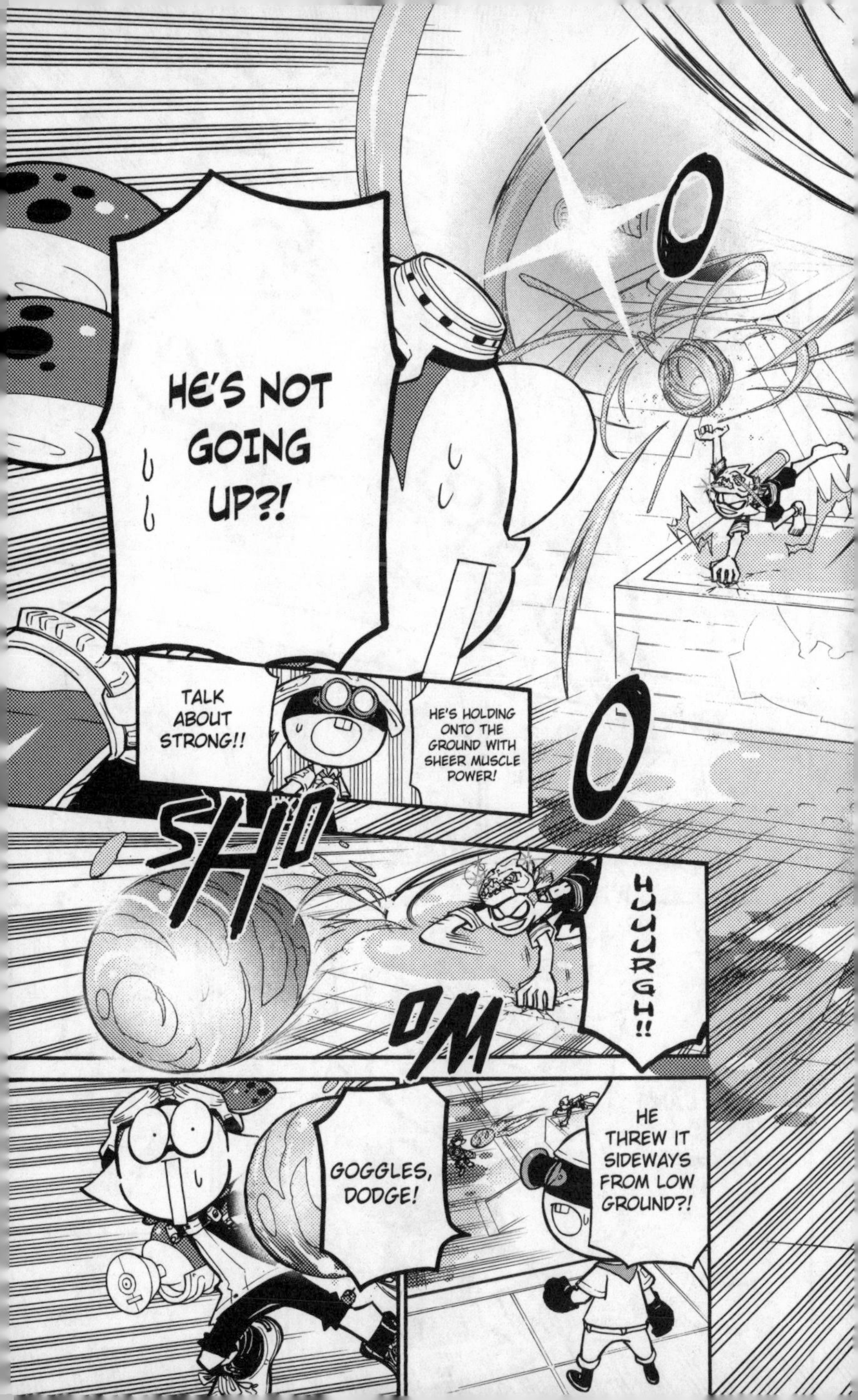
O
HE'S NOT GOING UP?!
HE'S HOLDING ONTO THE GROUND WITH SHEER MUSCLE POWER!
TALK ABOUT STRONG!!
O
HUUURGH!!
SHO
OM
HE THREW IT SIDEWAYS FROM LOW GROUND?!
GOGGLES, DODGE!

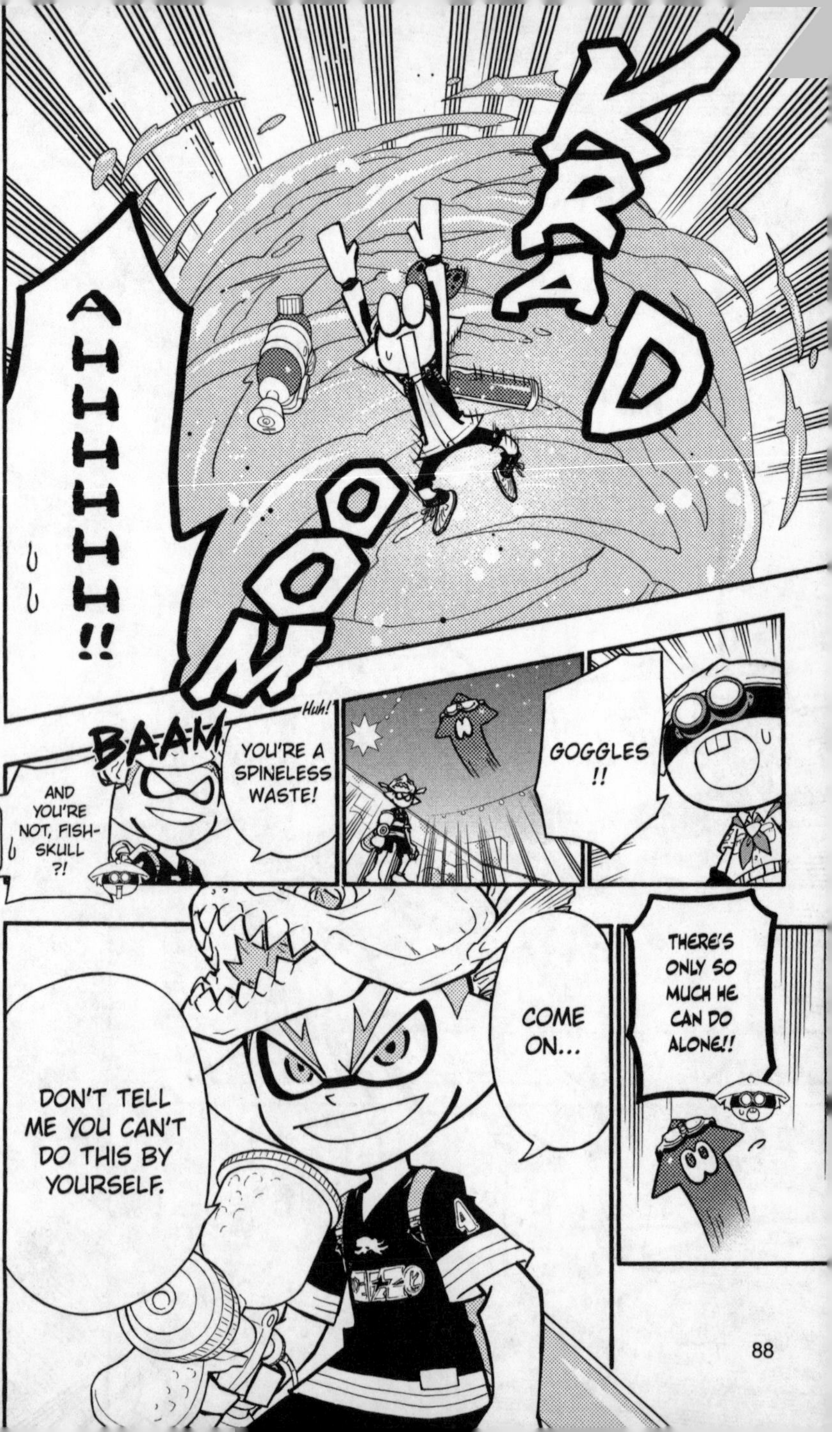
KRADOOM
AHHHHHH!!
GOGGLES!!
Huh!
YOU'RE A SPINELESS WASTE!
BAAM
AND YOU'RE NOT, FISH-SKULL?!
THERE'S ONLY SO MUCH HE CAN DO ALONE!!
COME ON...
DON'T TELL ME YOU CAN'T DO THIS BY YOURSELF.

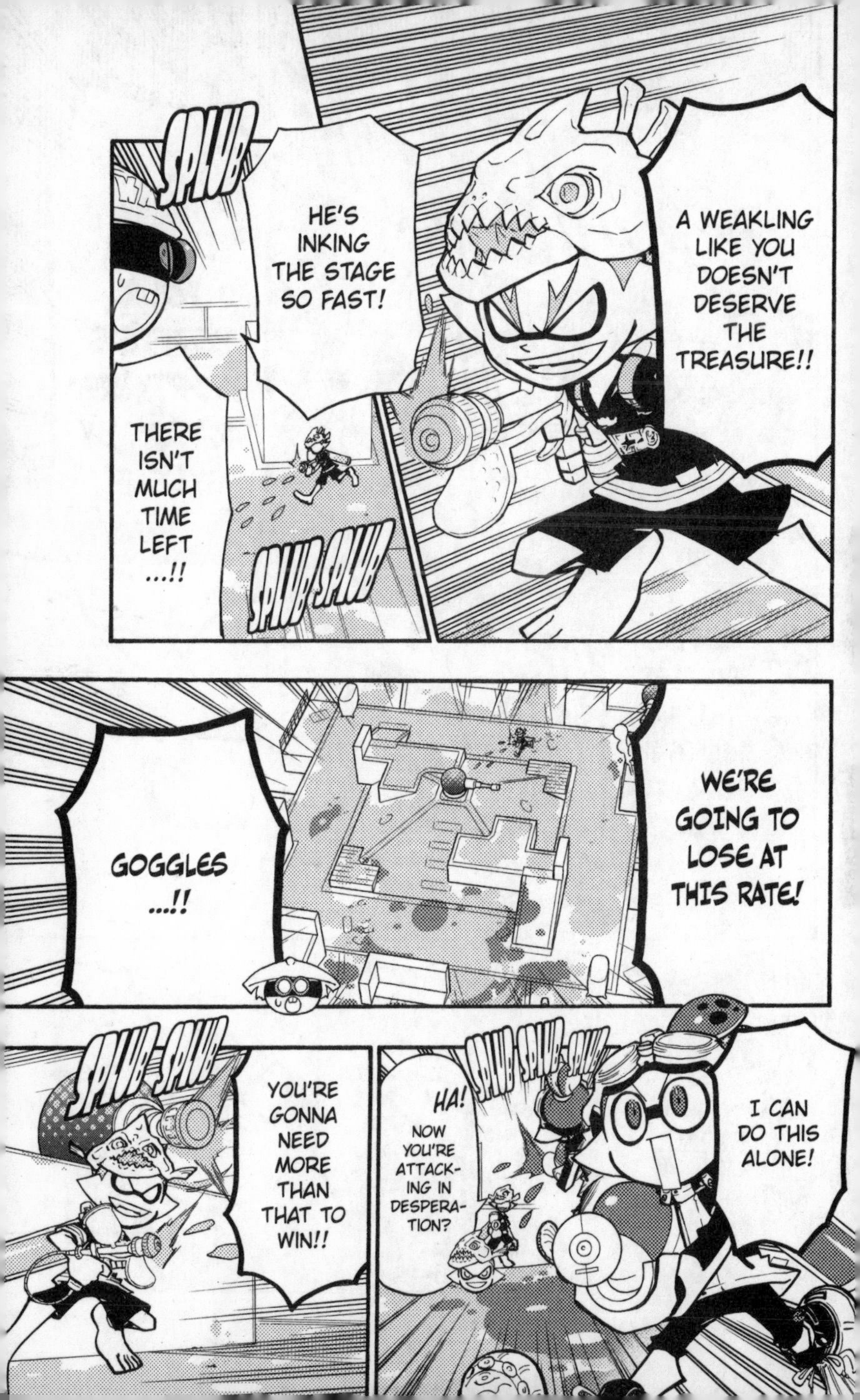
A WEAKLING LIKE YOU DOESN'T DESERVE THE TREASURE!!
SPLUB
HE'S INKING THE STAGE SO FAST!
THERE ISN'T MUCH TIME LEFT ...!!
SPLUB SPLUB
WE'RE GOING TO LOSE AT THIS RATE!
GOGGLES ...!!
I CAN DO THIS ALONE!
SPLUB SPLUB SPLUB
HA!
NOW YOU'RE ATTACKING IN DESPERATION?
SPLUB SPLUB
YOU'RE GONNA NEED MORE THAN THAT TO WIN!!

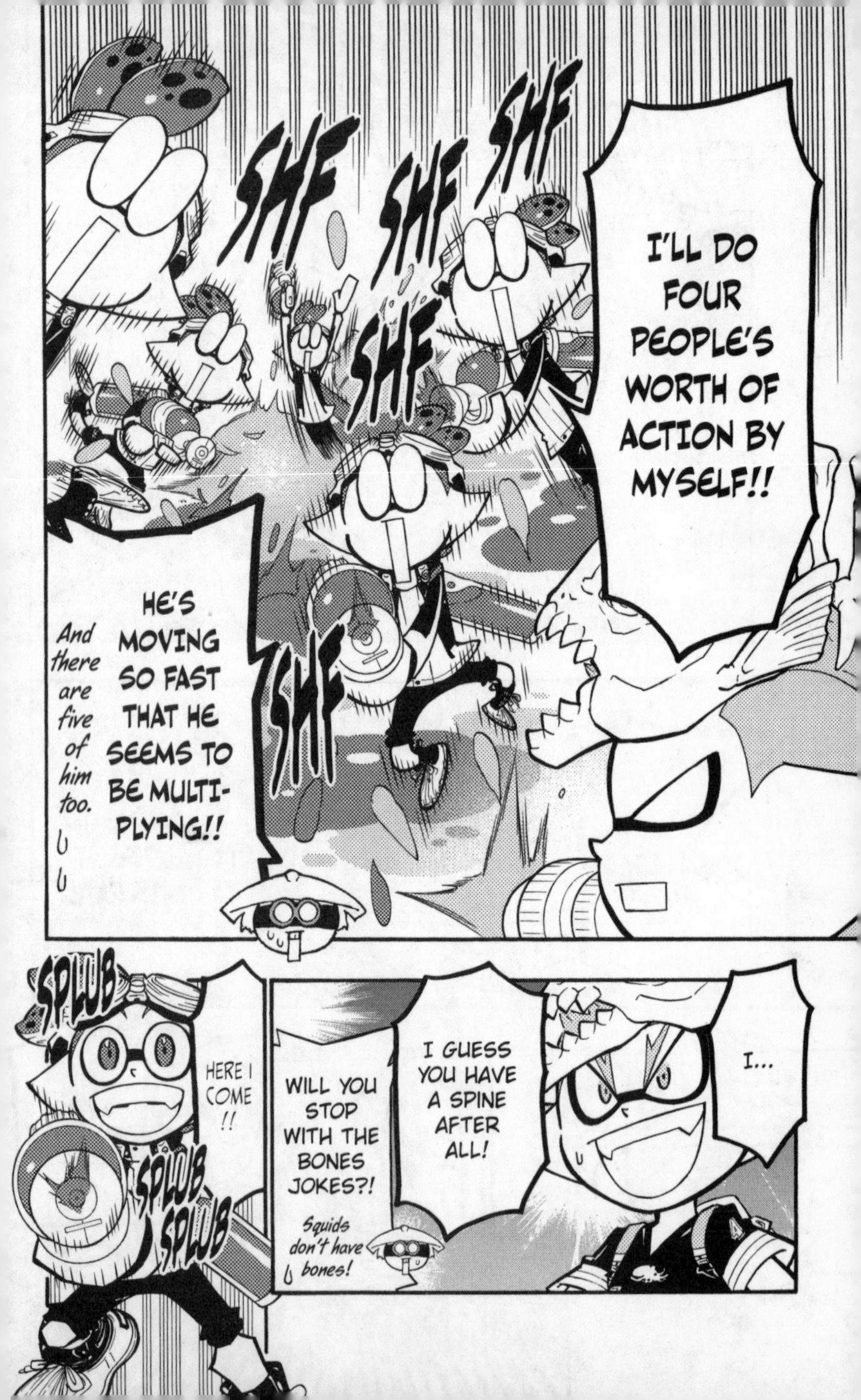
SHF SHF SHF
I'LL DO FOUR PEOPLE'S WORTH OF ACTION BY MYSELF!!
SHF
SHF
HE'S MOVING SO FAST THAT HE SEEMS TO BE MULTI-PLYING!!
And there are five of him too.
I...
I GUESS YOU HAVE A SPINE AFTER ALL!
WILL YOU STOP WITH THE BONES JOKES?!
Squids don't have bones!
SPLUB
HERE I COME!!
SPLUB SPLUB

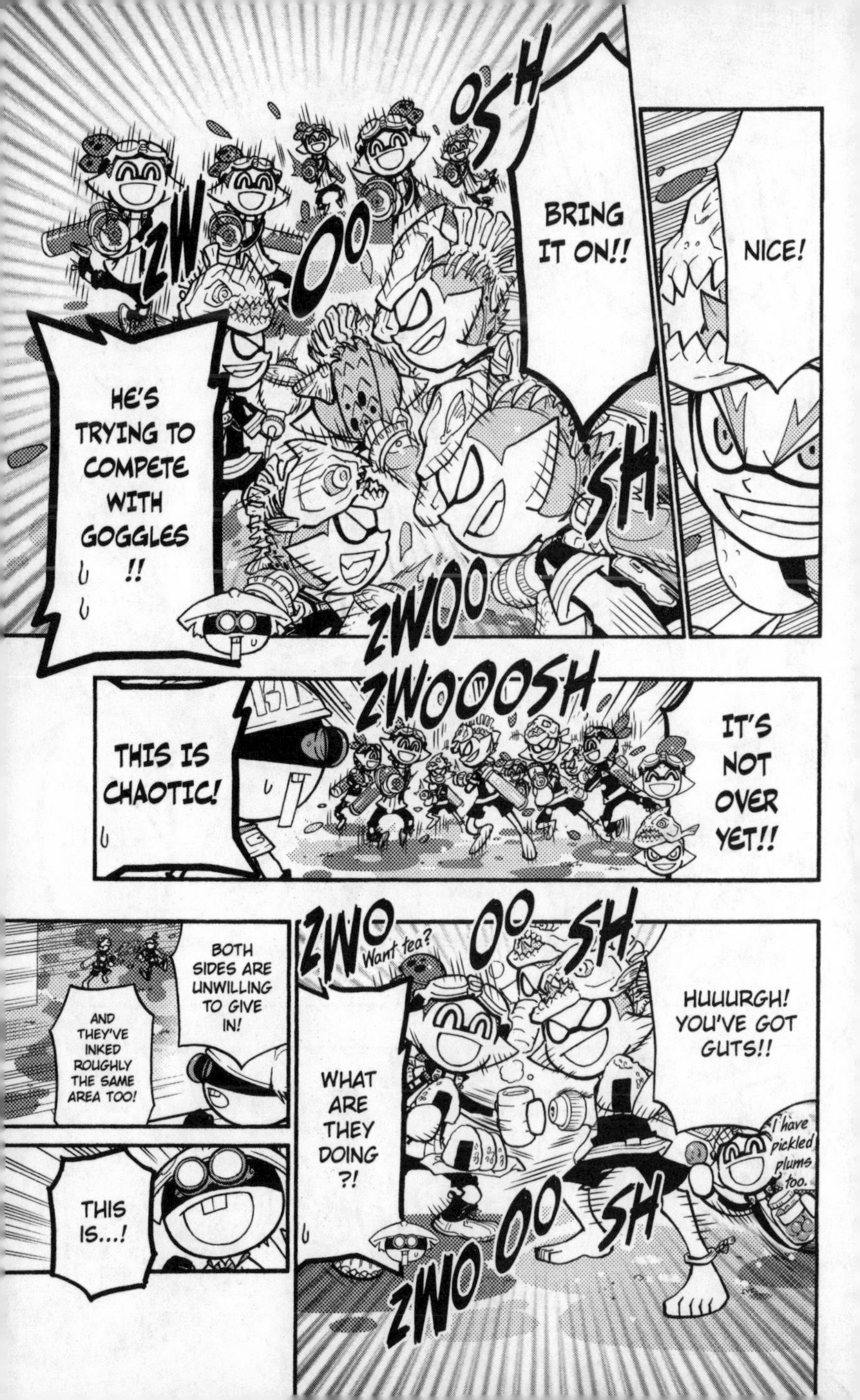
NICE!
BRING IT ON!!
ZWOOOSH
HE'S TRYING TO COMPETE WITH GOGGLES!!
SH
ZWOO
IT'S NOT OVER YET!!
ZWOOOSH
THIS IS CHAOTIC!
HUUURGH! YOU'VE GOT GUTS!!
ZWO OO SH
Want tea?
I have pickled plums too.
WHAT ARE THEY DOING?!
ZWO OO SH
BOTH SIDES ARE UNWILLING TO GIVE IN!
AND THEY'VE INKED ROUGHLY THE SAME AREA TOO!
THIS IS...!

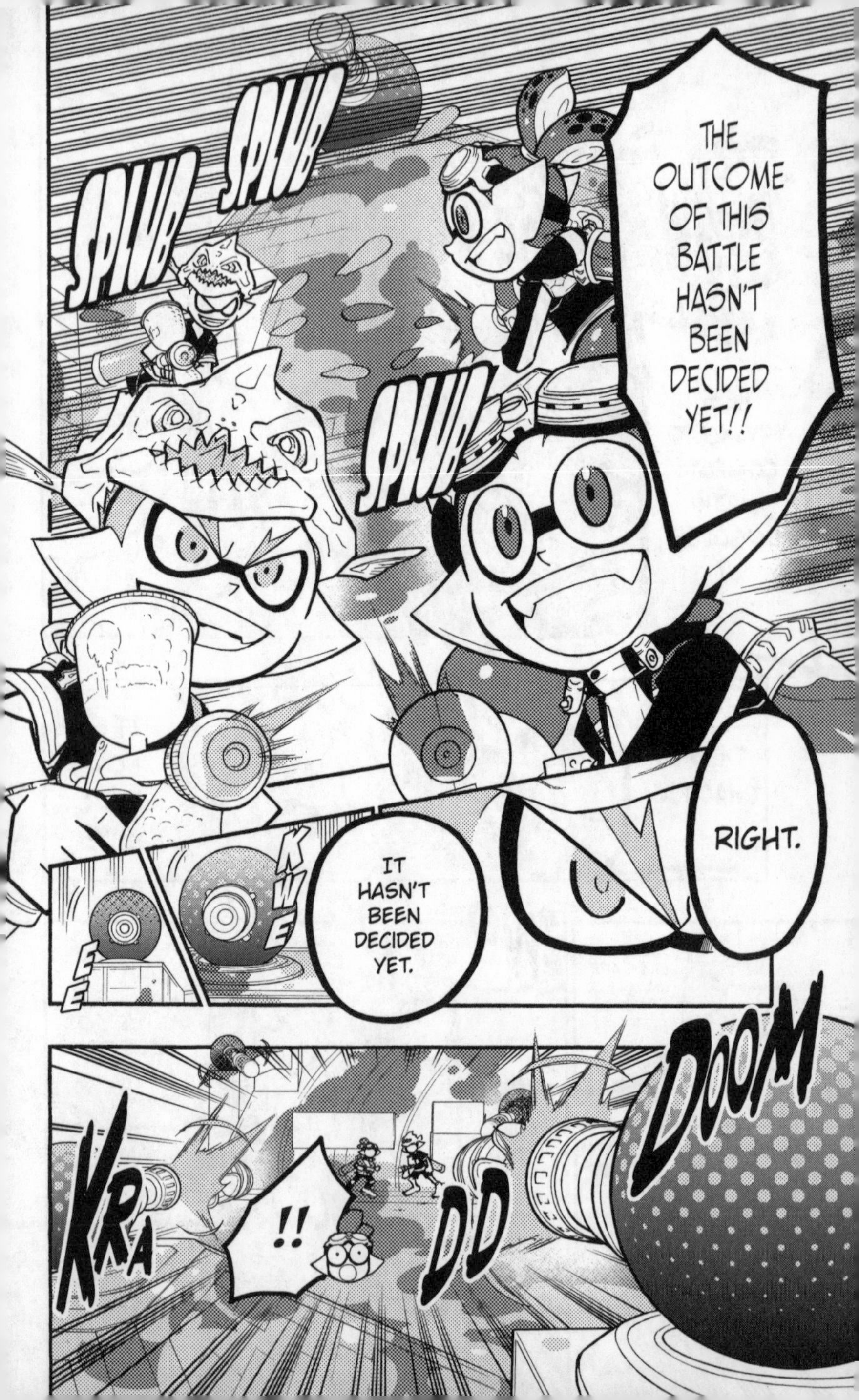
THE OUTCOME OF THIS BATTLE HASN'T BEEN DECIDED YET!!
SPLUB
SPLUB
SPLUB
RIGHT.
IT HASN'T BEEN DECIDED YET.
KWE
EE
DOOM
DD
!!
KRA

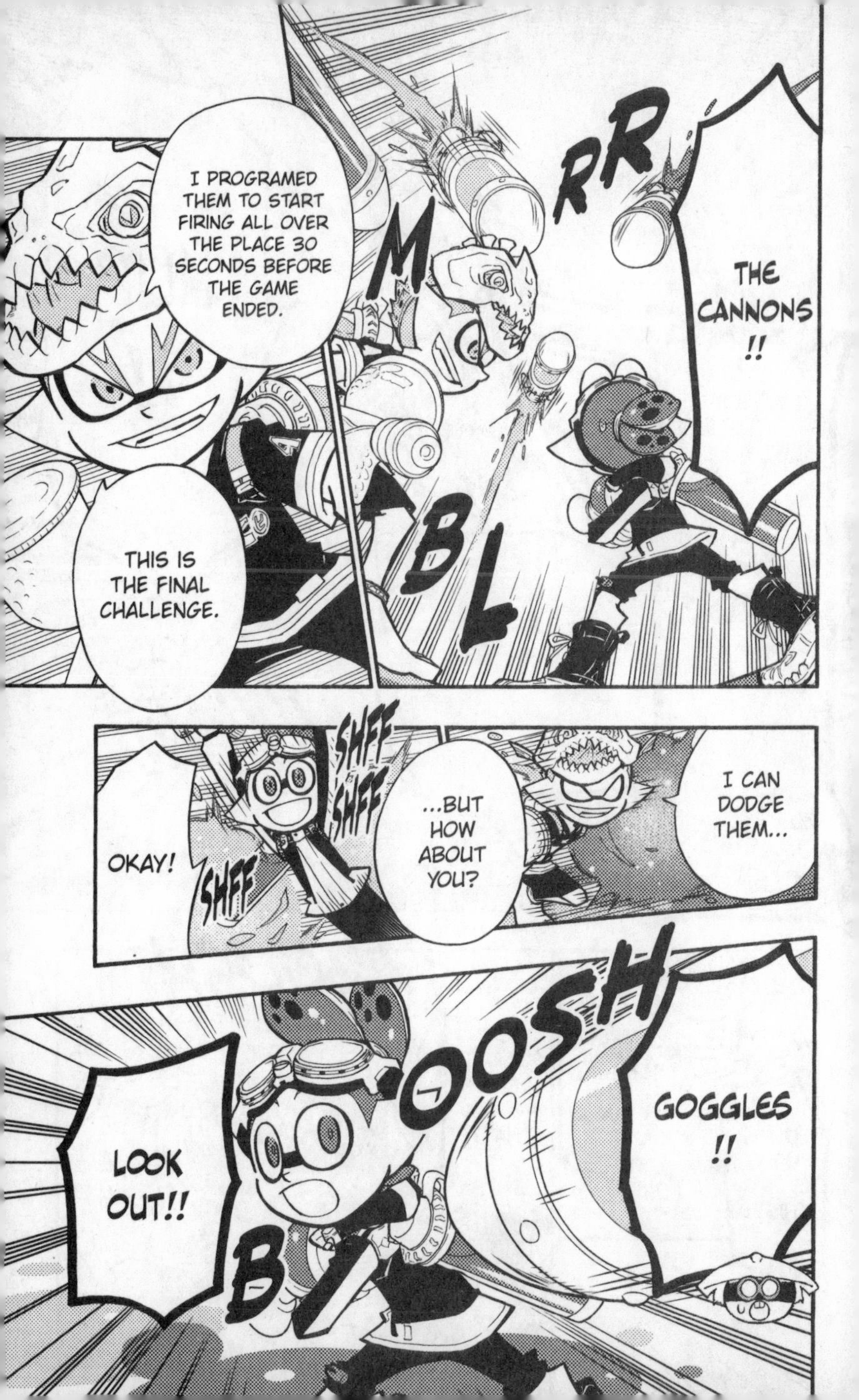
THE CANNONS !!
RRMBL
I PROGRAMED THEM TO START FIRING ALL OVER THE PLACE 30 SECONDS BEFORE THE GAME ENDED.
THIS IS THE FINAL CHALLENGE.
I CAN DODGE THEM...
...BUT HOW ABOUT YOU?
SHFF SHFF
OKAY!
SHFF
GOGGLES !!
BOOSH
LOOK OUT!!

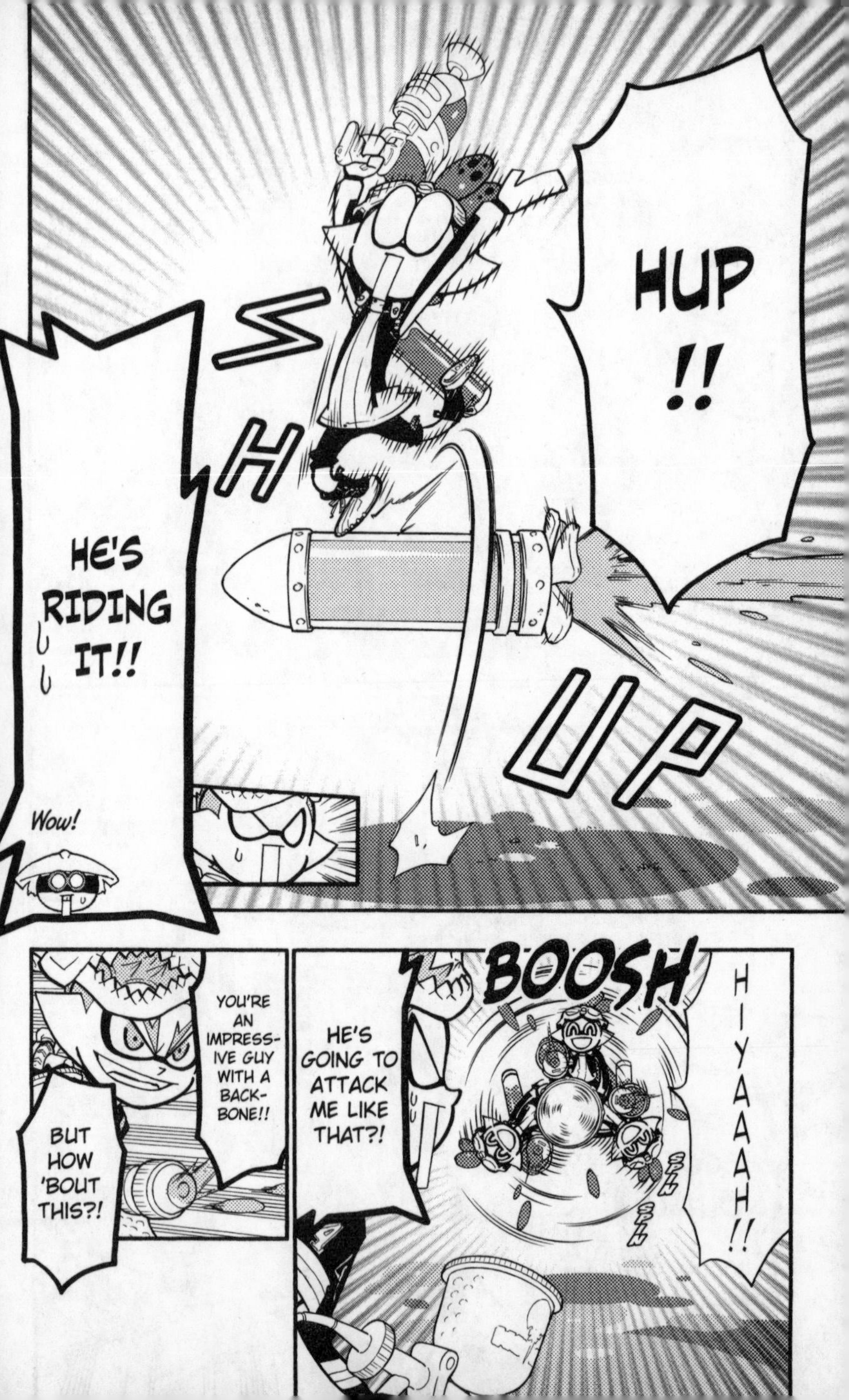
HUP!!
SH
UP
HE'S RIDING IT!!
Wow!
BOOSH
HIYAAAAH!!
SPIN SPIN
HE'S GOING TO ATTACK ME LIKE THAT?!
YOU'RE AN IMPRESSIVE GUY WITH A BACKBONE!!
BUT HOW 'BOUT THIS?!

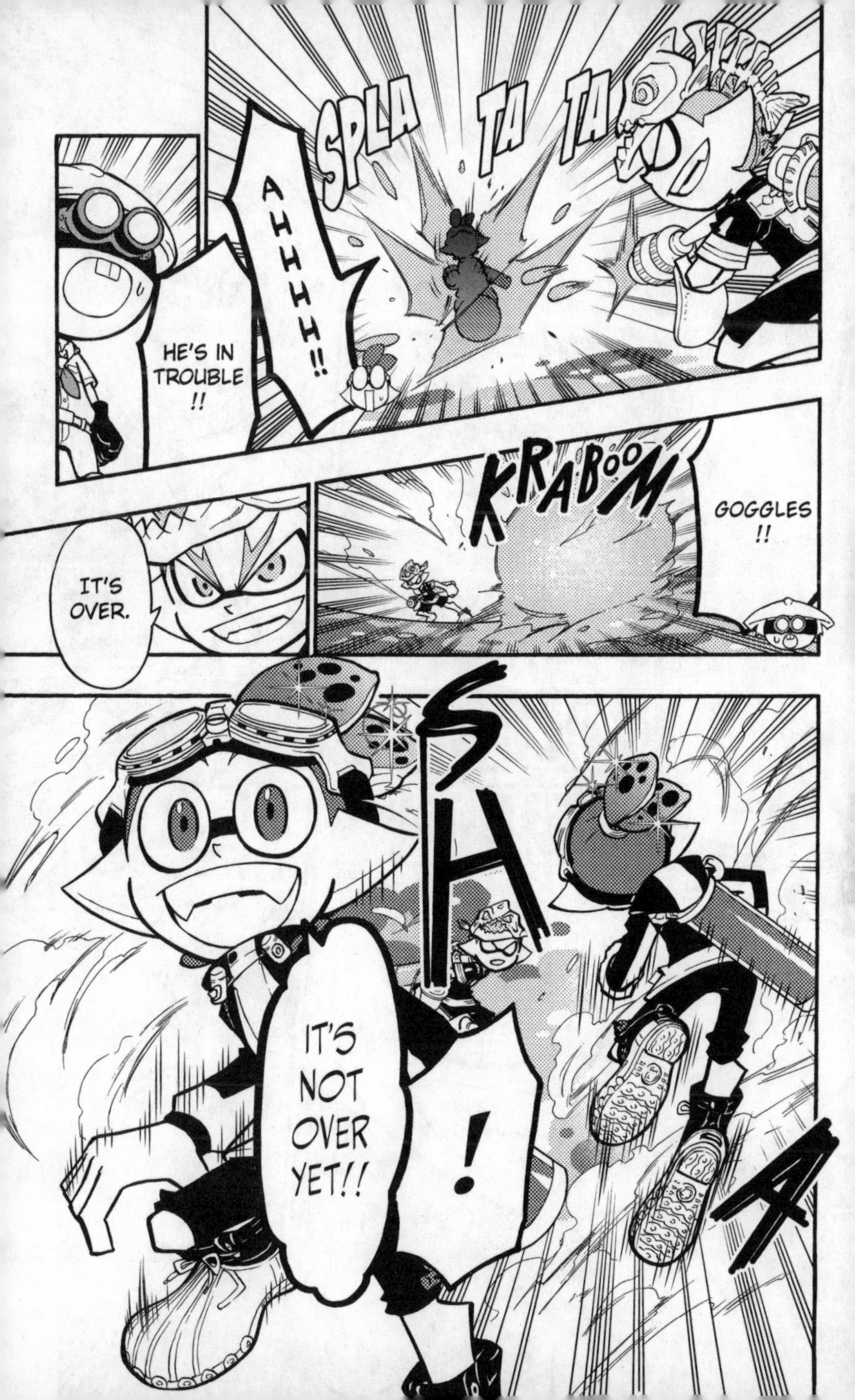
SPLA TA TA
AHHHH!!
HE'S IN TROUBLE!!
KRABOOM
GOGGLES!!
IT'S OVER.
SHA
!
IT'S NOT OVER YET!!

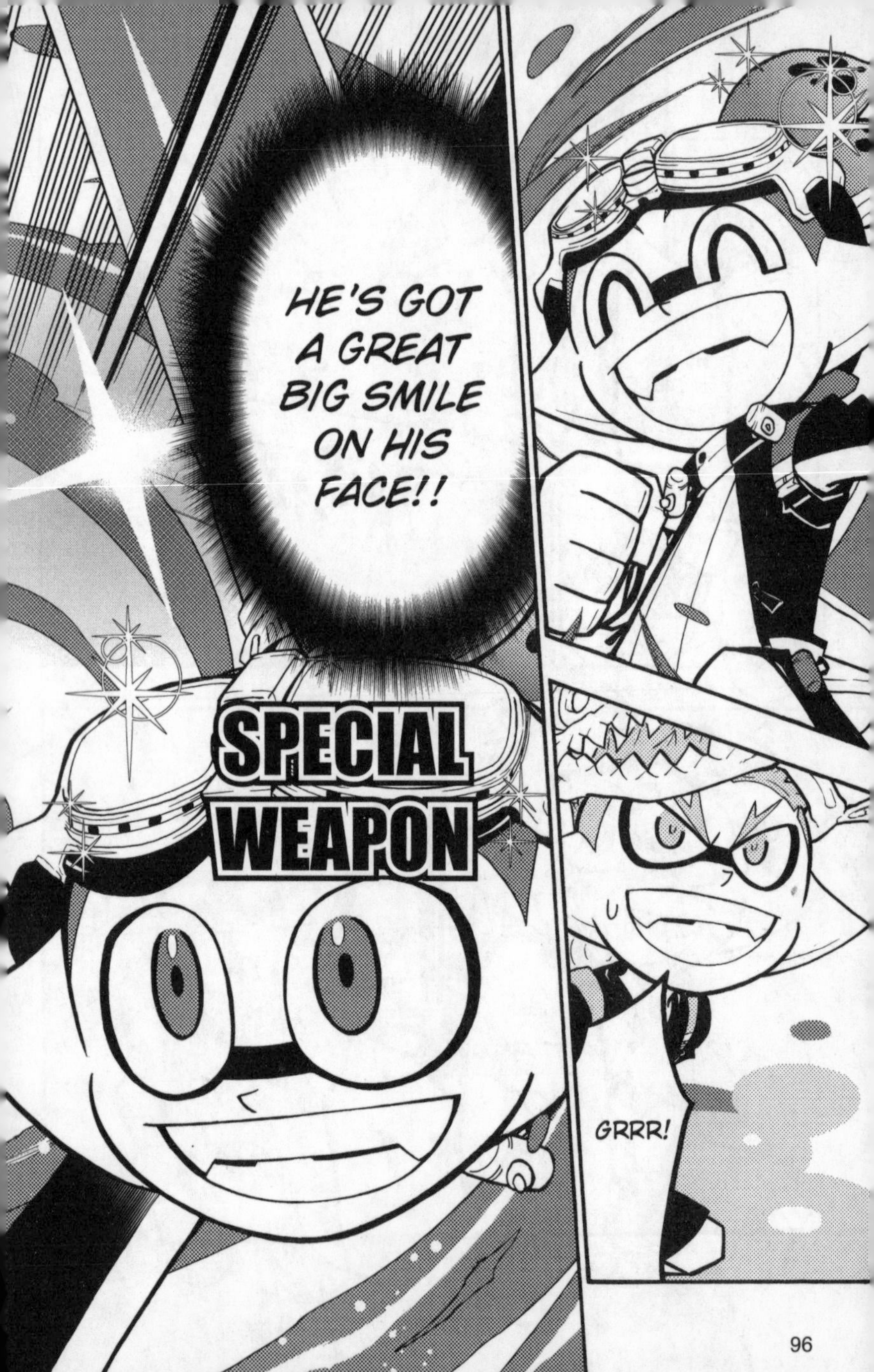
GRRR!
HE'S GOT A GREAT BIG SMILE ON HIS FACE!!
SPECIAL WEAPON

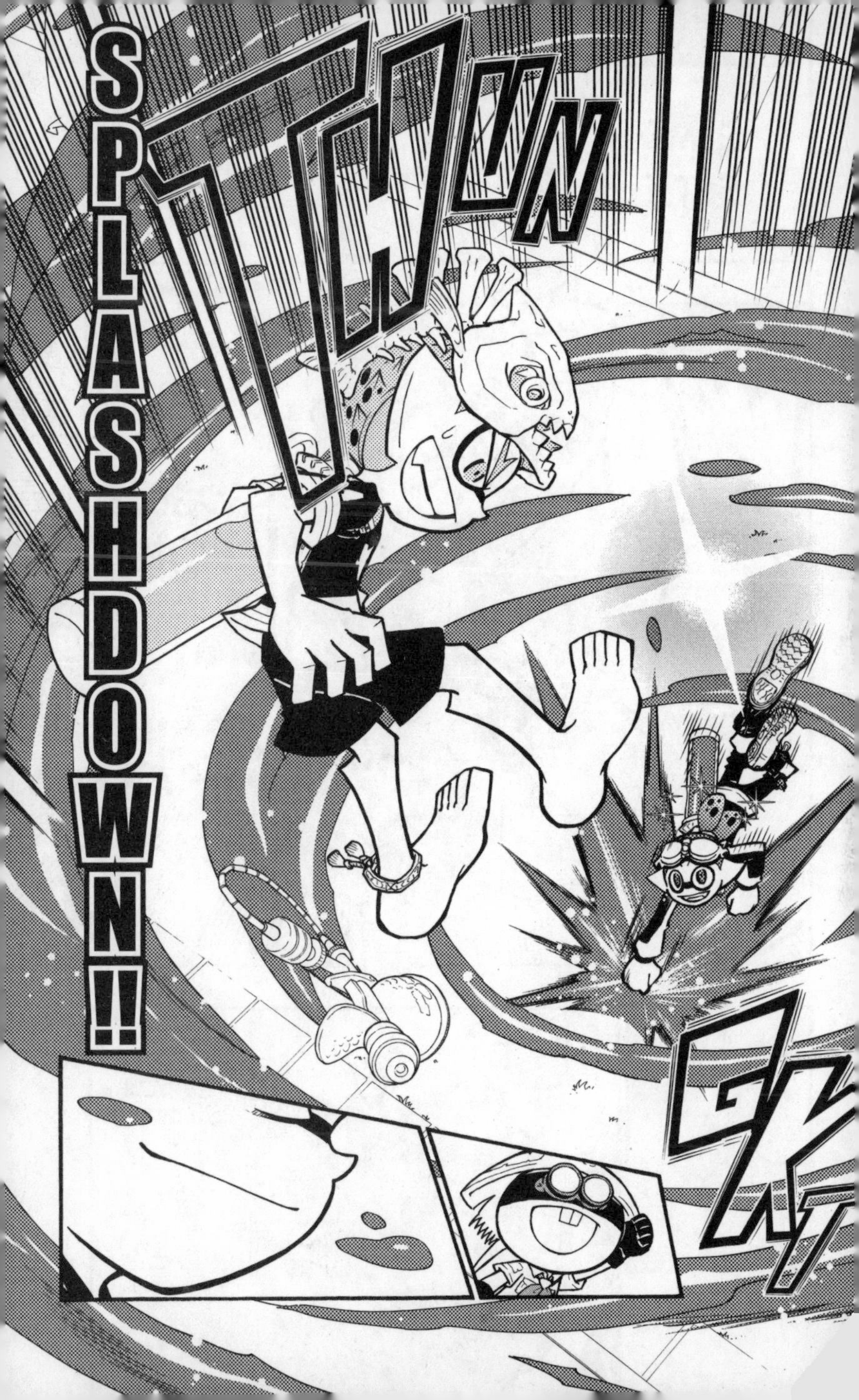
TCHUN
SPLASHDOWN!!
GZT

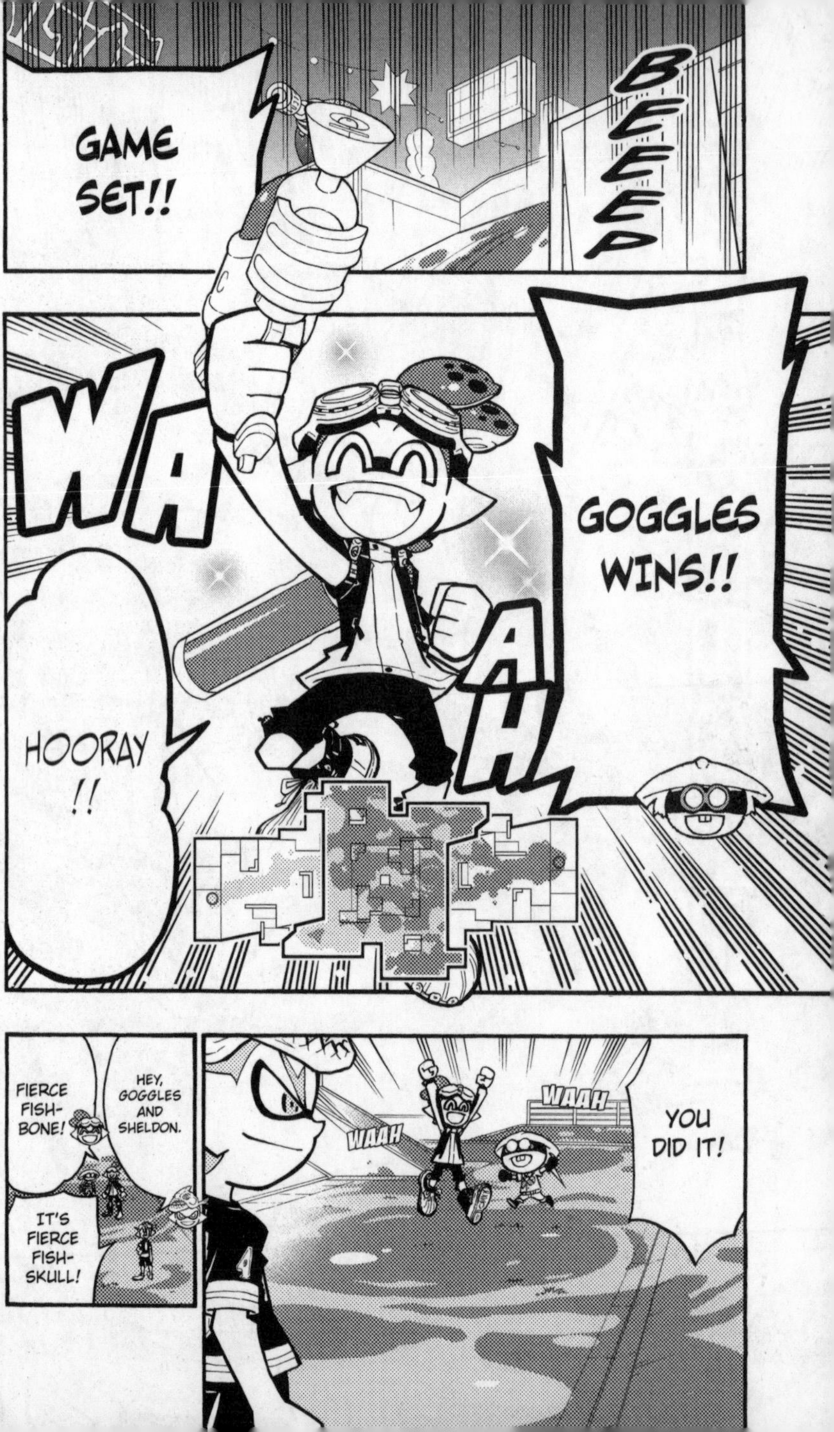
BEEEP
GAME SET!!
GOGGLES WINS!!
WAAAH
HOORAY!!
YOU DID IT!
WAAH
WAAH
HEY, GOGGLES AND SHELDON.
FIERCE FISH-BONE!
IT'S FIERCE FISH-SKULL!

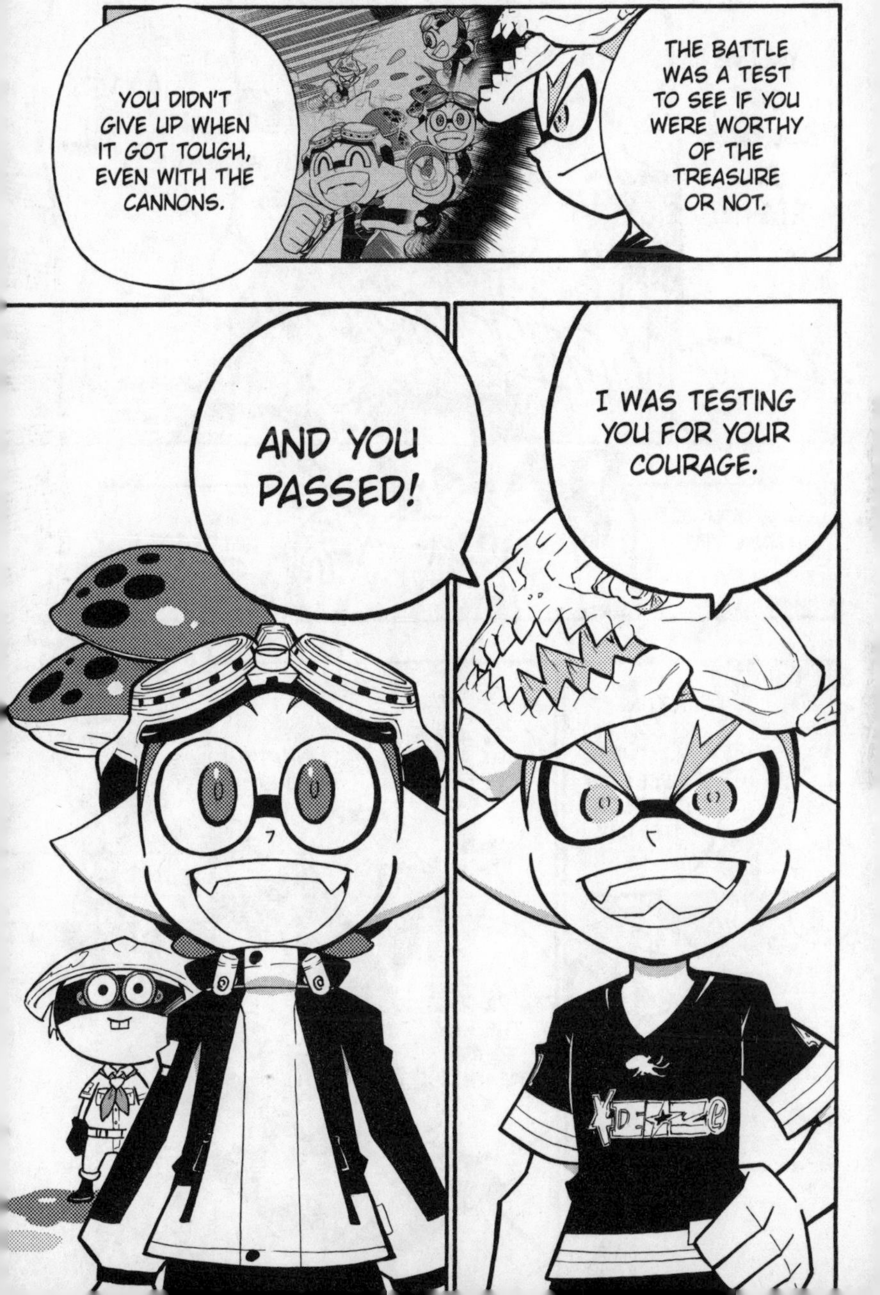
THE BATTLE WAS A TEST TO SEE IF YOU WERE WORTHY OF THE TREASURE OR NOT.
YOU DIDN'T GIVE UP WHEN IT GOT TOUGH, EVEN WITH THE CANNONS.
I WAS TESTING YOU FOR YOUR COURAGE.
AND YOU PASSED!

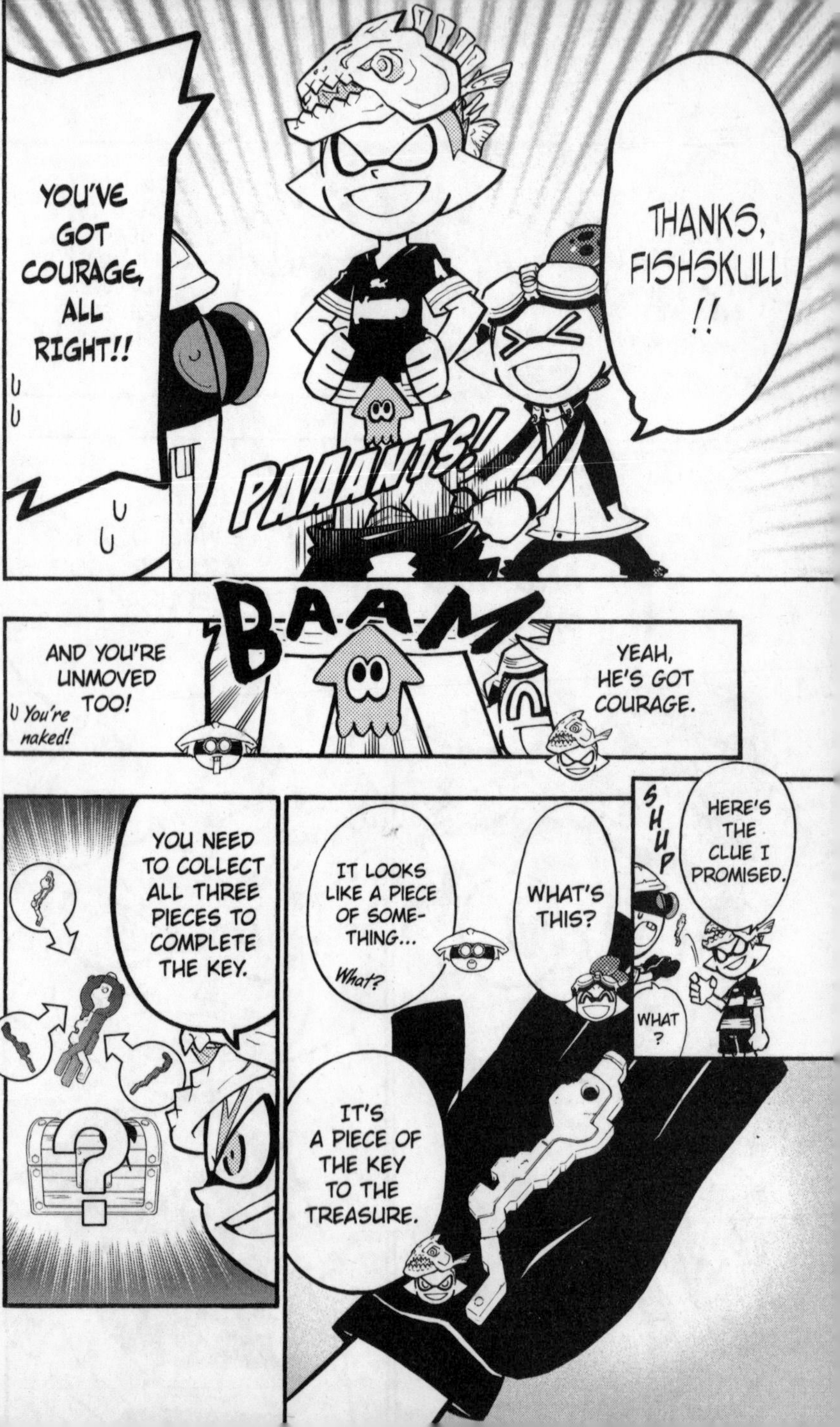
THANKS, FISHSKULL!!
PAAANTS!
YOU'VE GOT COURAGE, ALL RIGHT!!
YEAH, HE'S GOT COURAGE.
BAAM
AND YOU'RE UNMOVED TOO!
You're naked!
SHUP
HERE'S THE CLUE I PROMISED.
WHAT?
WHAT'S THIS?
IT LOOKS LIKE A PIECE OF SOME-THING...
What?
IT'S A PIECE OF THE KEY TO THE TREASURE.
YOU NEED TO COLLECT ALL THREE PIECES TO COMPLETE THE KEY.

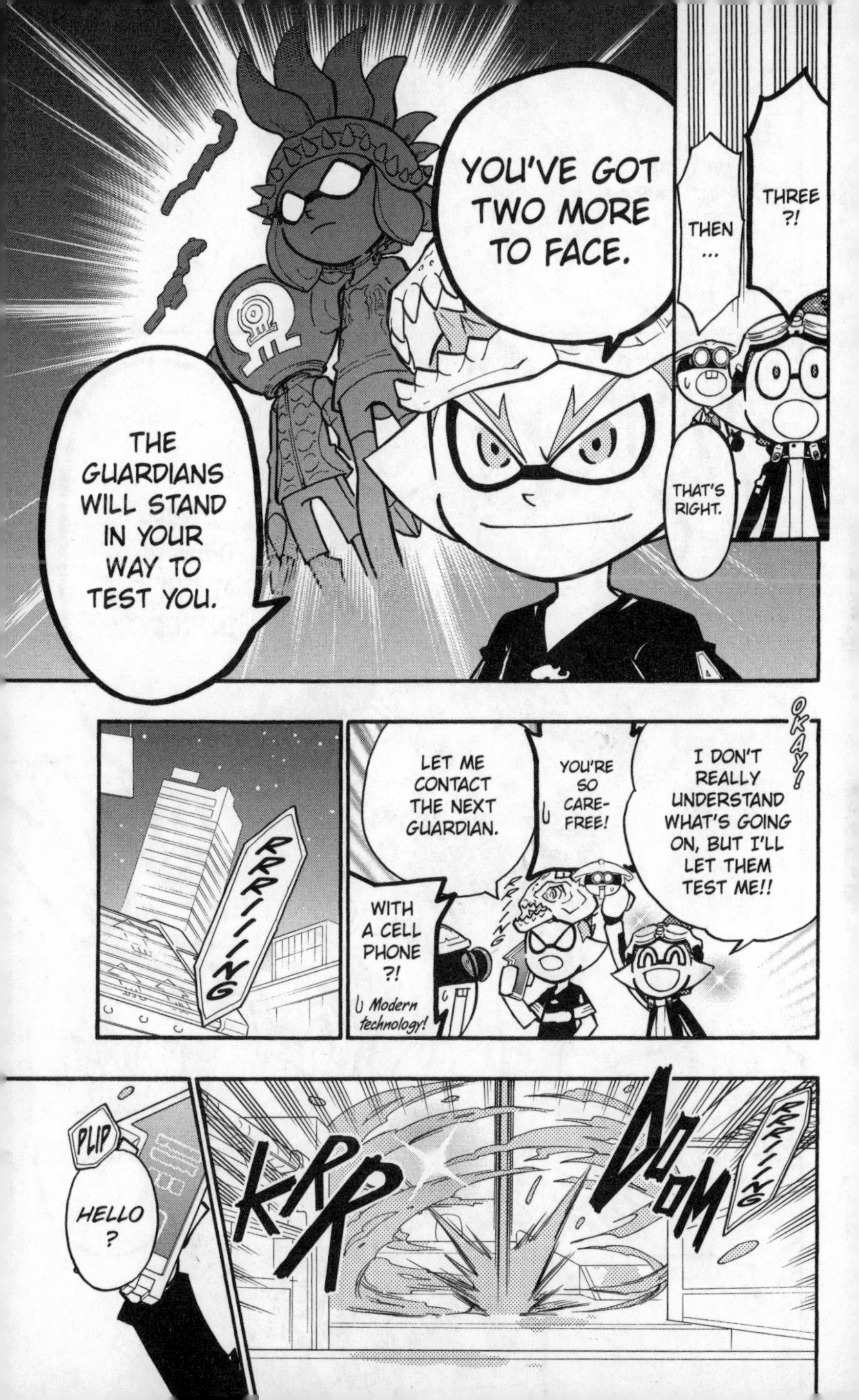
THREE?!
THEN...
THAT'S RIGHT.
YOU'VE GOT TWO MORE TO FACE.
THE GUARDIANS WILL STAND IN YOUR WAY TO TEST YOU.
OKAY!
I DON'T REALLY UNDERSTAND WHAT'S GOING ON, BUT I'LL LET THEM TEST ME!!
YOU'RE SO CARE-FREE!
LET ME CONTACT THE NEXT GUARDIAN.
WITH A CELL PHONE?!
Modern technology!
RRRIIIING
RRRIIIING
DOOM
KRP
PLIP
HELLO?

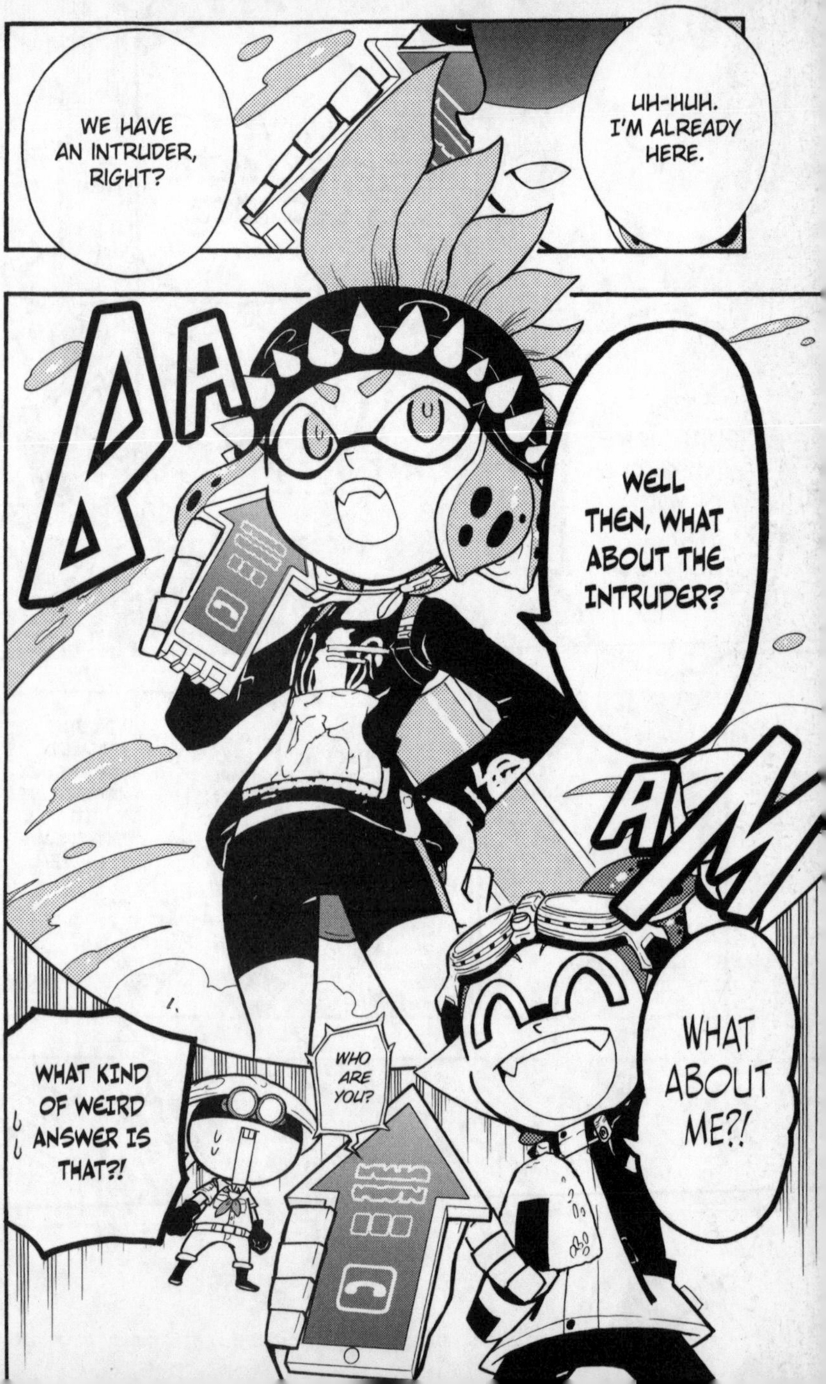
UH-HUH. I'M ALREADY HERE.
WE HAVE AN INTRUDER, RIGHT?
BAAM
WELL THEN, WHAT ABOUT THE INTRUDER?
WHAT ABOUT ME?!
WHO ARE YOU?
WHAT KIND OF WEIRD ANSWER IS THAT?!

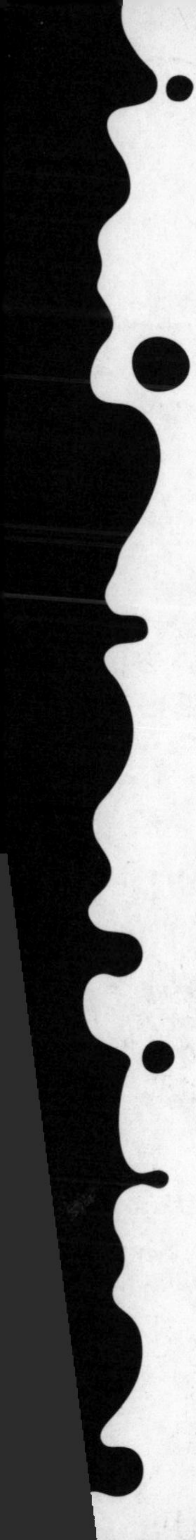

Meanwhile,
back at
Ammo Knights...

Why do
I have to
do this...?

← Watching over
the shop.

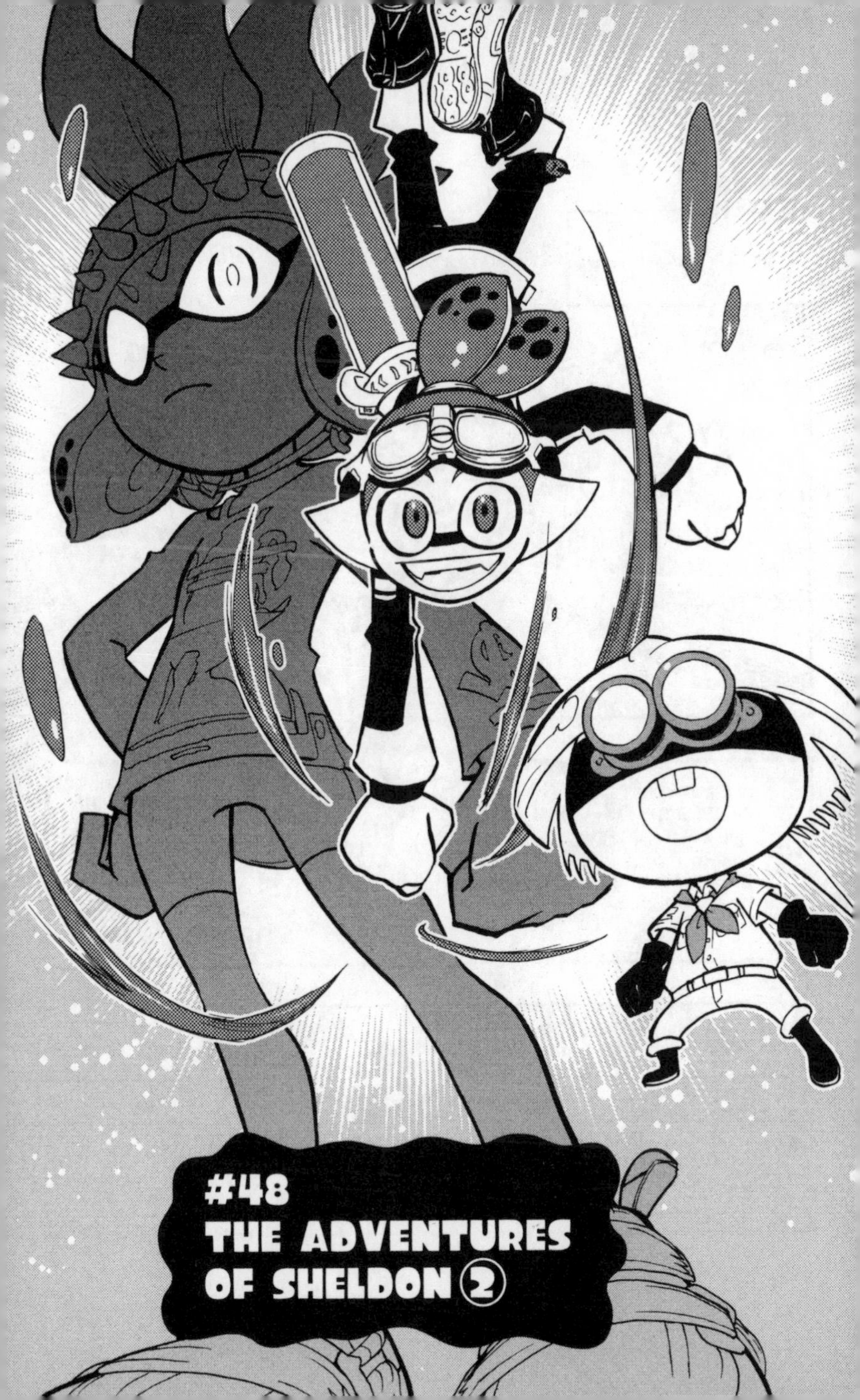
#48
THE ADVENTURES
OF SHELDON ②

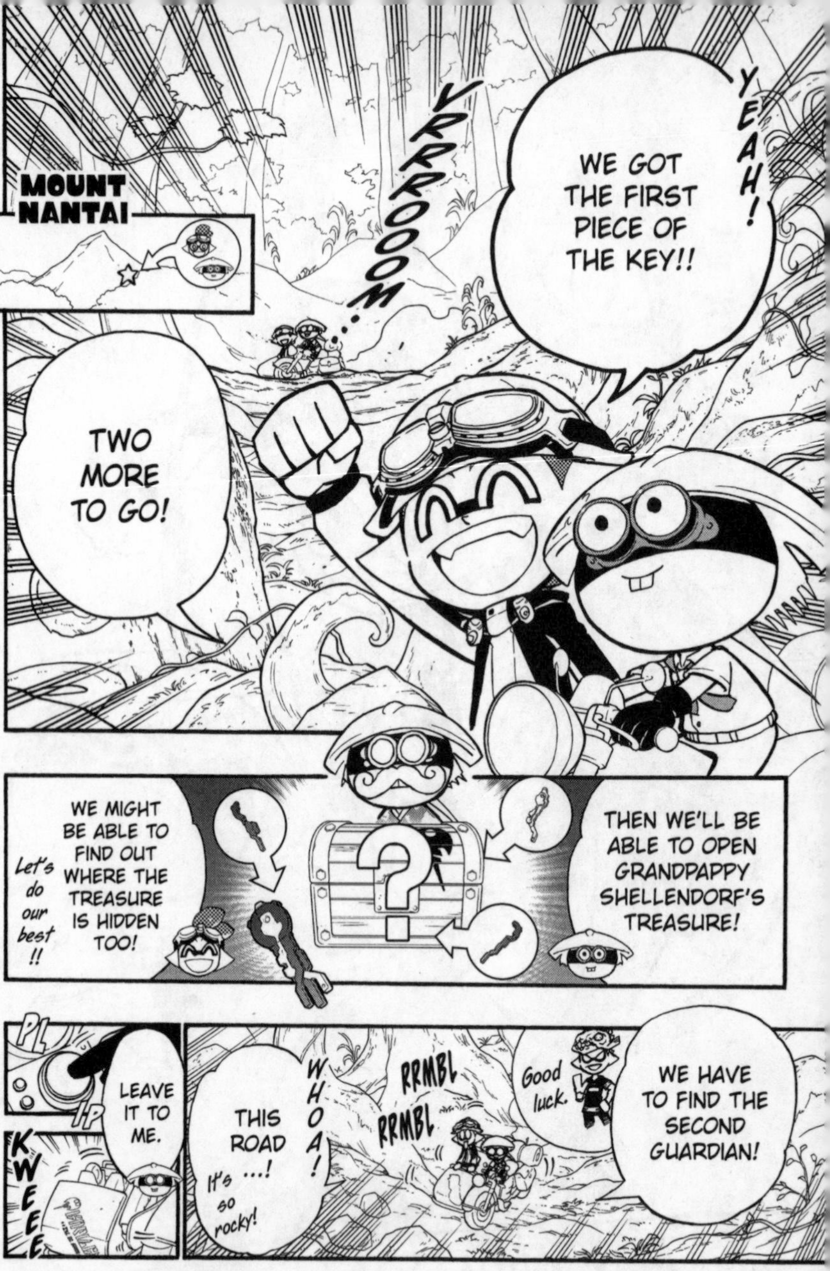
YEAH!
WE GOT THE FIRST PIECE OF THE KEY!!
VRRROOOOM...
MOUNT NANTAI
TWO MORE TO GO!
THEN WE'LL BE ABLE TO OPEN GRANDPAPPY SHELLENDORF'S TREASURE!
WE MIGHT BE ABLE TO FIND OUT WHERE THE TREASURE IS HIDDEN TOO!
Let's do our best!!
WE HAVE TO FIND THE SECOND GUARDIAN!
Good luck.
RRMBL
RRMBL
WHOA!
THIS ROAD ...!
It's so rocky!
LEAVE IT TO ME.
KWEEE

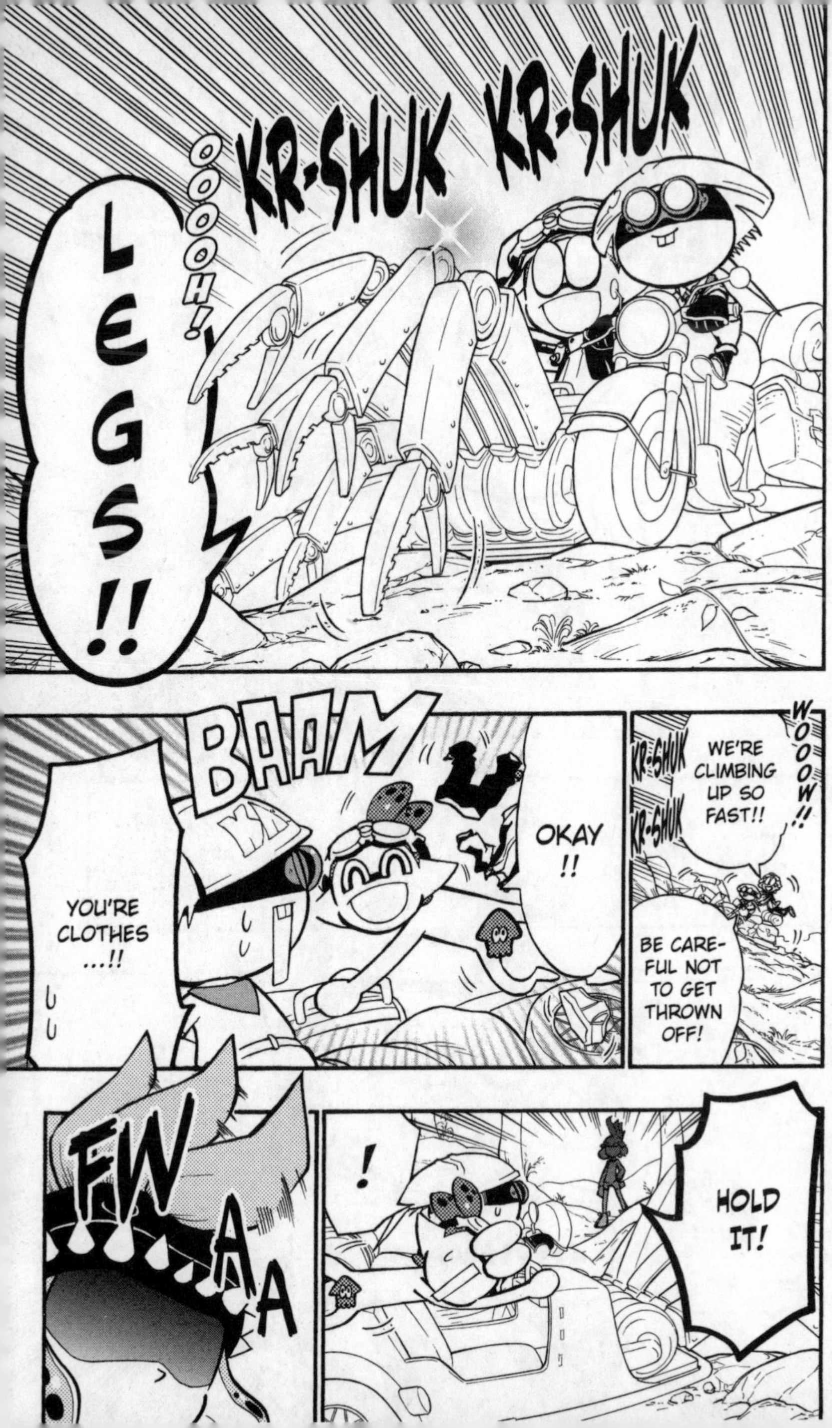
KR-SHUK KR-SHUK
OOOOOH!
LEGS!!
WOOOOW!!
WE'RE CLIMBING UP SO FAST!!
KR-SHUK
KR-SHUK
BE CARE-FUL NOT TO GET THROWN OFF!
BAAM
OKAY!!
YOU'RE CLOTHES...!!
HOLD IT!
!
FWAAA

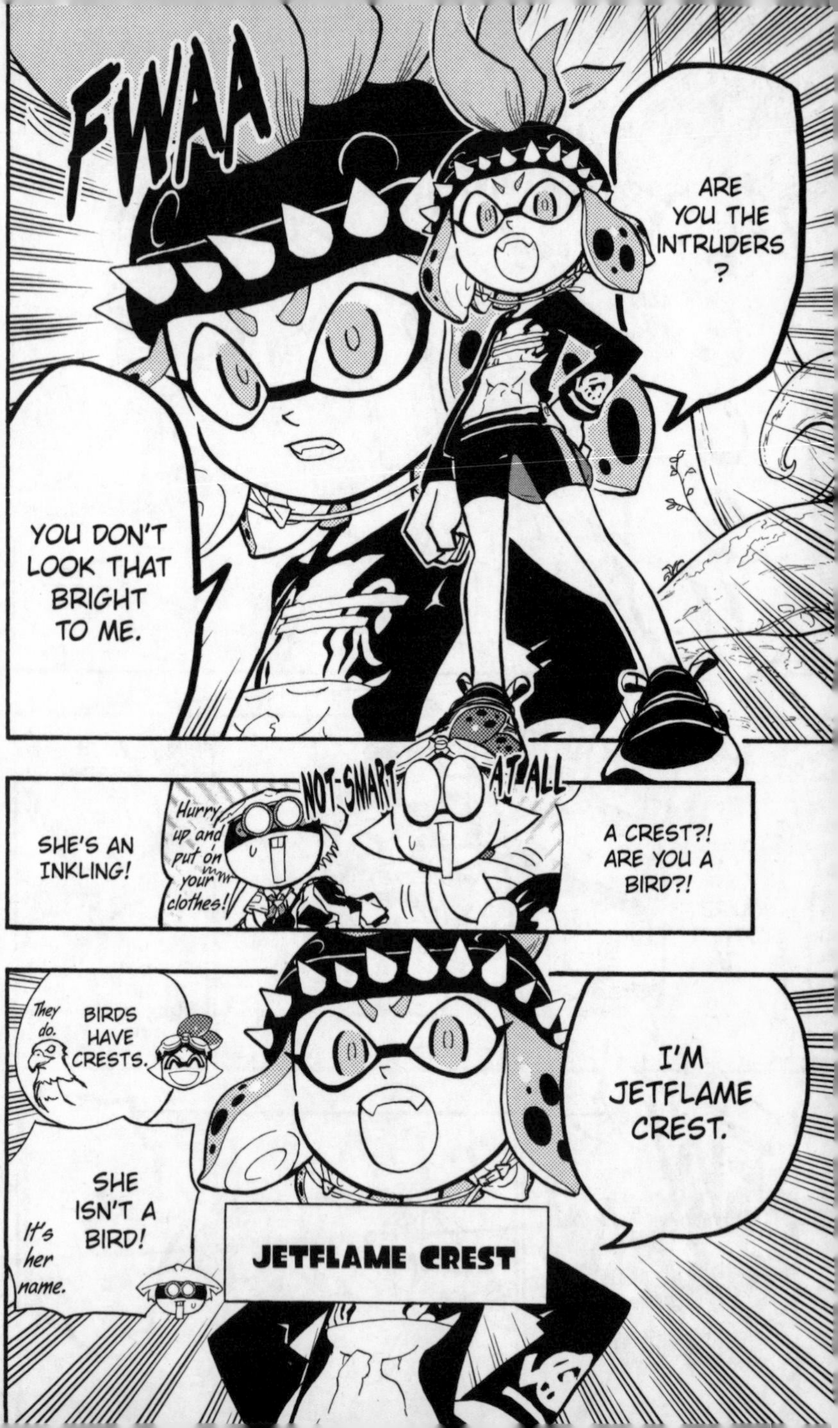
FWAA
ARE YOU THE INTRUDERS?
YOU DON'T LOOK THAT BRIGHT TO ME.
A CREST?! ARE YOU A BIRD?!
NOT-SMART AT ALL
Hurry up and put on your clothes!
SHE'S AN INKLING!
I'M JETFLAME CREST.
JETFLAME CREST
BIRDS HAVE CRESTS.
They do.
SHE ISN'T A BIRD!
It's her name.

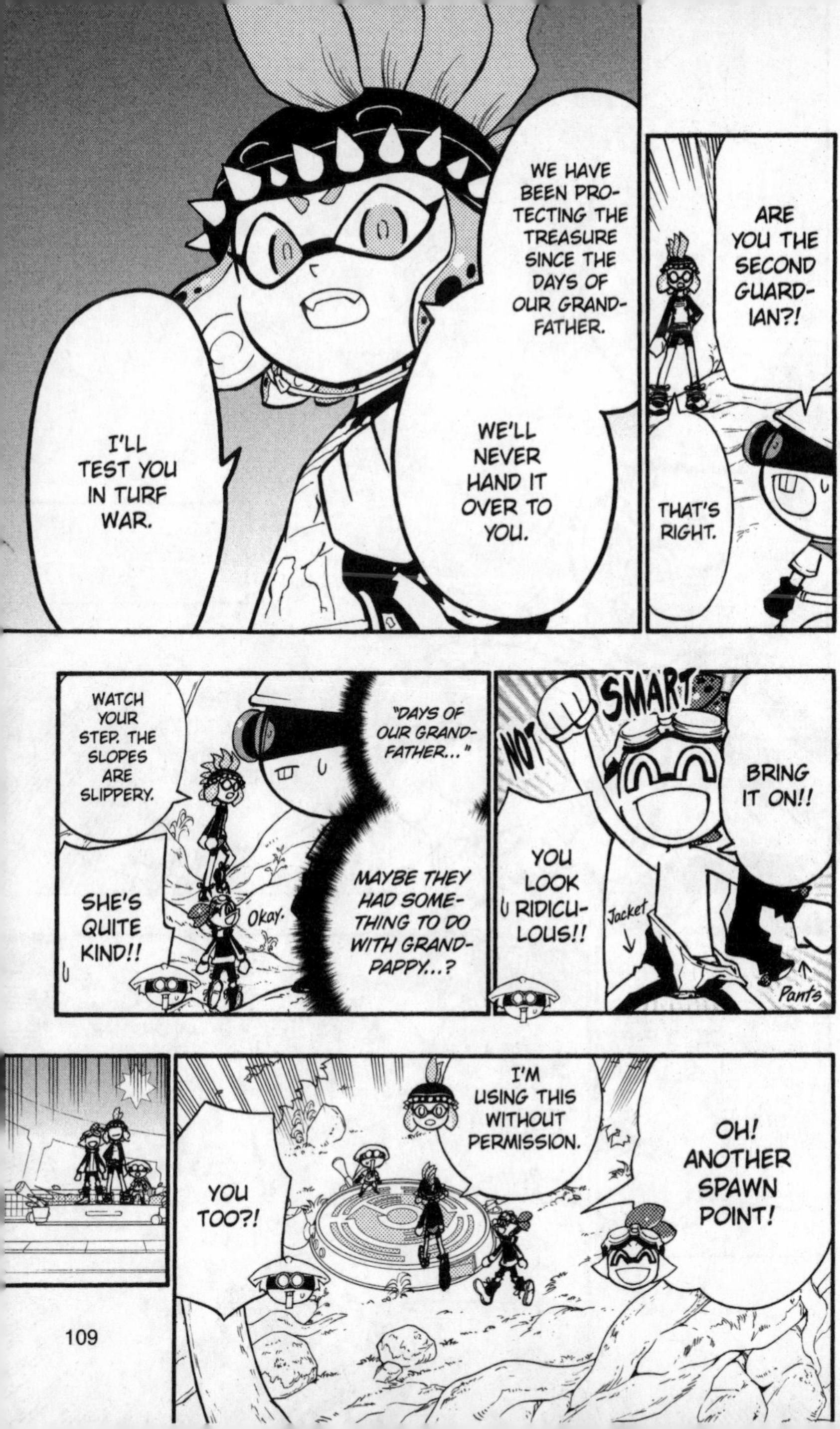
ARE YOU THE SECOND GUARDIAN?!
THAT'S RIGHT.
WE HAVE BEEN PROTECTING THE TREASURE SINCE THE DAYS OF OUR GRANDFATHER.
WE'LL NEVER HAND IT OVER TO YOU.
I'LL TEST YOU IN TURF WAR.
BRING IT ON!!
SMART
NOT
YOU LOOK RIDICULOUS!!
Jacket
Pants
"DAYS OF OUR GRANDFATHER..."
WATCH YOUR STEP. THE SLOPES ARE SLIPPERY.
MAYBE THEY HAD SOMETHING TO DO WITH GRANDPAPPY...?
Okay.
SHE'S QUITE KIND!!
OH! ANOTHER SPAWN POINT!
I'M USING THIS WITHOUT PERMISSION.
YOU TOO?!

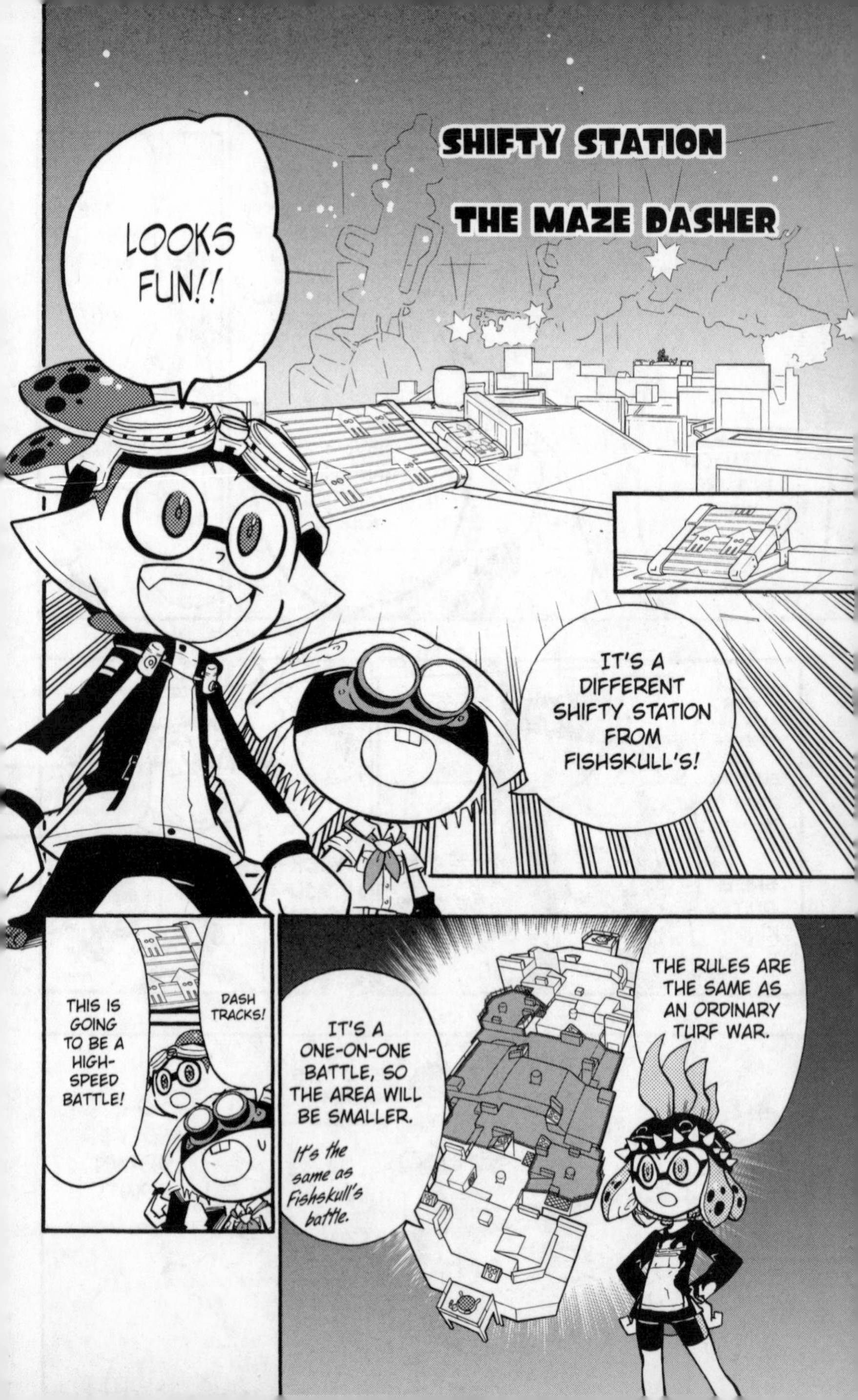

SHIFTY STATION
THE MAZE DASHER
LOOKS FUN!!
IT'S A DIFFERENT SHIFTY STATION FROM FISHSKULL'S!
THE RULES ARE THE SAME AS AN ORDINARY TURF WAR.
IT'S A ONE-ON-ONE BATTLE, SO THE AREA WILL BE SMALLER.
It's the same as Fishskull's battle.
DASH TRACKS!
THIS IS GOING TO BE A HIGH-SPEED BATTLE!

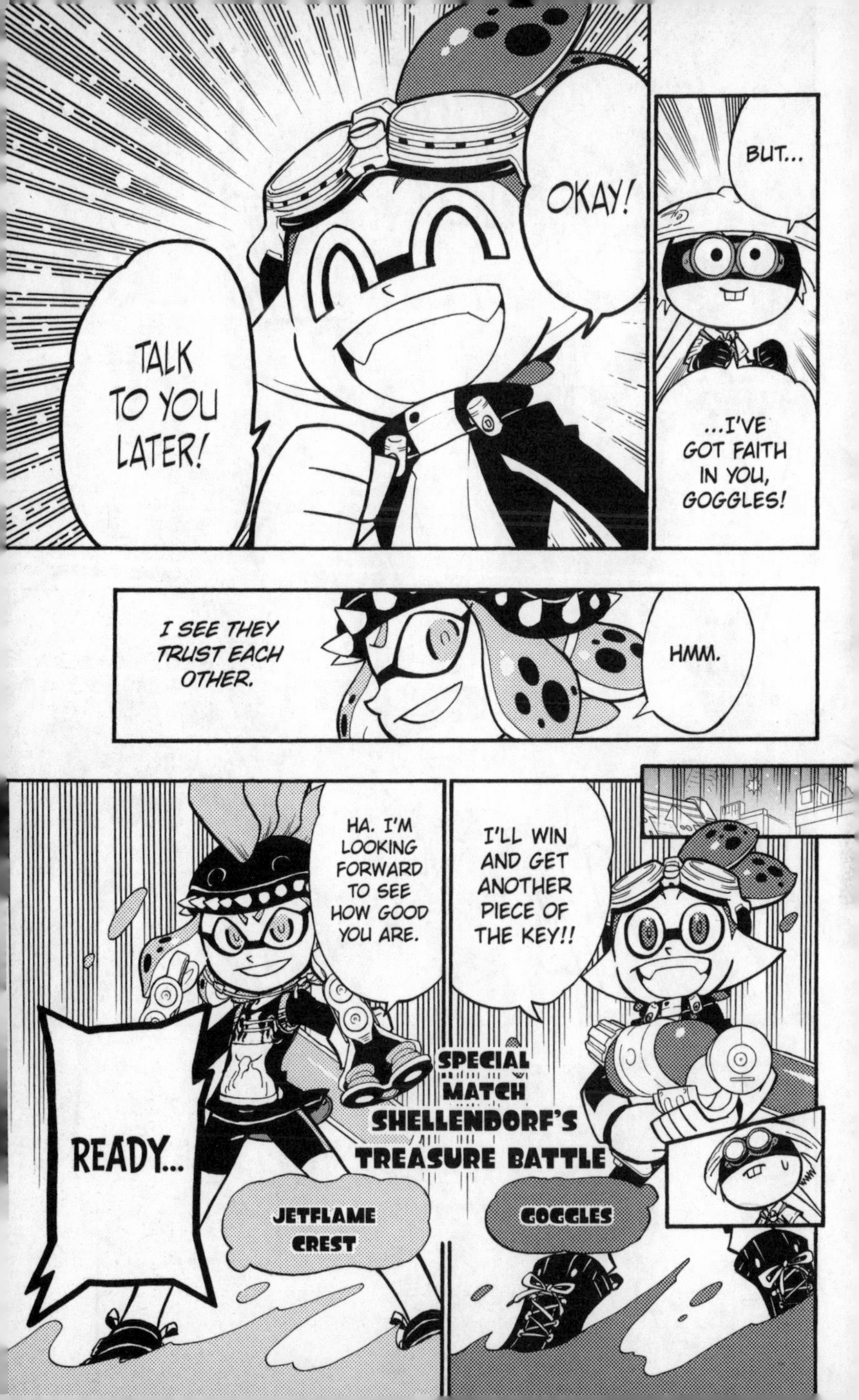
BUT...
...I'VE GOT FAITH IN YOU, GOGGLES!
OKAY!
TALK TO YOU LATER!
HMM.
I SEE THEY TRUST EACH OTHER.
I'LL WIN AND GET ANOTHER PIECE OF THE KEY!!
HA. I'M LOOKING FORWARD TO SEE HOW GOOD YOU ARE.
SPECIAL MATCH SHELLENDORF'S TREASURE BATTLE
GOGGLES
JETFLAME CREST
READY...

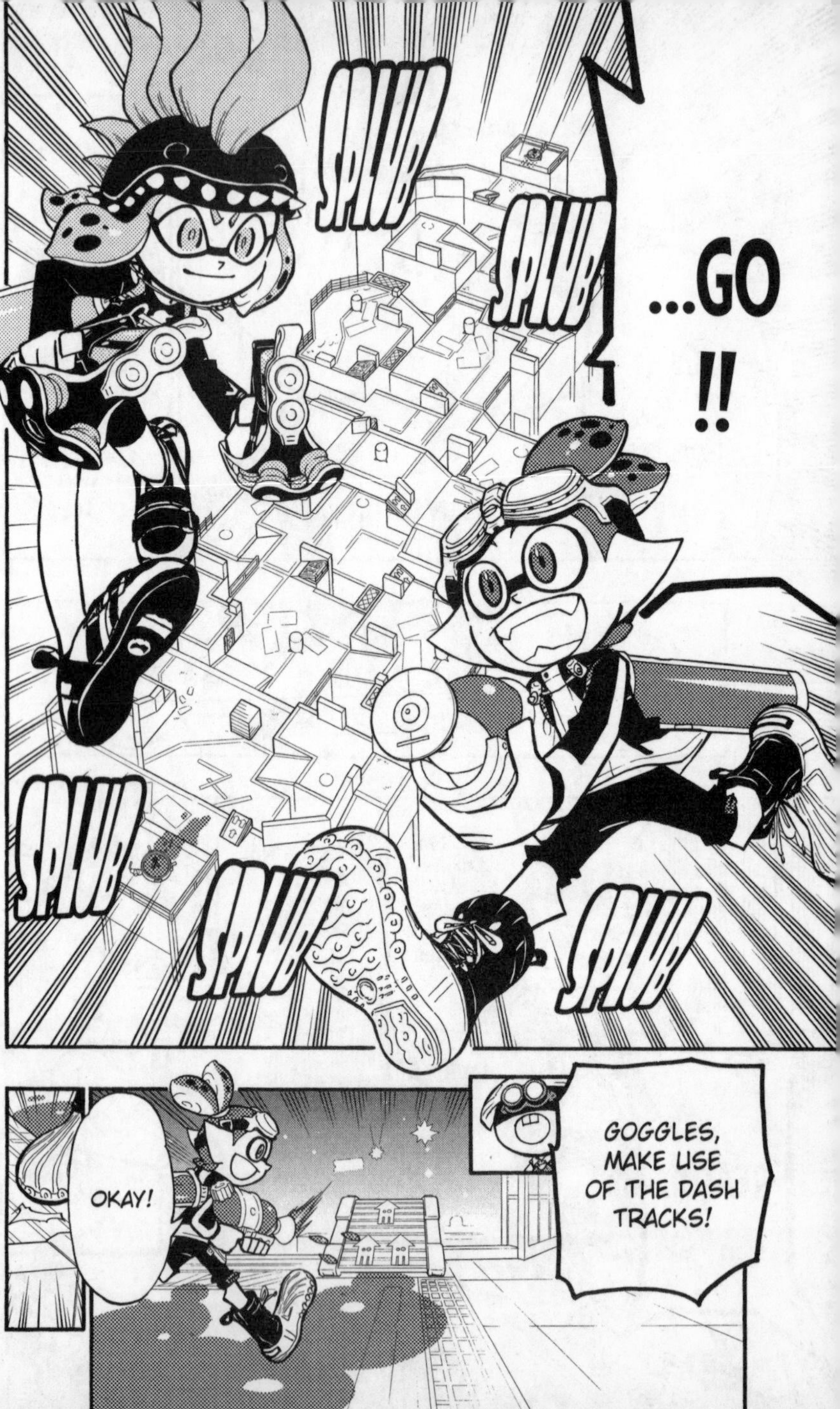
...GO!!
SPLUB
SPLUB
SPLUB
SPLUB
SPLUB
GOGGLES, MAKE USE OF THE DASH TRACKS!
OKAY!

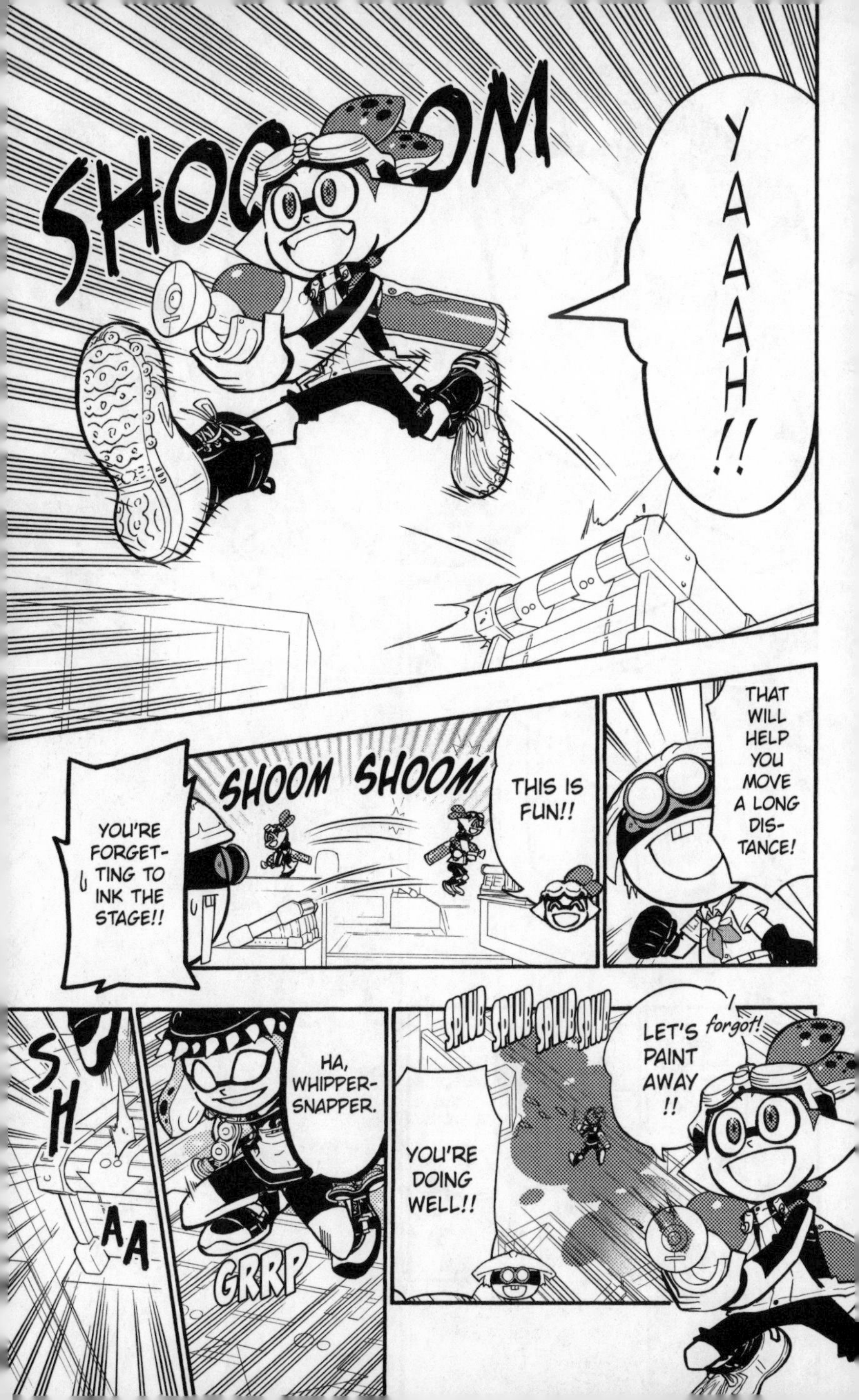
YAAAH!!
SHOOOM
THAT WILL HELP YOU MOVE A LONG DIS-TANCE!
THIS IS FUN!!
SHOOM SHOOM
YOU'RE FORGET-TING TO INK THE STAGE!!
I forgot!
LET'S PAINT AWAY!!
SPLUB SPLUB SPLUB SPLUB
YOU'RE DOING WELL!!
HA, WHIPPER-SNAPPER.
GRRP
SHHAA

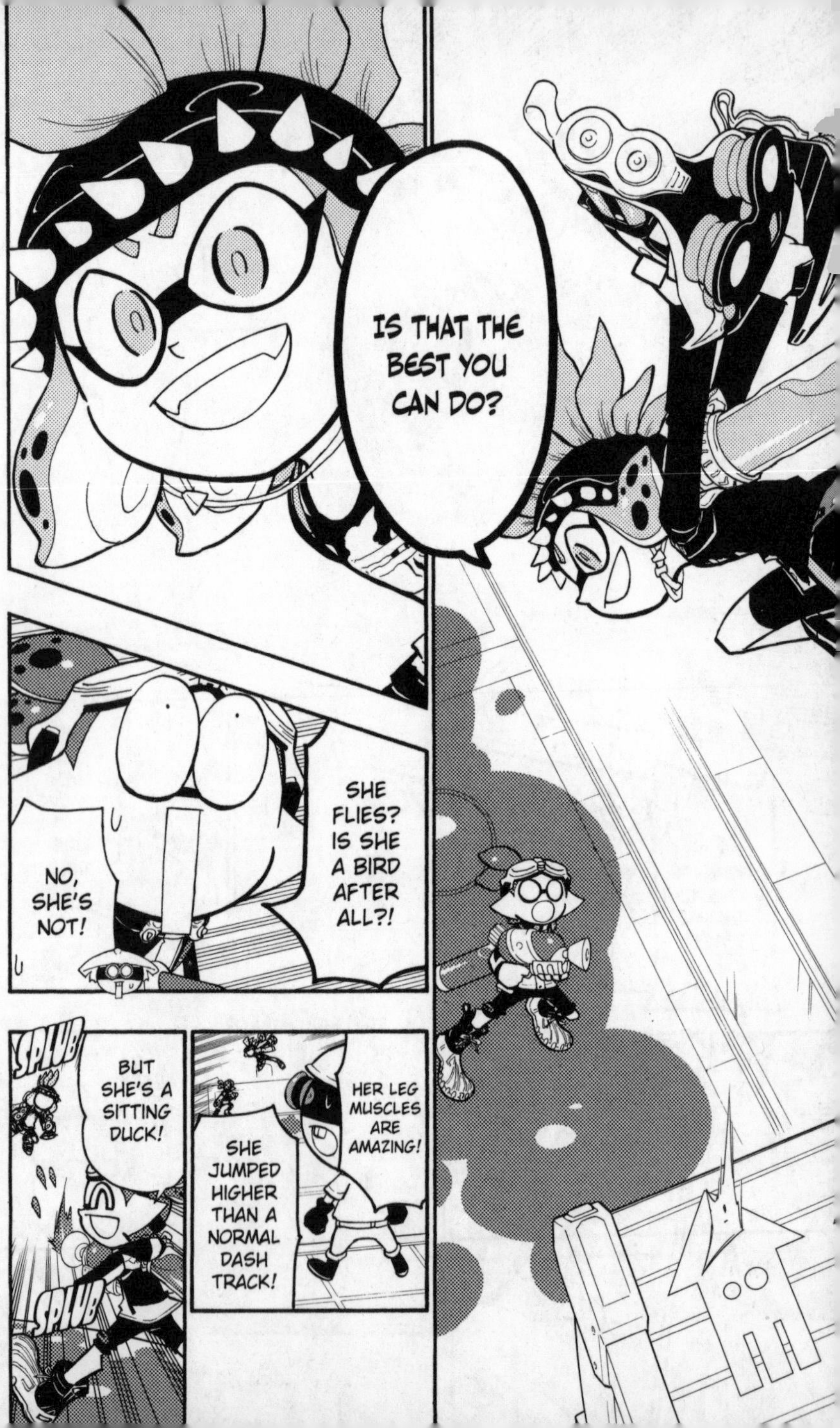
IS THAT THE BEST YOU CAN DO?
SHE FLIES? IS SHE A BIRD AFTER ALL?!
NO, SHE'S NOT!
HER LEG MUSCLES ARE AMAZING!
SHE JUMPED HIGHER THAN A NORMAL DASH TRACK!
SPLUB
BUT SHE'S A SITTING DUCK!
SPLUB

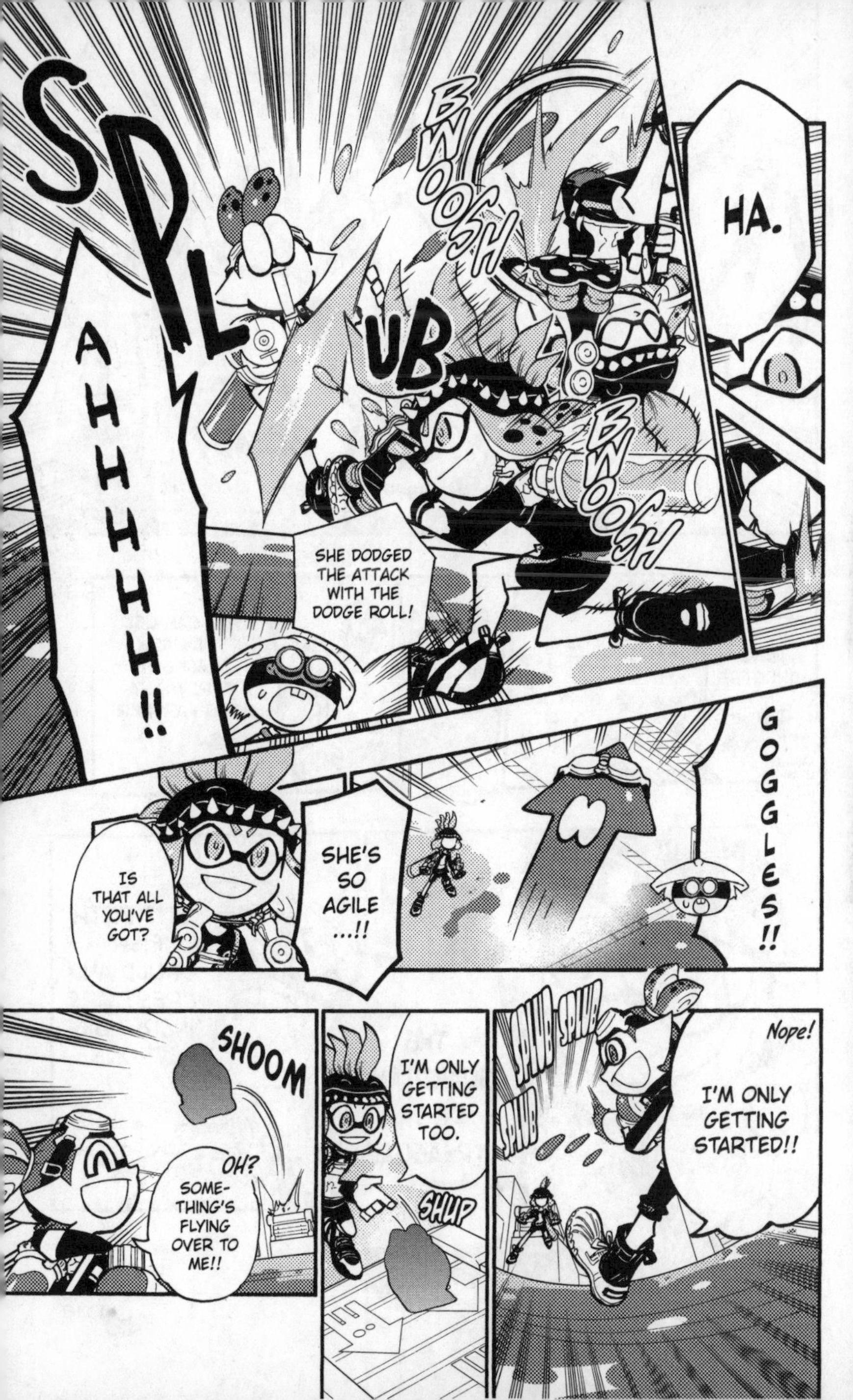
HA.
BWOOSH
SPLUB
BWOOSH
SHE DODGED THE ATTACK WITH THE DODGE ROLL!
AHHHHH!!
GOGGLES!!
SHE'S SO AGILE...!!
IS THAT ALL YOU'VE GOT?
Nope!
I'M ONLY GETTING STARTED!!
SPLUB SPLUB SPLUB
I'M ONLY GETTING STARTED TOO.
SHUP
SHOOM
OH?
SOME-THING'S FLYING OVER TO ME!!

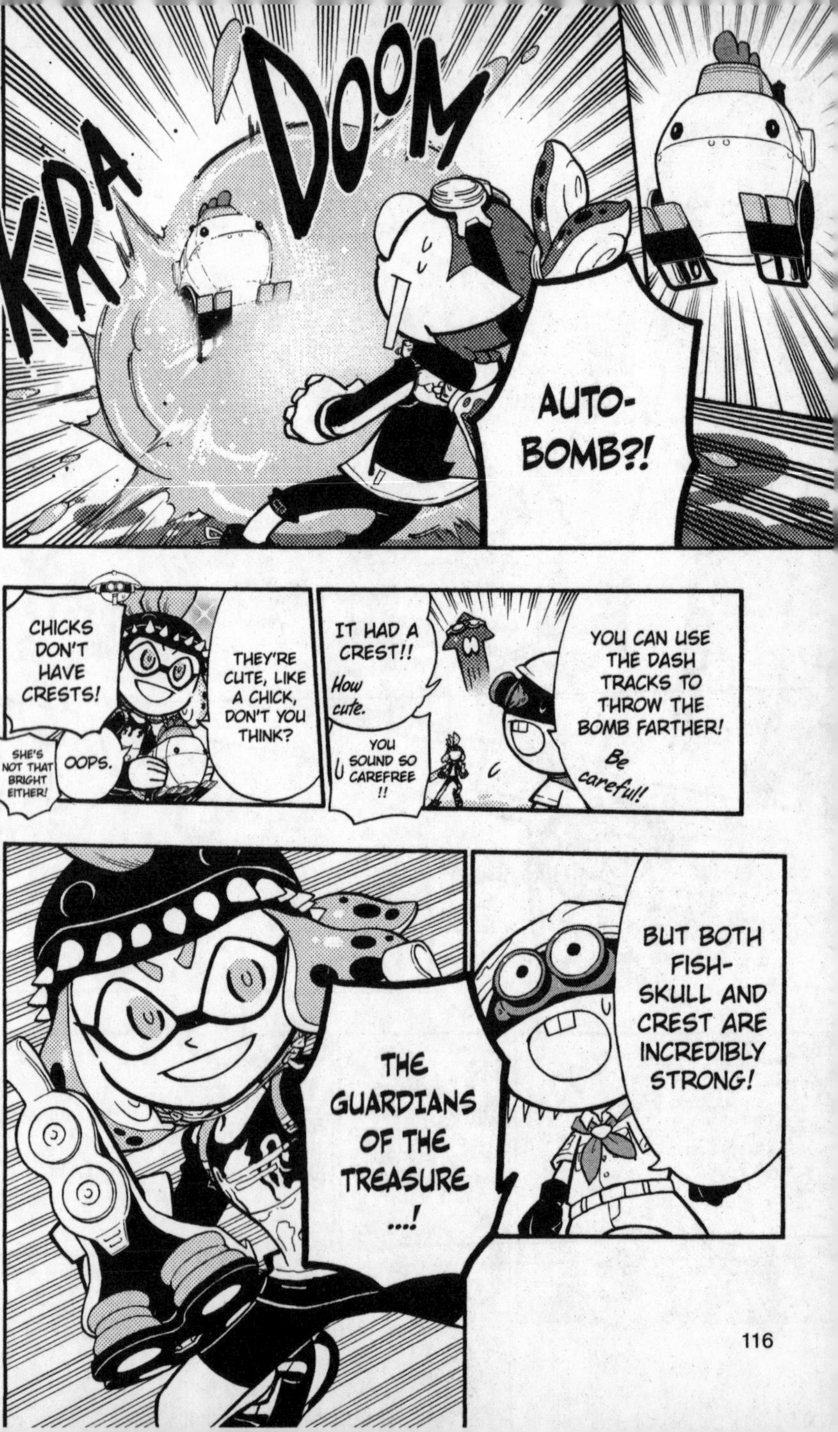
KRA-DOOM
AUTO-BOMB?!
YOU CAN USE THE DASH TRACKS TO THROW THE BOMB FARTHER!
Be careful!!
IT HAD A CREST!!
How cute.
YOU SOUND SO CAREFREE!!
THEY'RE CUTE, LIKE A CHICK, DON'T YOU THINK?
CHICKS DON'T HAVE CRESTS!
OOPS.
SHE'S NOT THAT BRIGHT EITHER!
BUT BOTH FISH-SKULL AND CREST ARE INCREDIBLY STRONG!
THE GUARDIANS OF THE TREASURE ...!

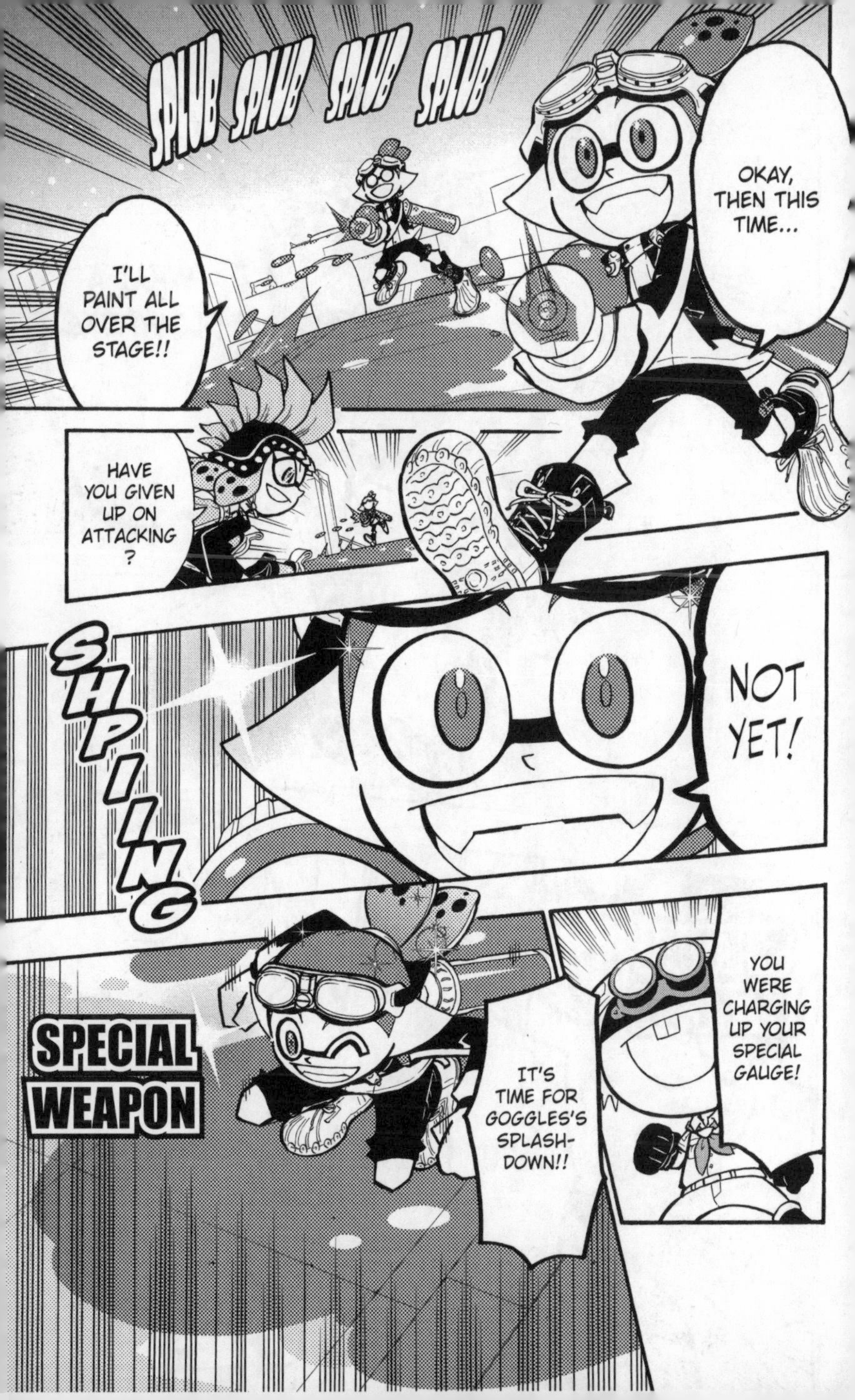
SPLUB SPLUB SPLUB SPLUB
OKAY, THEN THIS TIME...
I'LL PAINT ALL OVER THE STAGE!!
HAVE YOU GIVEN UP ON ATTACKING?
NOT YET!
SHPIIING
YOU WERE CHARGING UP YOUR SPECIAL GAUGE!
IT'S TIME FOR GOGGLES'S SPLASH-DOWN!!
SPECIAL WEAPON

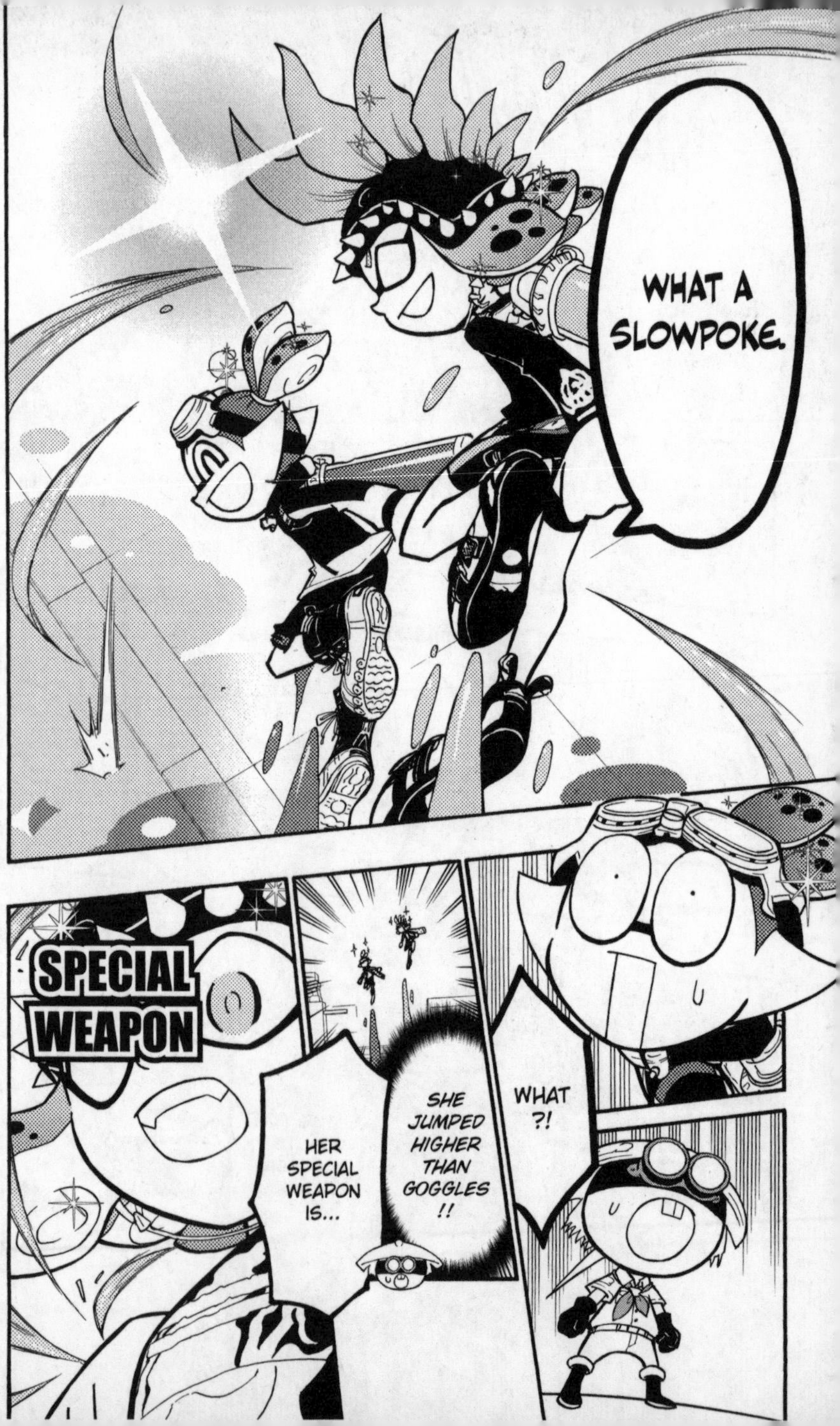
WHAT A SLOWPOKE.
WHAT ?!
SHE JUMPED HIGHER THAN GOGGLES !!
HER SPECIAL WEAPON IS...
SPECIAL WEAPON

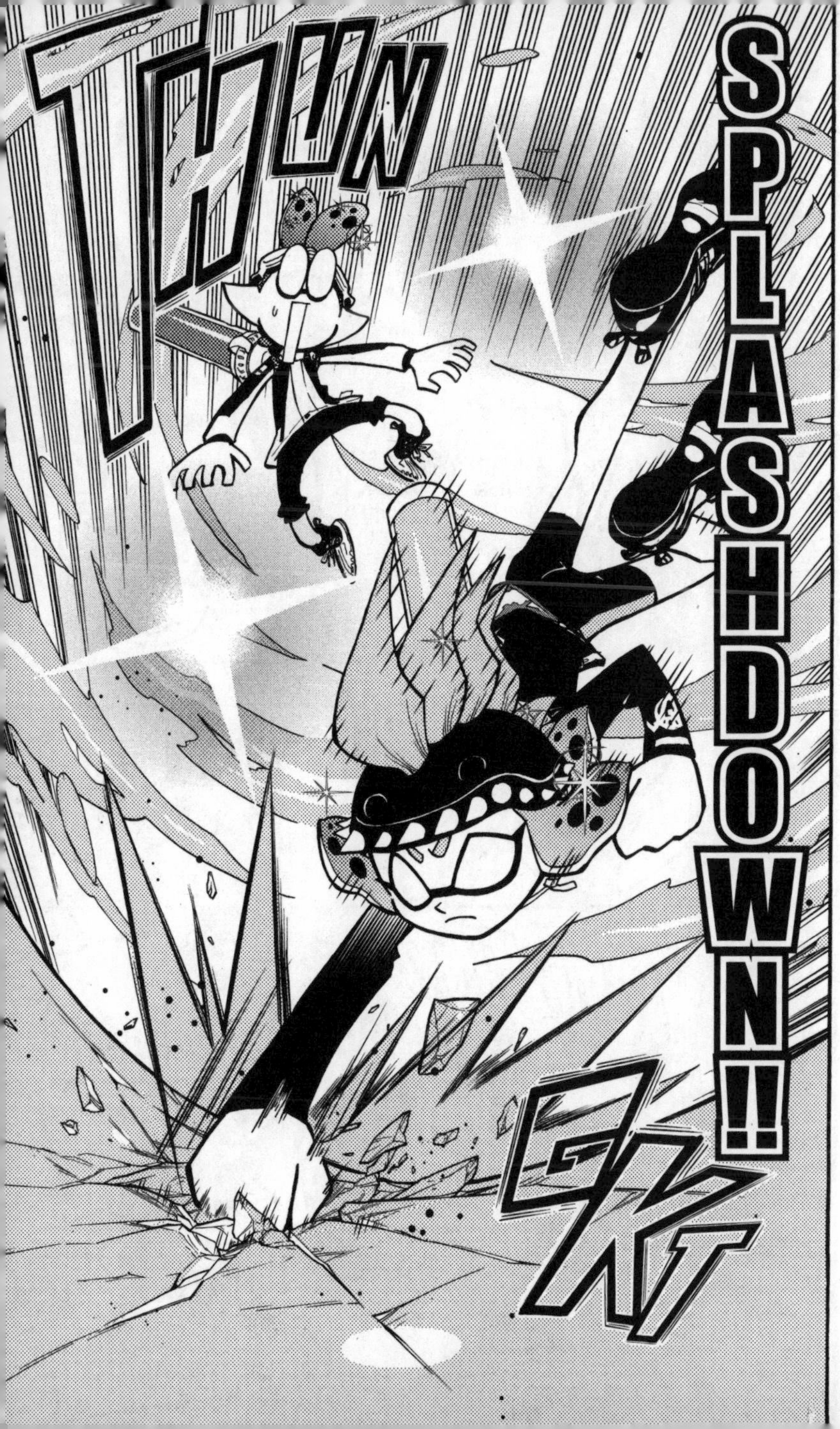
SPLASHDOWN!!
THUN

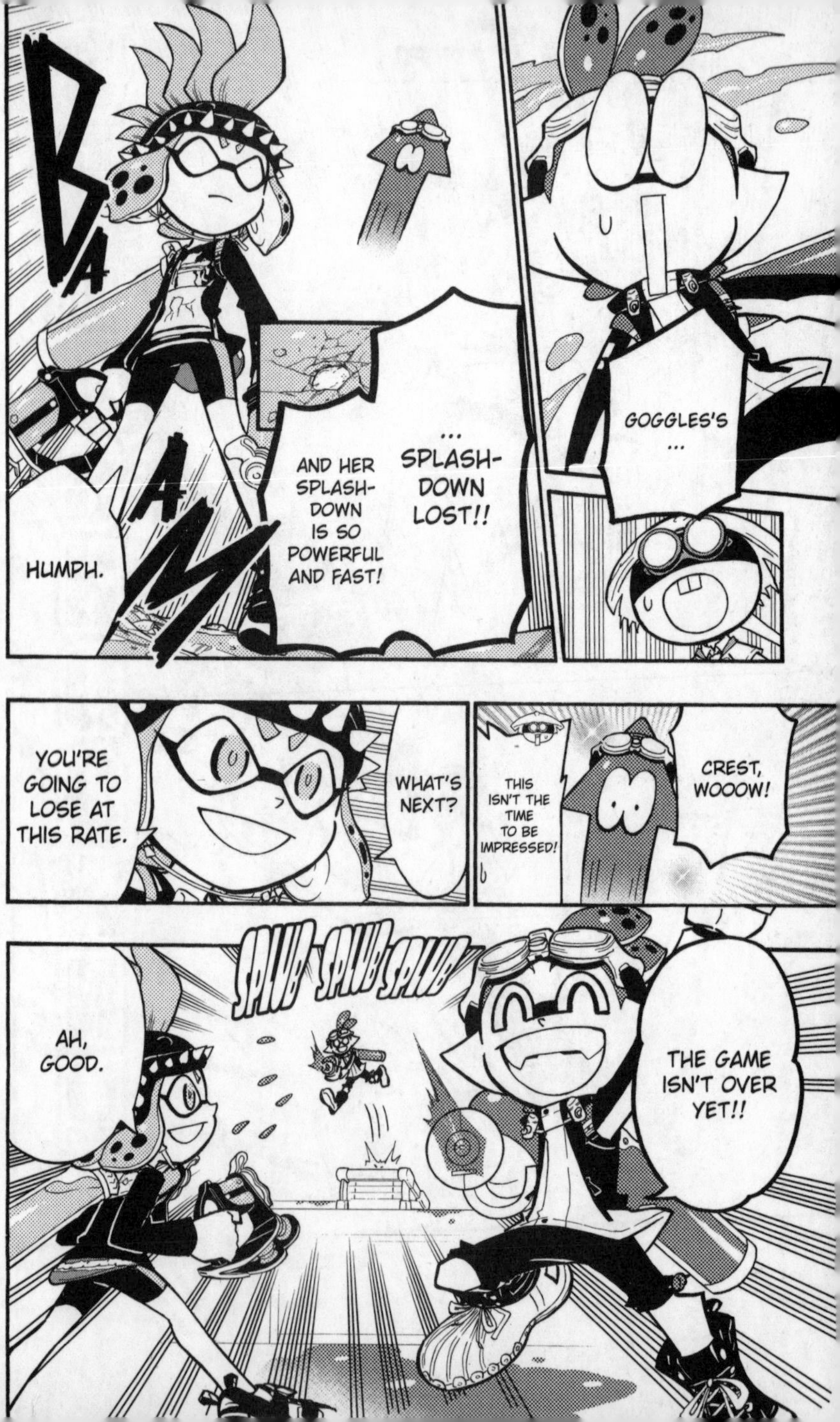
GOGGLES'S ...
... SPLASH-DOWN LOST!!
AND HER SPLASH-DOWN IS SO POWERFUL AND FAST!
BAM
HUMPH.
CREST, WOOOW!
THIS ISN'T THE TIME TO BE IMPRESSED!
WHAT'S NEXT?
YOU'RE GOING TO LOSE AT THIS RATE.
THE GAME ISN'T OVER YET!!
SPLUB SPLUB SPLUB
AH, GOOD.

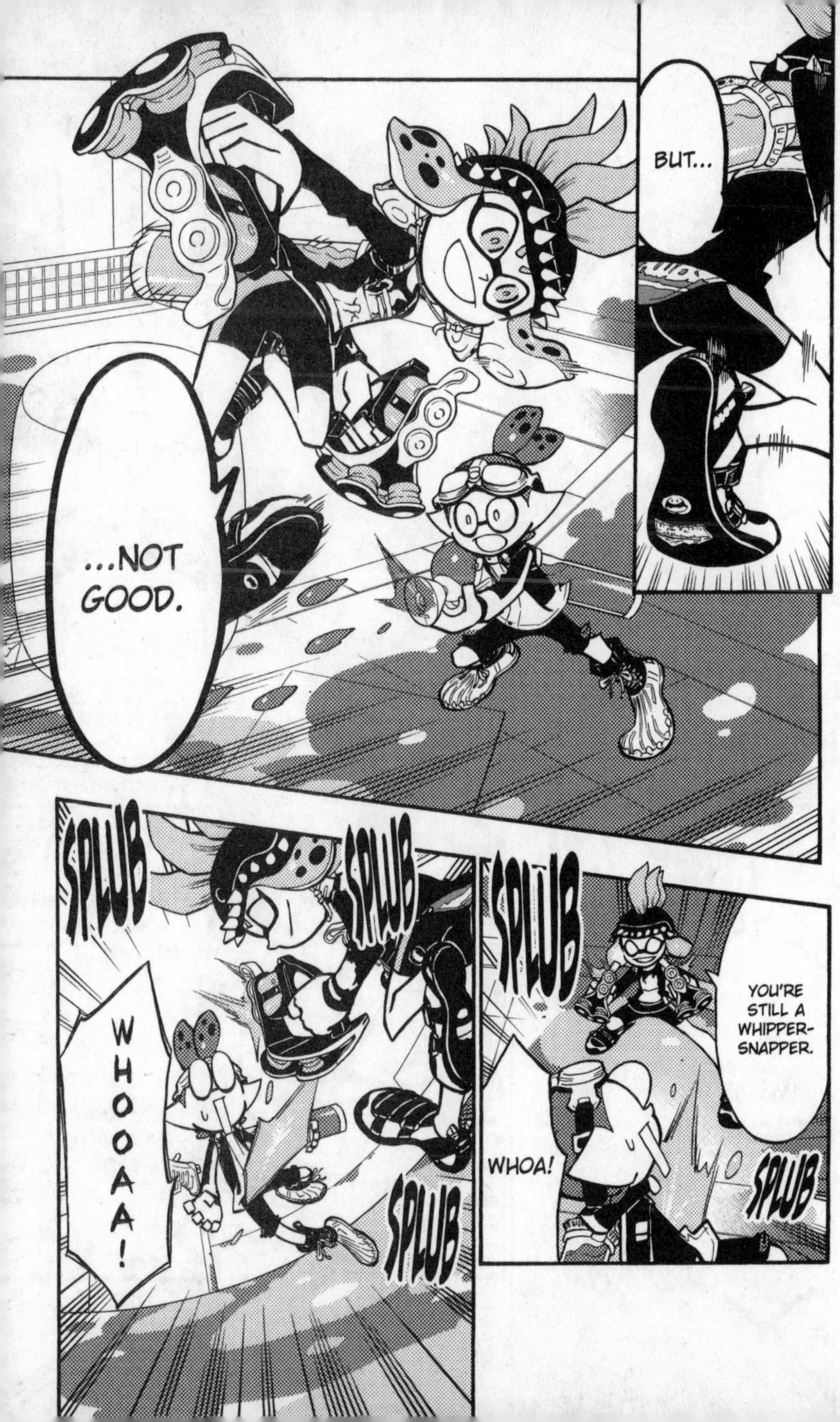
BUT...
...NOT GOOD.
SPLUB
YOU'RE STILL A WHIPPER-SNAPPER.
WHOA!
SPLUB
SPLUB
SPLUB
WHOOAA!
SPLUB

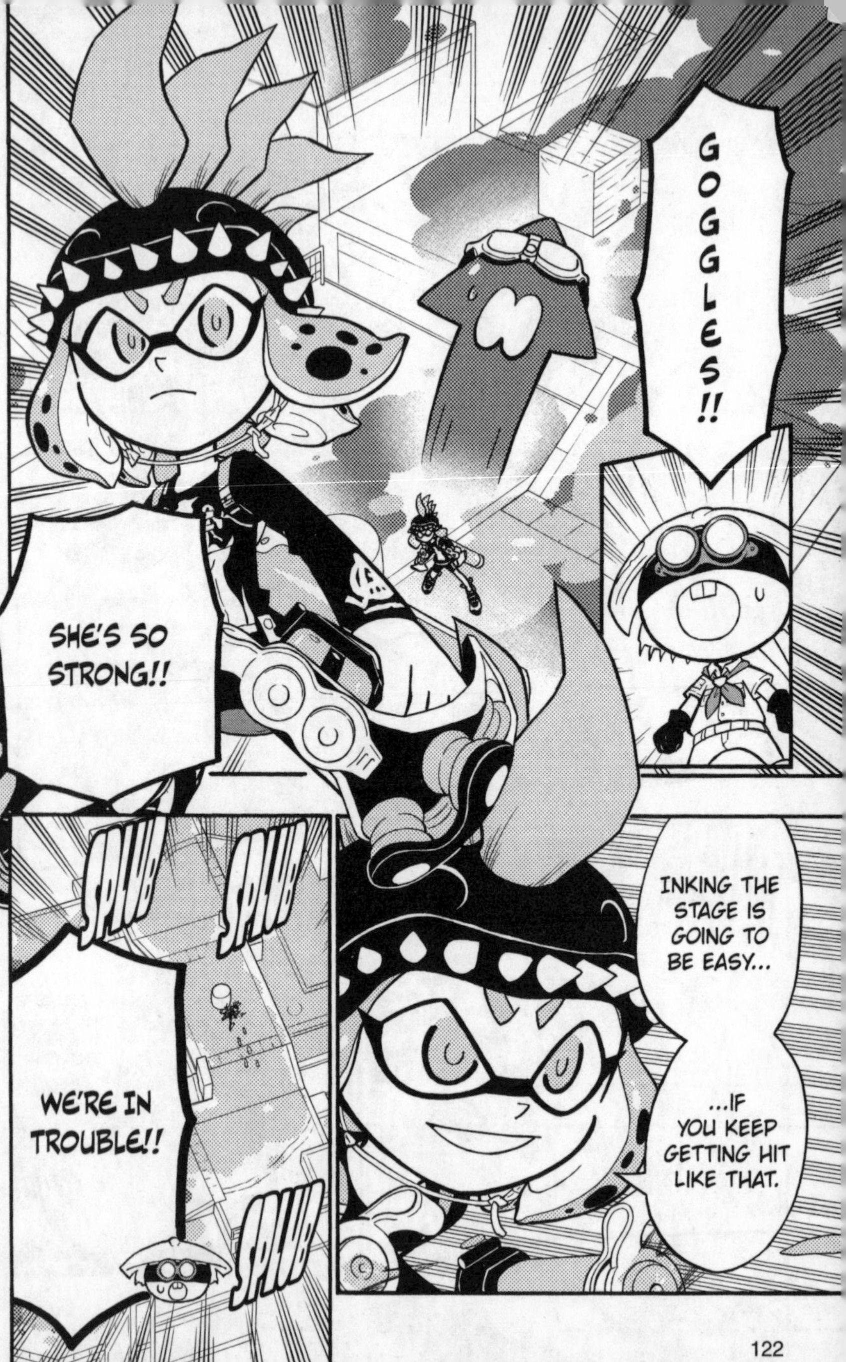
GOGGLES!!
SHE'S SO STRONG!!
INKING THE STAGE IS GOING TO BE EASY...
...IF YOU KEEP GETTING HIT LIKE THAT.
SPLUB
SPLUB
WE'RE IN TROUBLE!!
SPLUB

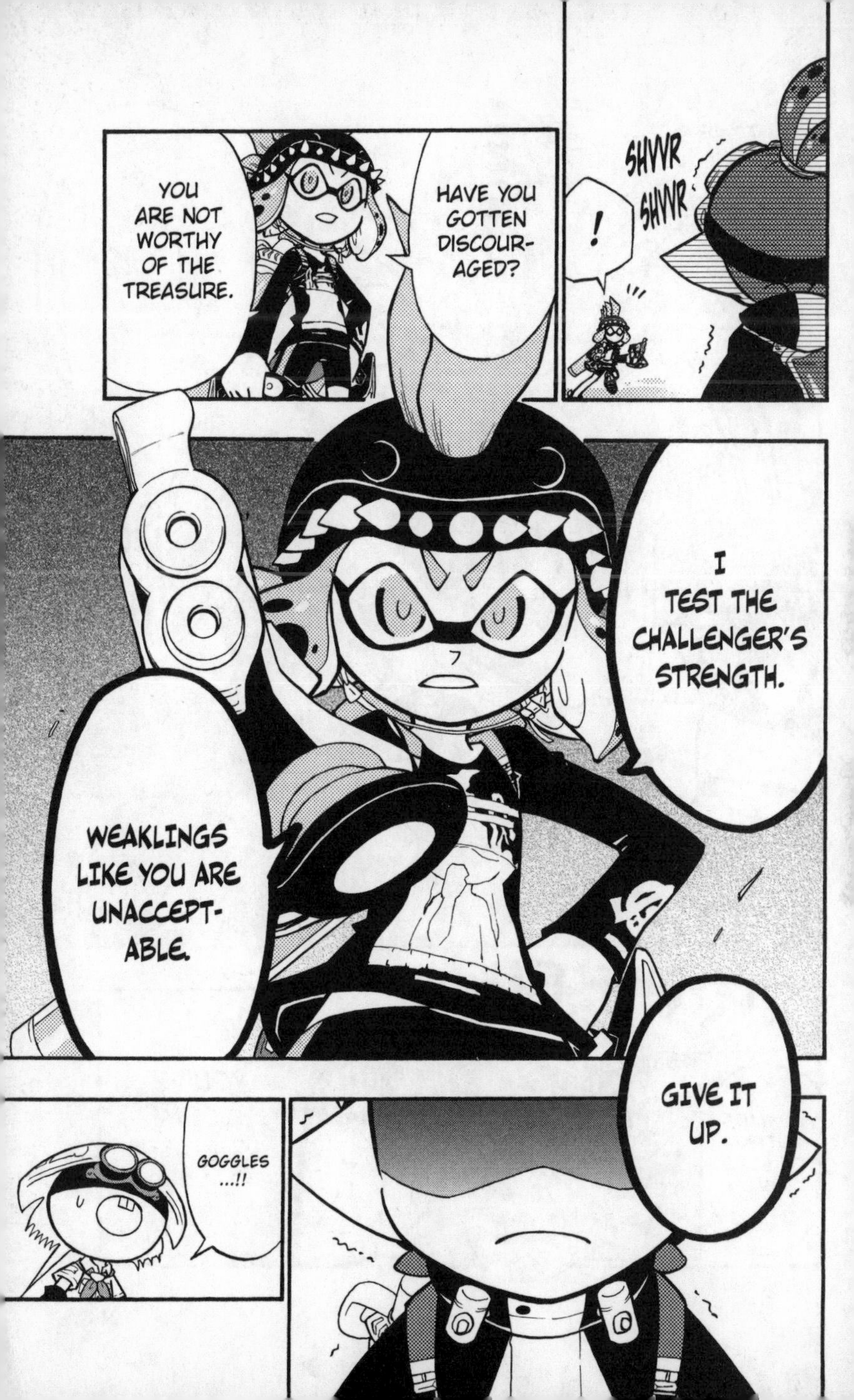
SHVVR SHVVR
!
HAVE YOU GOTTEN DISCOUR-AGED?
YOU ARE NOT WORTHY OF THE TREASURE.
I TEST THE CHALLENGER'S STRENGTH.
WEAKLINGS LIKE YOU ARE UNACCEPT-ABLE.
GIVE IT UP.
GOGGLES ...!!

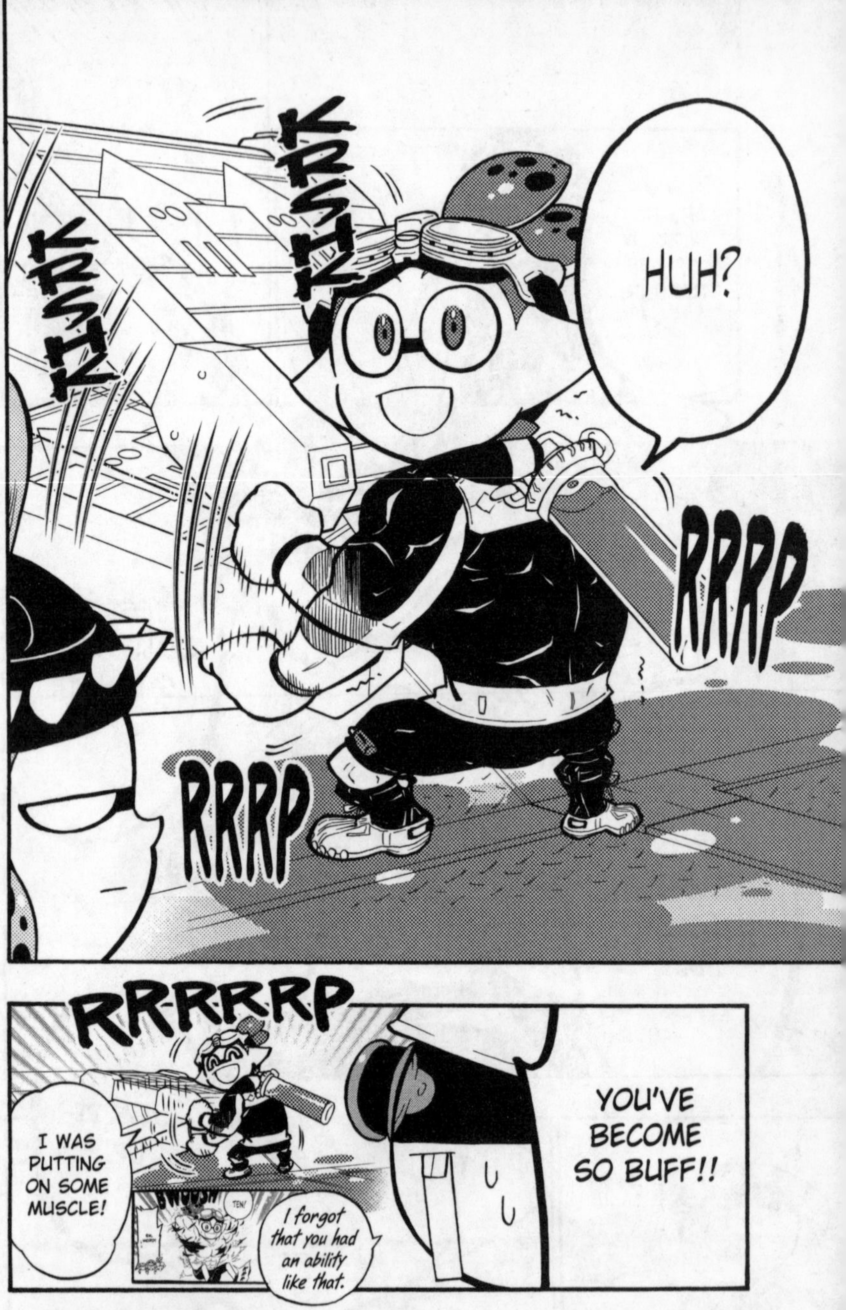
HUH?
KRSH
KRSH
RRRP
RRRP
YOU'VE BECOME SO BUFF!!
RRRRRP
I WAS PUTTING ON SOME MUSCLE!
I forgot that you had an ability like that.

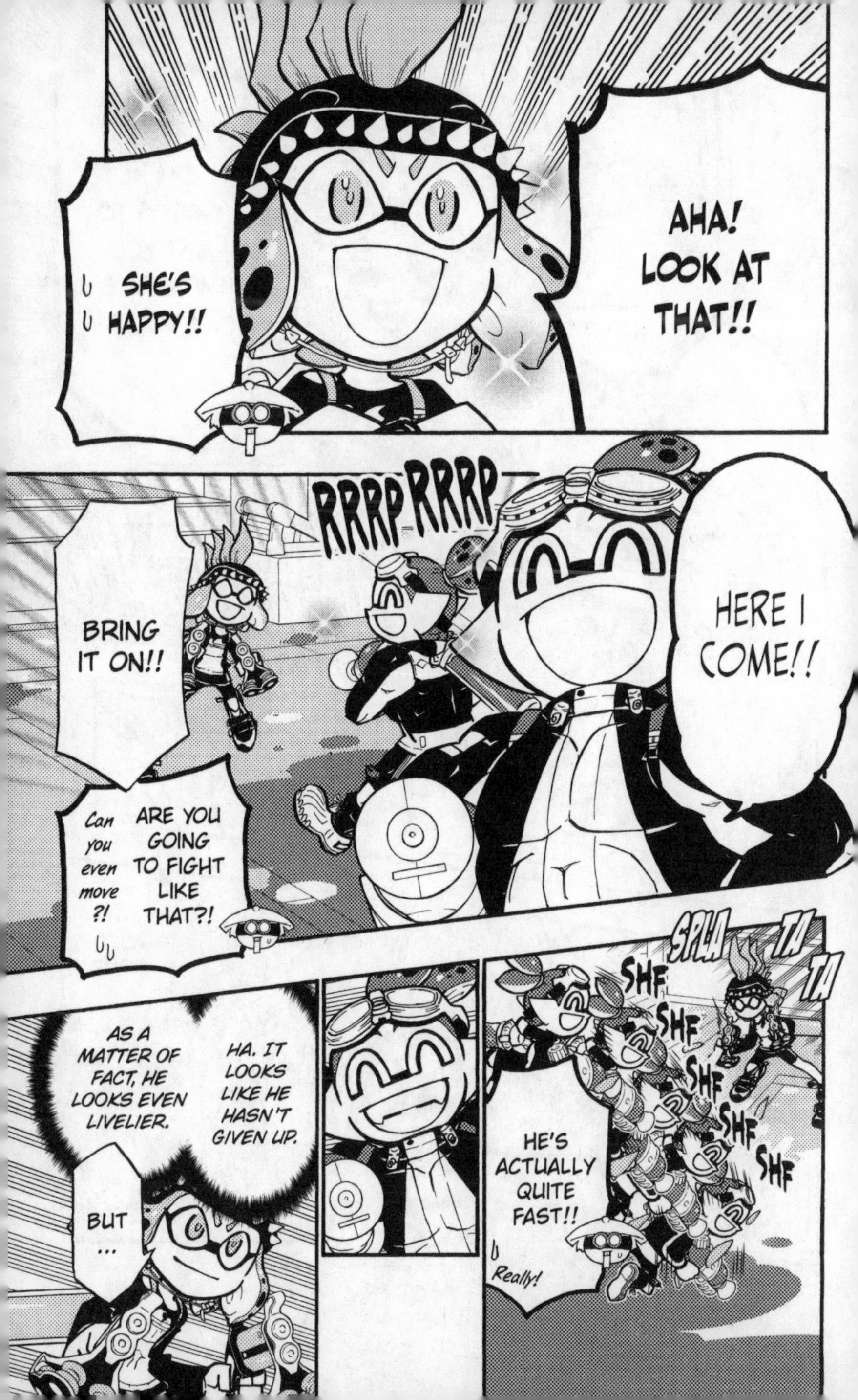
AHA! LOOK AT THAT!!
SHE'S HAPPY!!
HERE I COME!!
RRRP RRRP
BRING IT ON!!
ARE YOU GOING TO FIGHT LIKE THAT?!
Can you even move?!
SPLA TA TA
SHF SHF SHF SHF SHF SHF
HE'S ACTUALLY QUITE FAST!!
Really!
HA. IT LOOKS LIKE HE HASN'T GIVEN UP.
AS A MATTER OF FACT, HE LOOKS EVEN LIVELIER.
BUT...

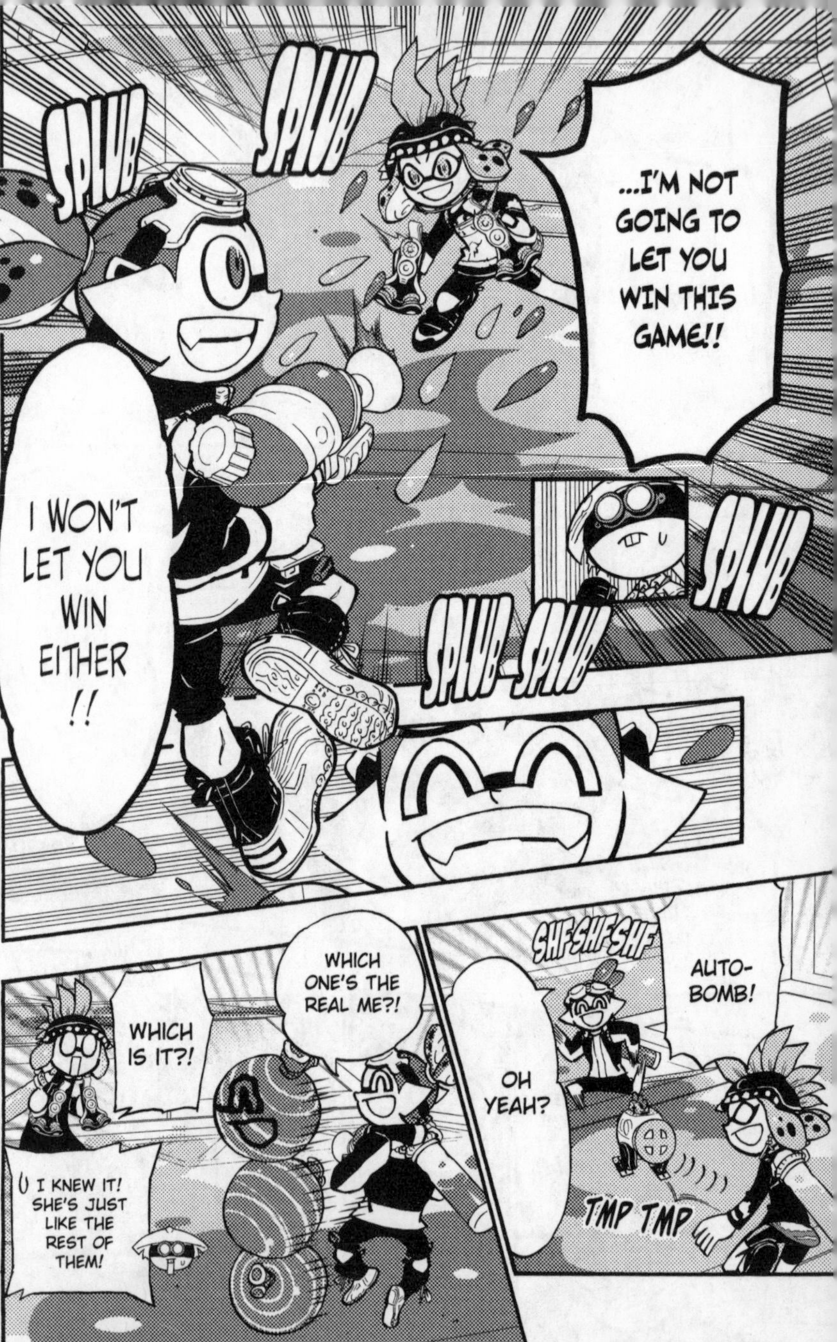
SPLVB
SPLVB
...I'M NOT GOING TO LET YOU WIN THIS GAME!!
I WON'T LET YOU WIN EITHER!!
SPLVB
SPLVB SPLVB
SHF SHF SHF
AUTO-BOMB!
OH YEAH?
TMP TMP
WHICH ONE'S THE REAL ME?!
WHICH IS IT?!
I KNEW IT! SHE'S JUST LIKE THE REST OF THEM!

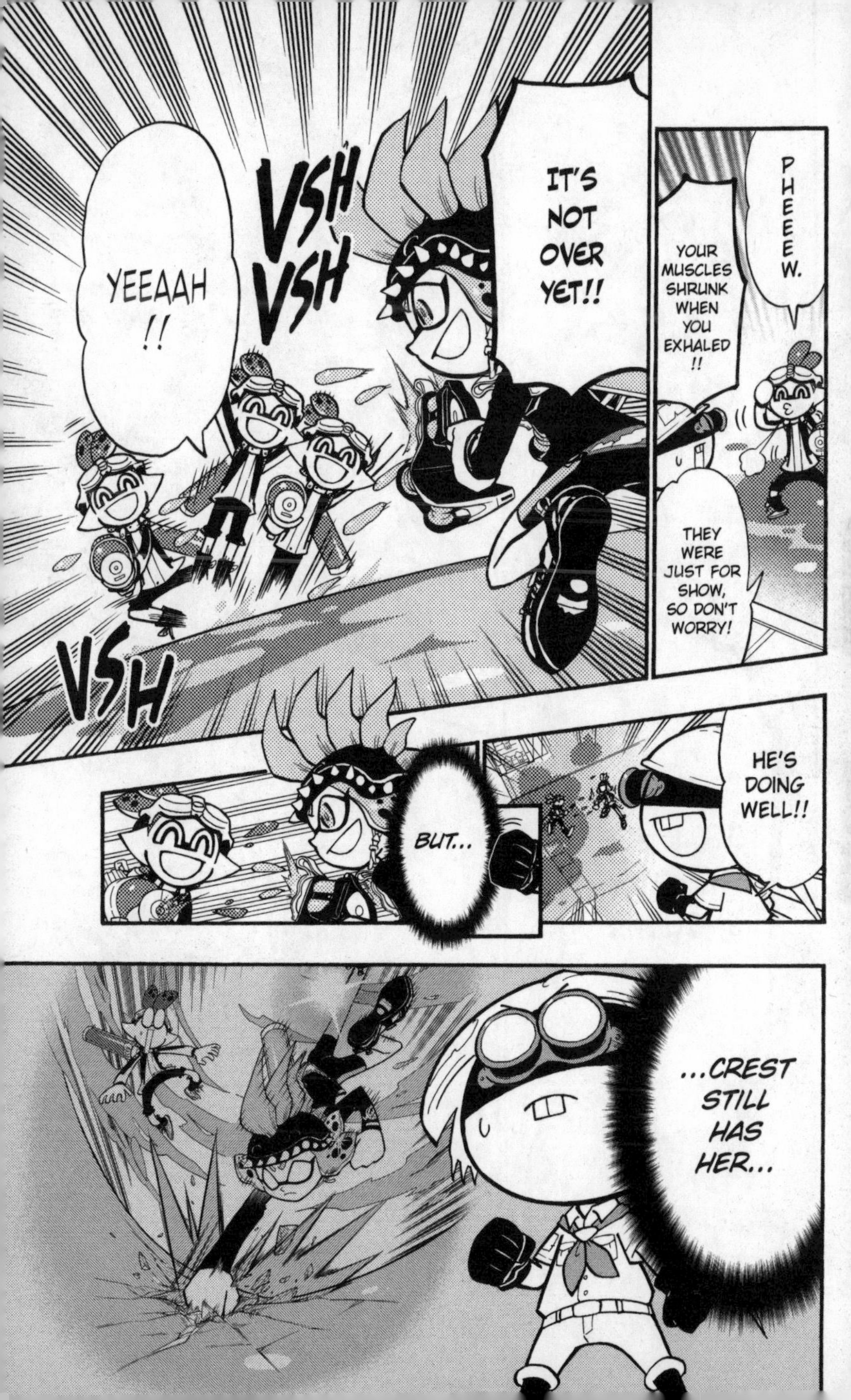
PHEEEW.
YOUR MUSCLES SHRUNK WHEN YOU EXHALED!!
THEY WERE JUST FOR SHOW, SO DON'T WORRY!
IT'S NOT OVER YET!!
VSH VSH
YEEAAH!!
VSH
HE'S DOING WELL!!
BUT...
...CREST STILL HAS HER...

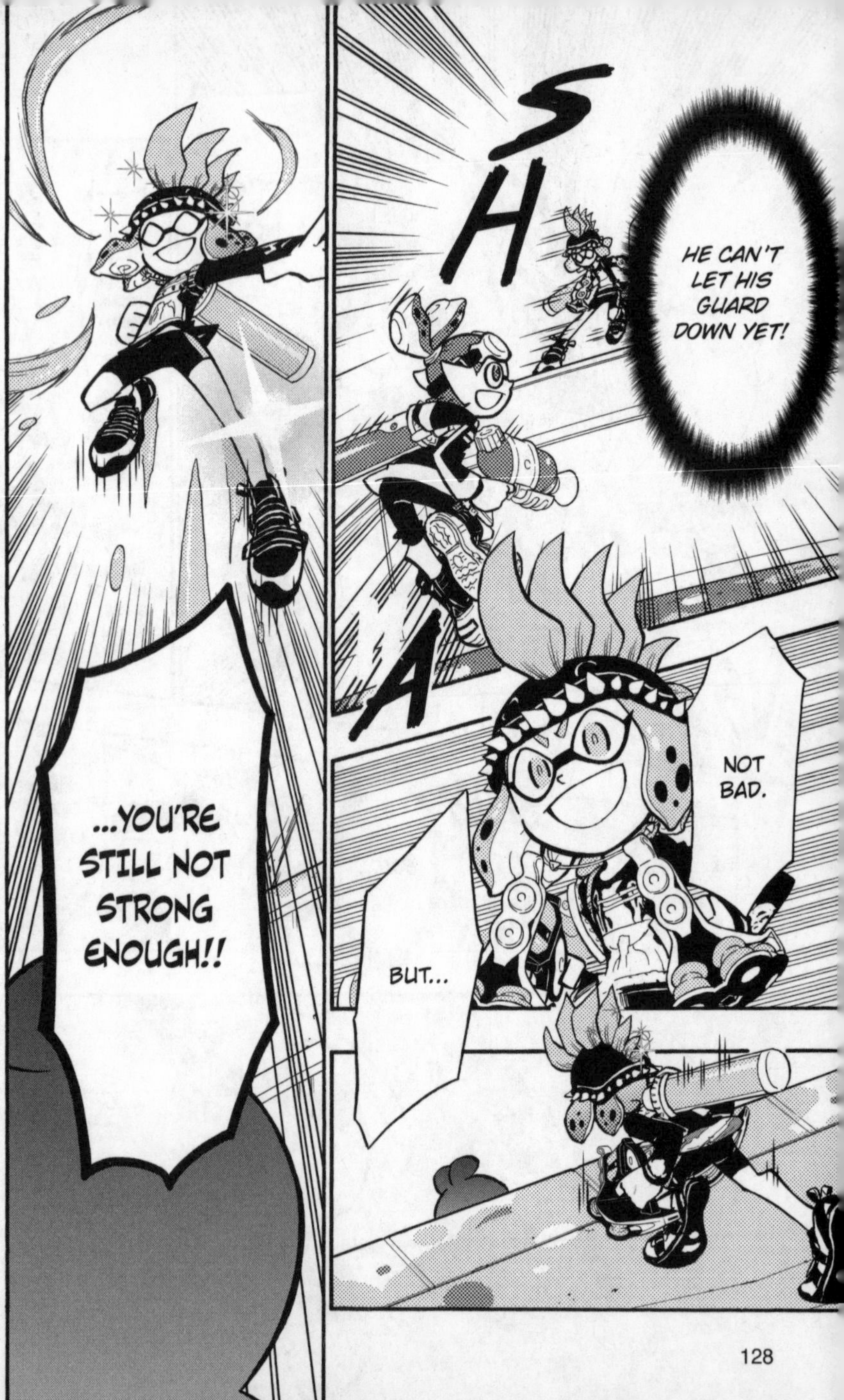
SHA
HE CAN'T LET HIS GUARD DOWN YET!
NOT BAD.
BUT...
...YOU'RE STILL NOT STRONG ENOUGH!!

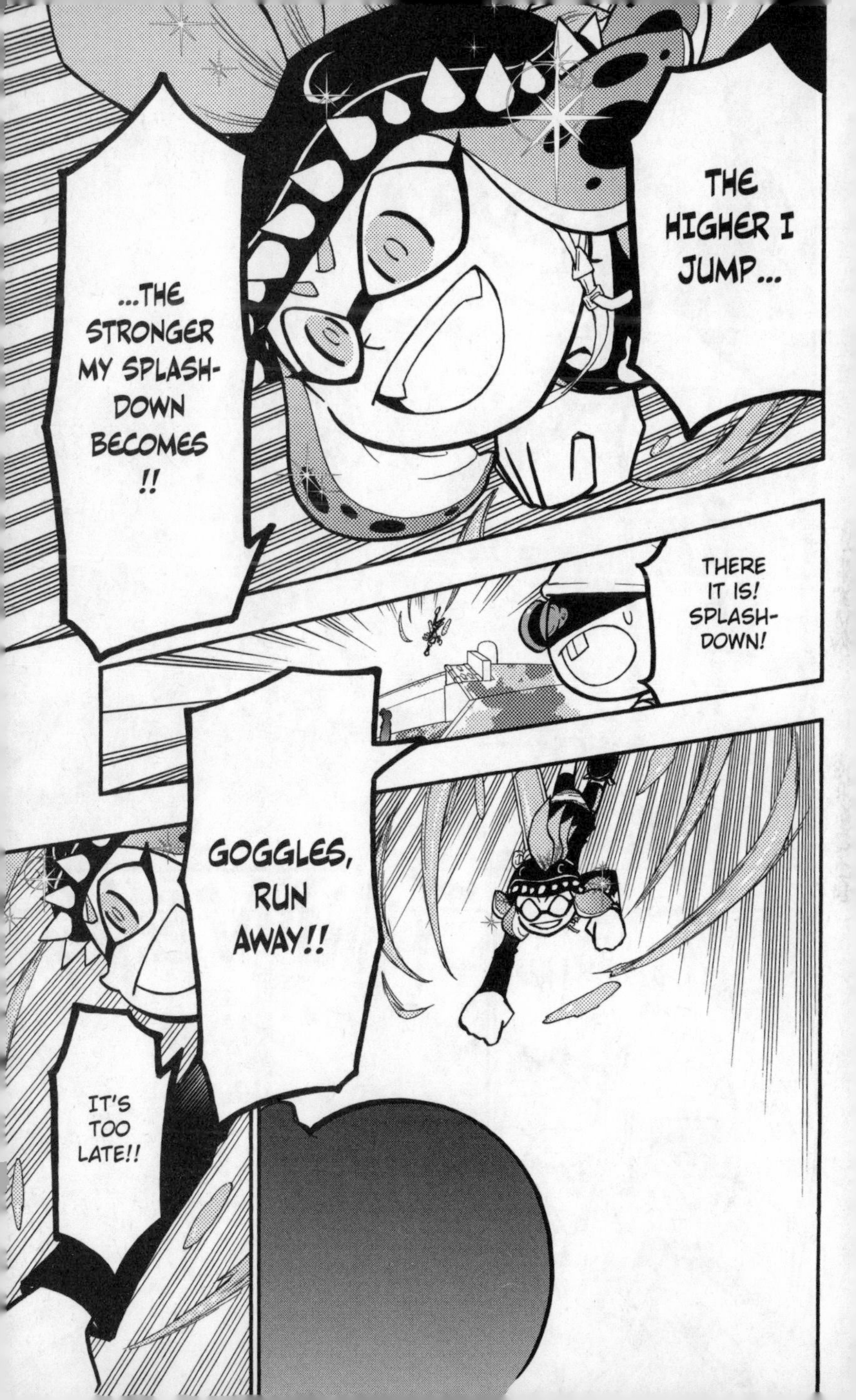
THE HIGHER I JUMP...
...THE STRONGER MY SPLASH-DOWN BECOMES!!
THERE IT IS! SPLASH-DOWN!
GOGGLES, RUN AWAY!!
IT'S TOO LATE!!

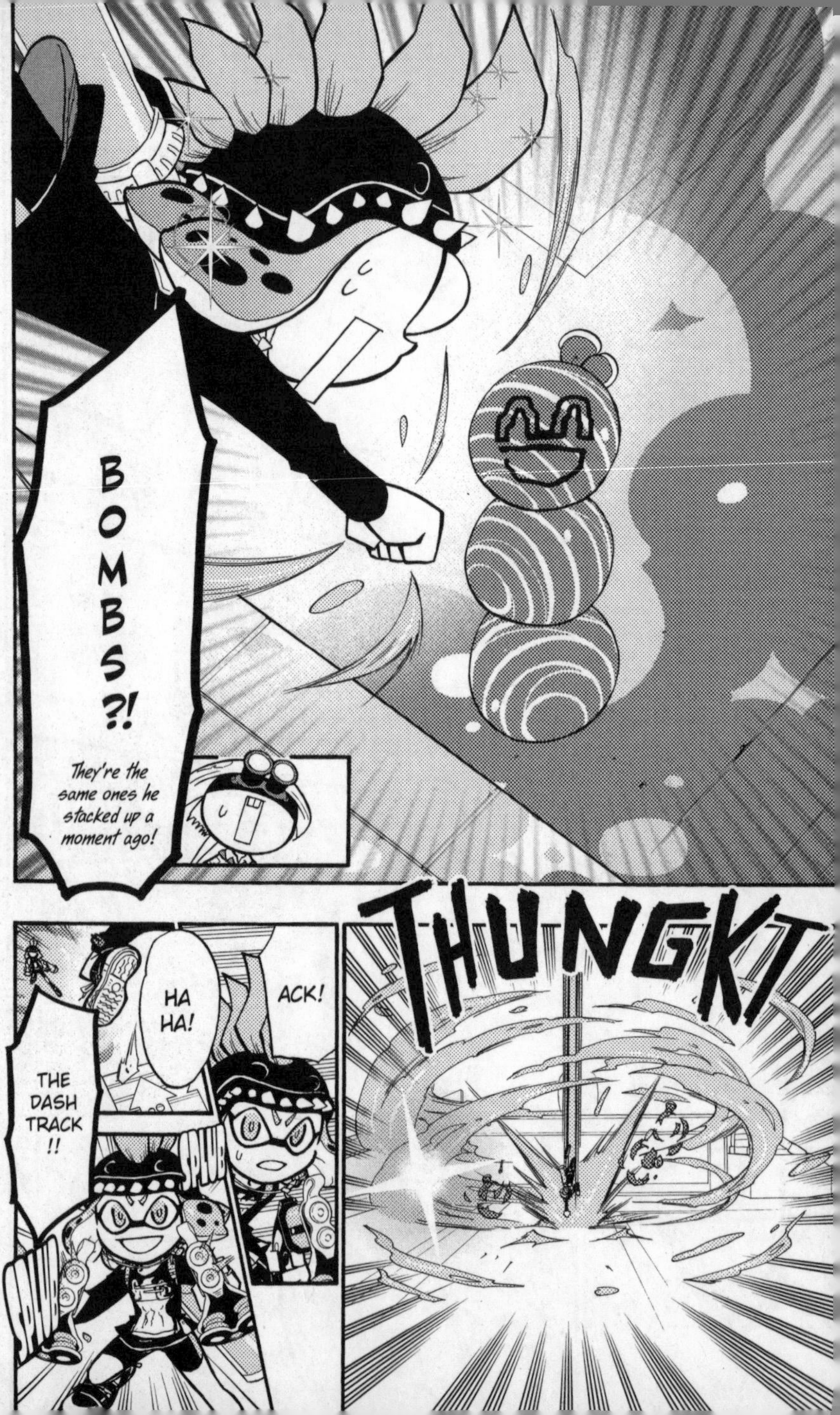

BOMBS?!
They're the same ones he stacked up a moment ago!
THUNGK!
ACK!
HA HA!
THE DASH TRACK!!
SPLUB
SPLUB
SPLUB

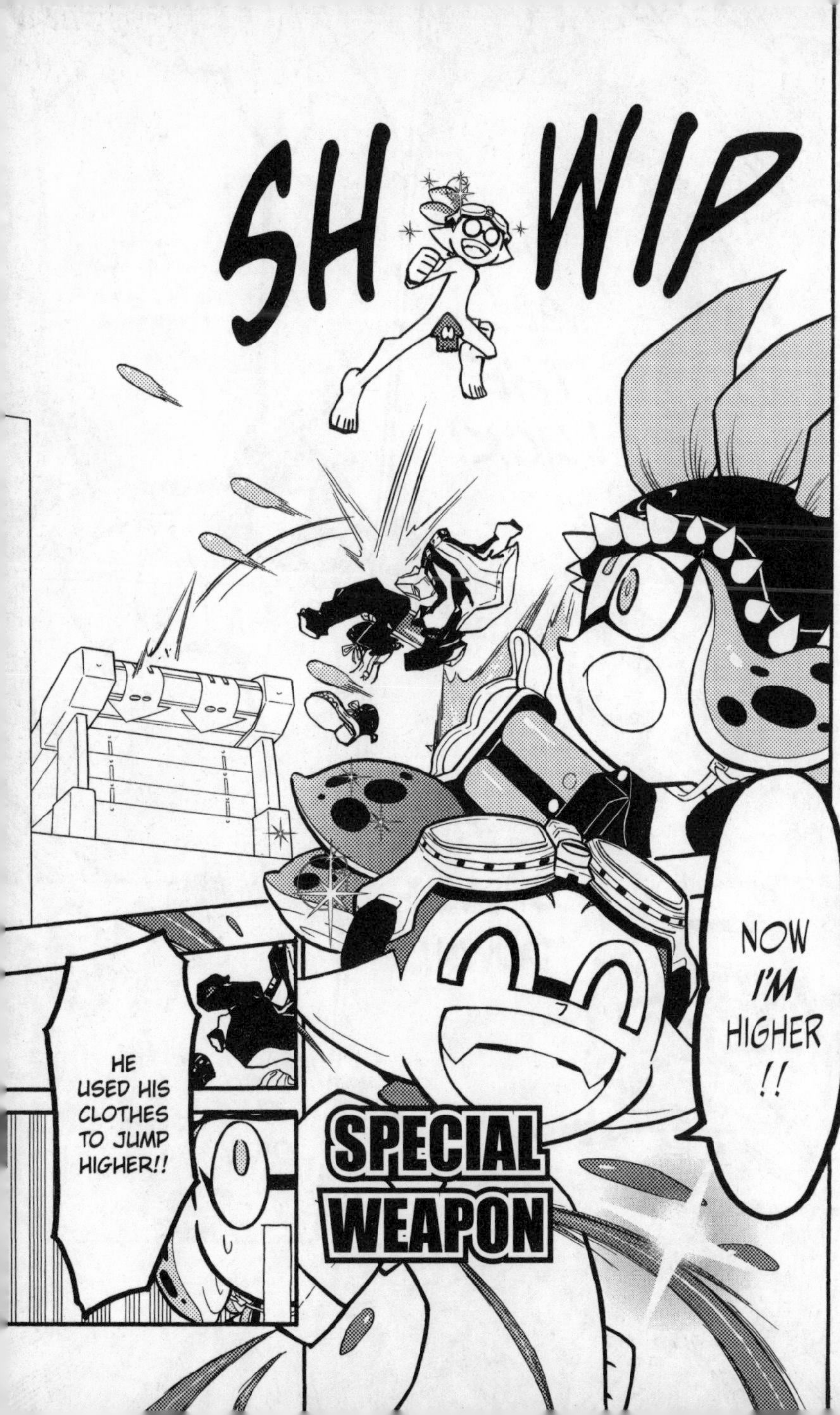
SHWIP
NOW I'M HIGHER!!
SPECIAL WEAPON
HE USED HIS CLOTHES TO JUMP HIGHER!!

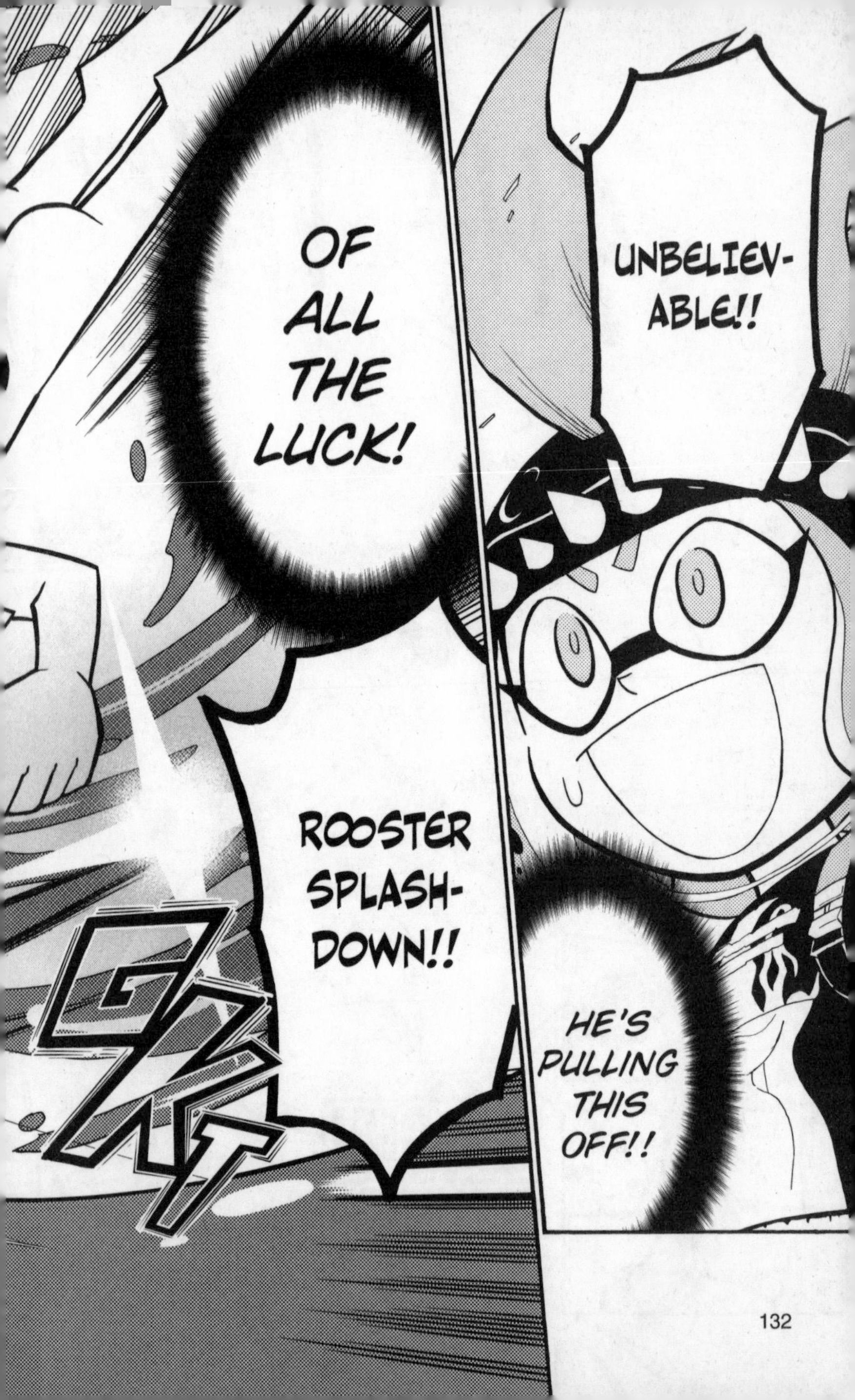
UNBELIEV-ABLE!!
HE'S PULLING THIS OFF!!
OF ALL THE LUCK!
ROOSTER SPLASH-DOWN!!

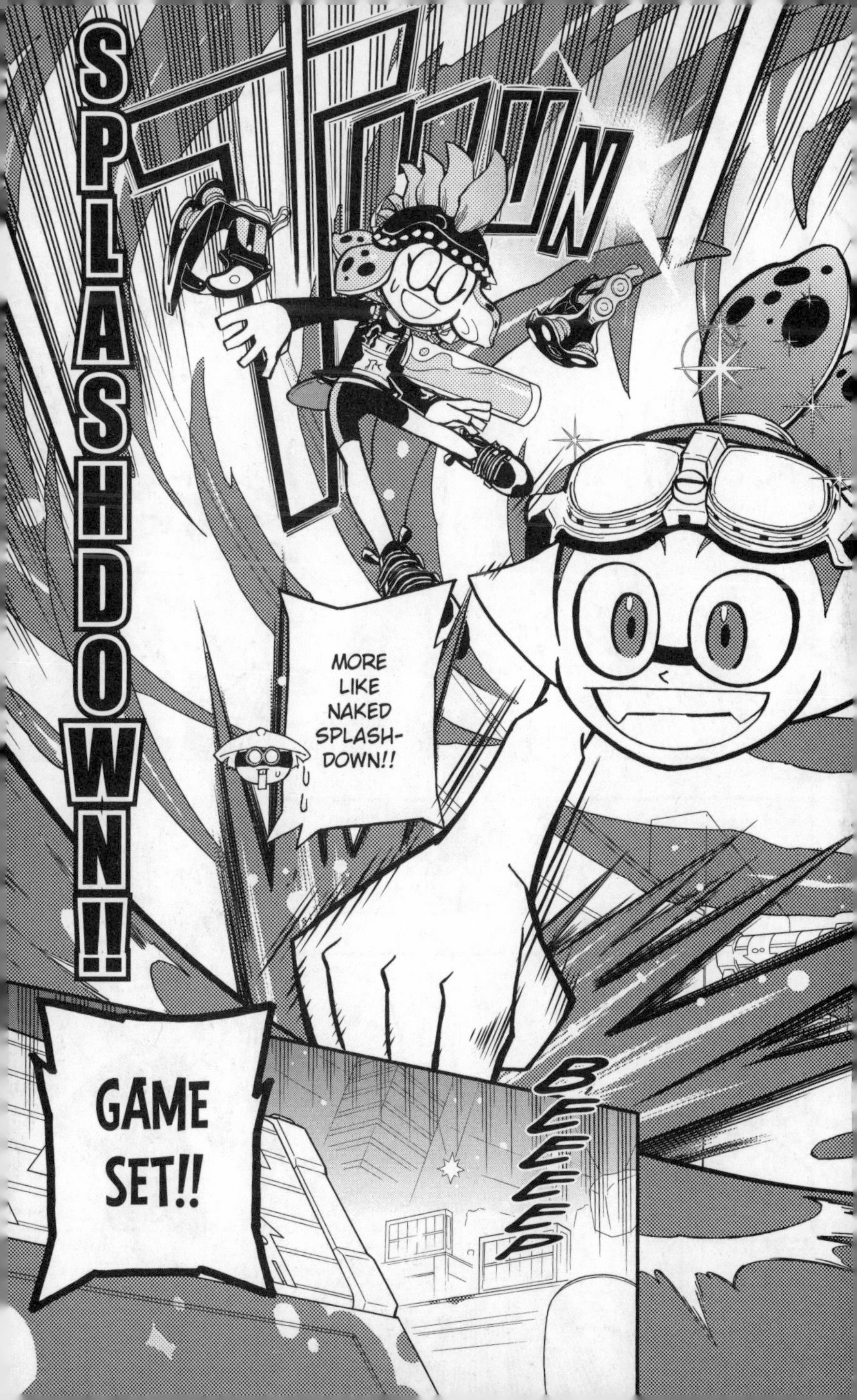
SPLASHDOWN!!
MORE LIKE NAKED SPLASH-DOWN!!
BEEEEP
GAME SET!!

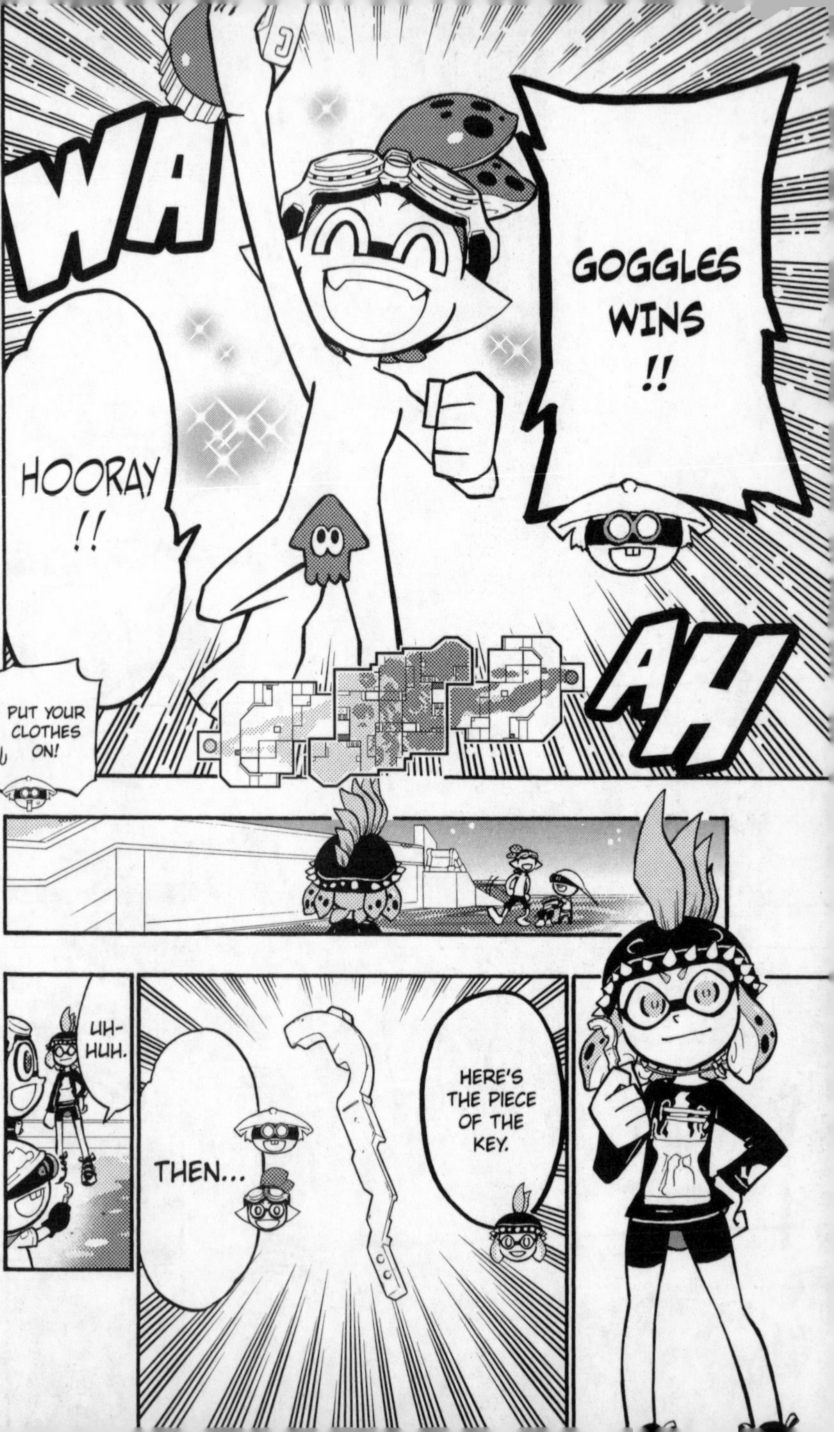
GOGGLES WINS !!
WA
HOORAY !!
AH
PUT YOUR CLOTHES ON!
HERE'S THE PIECE OF THE KEY.
THEN...
UH-HUH.

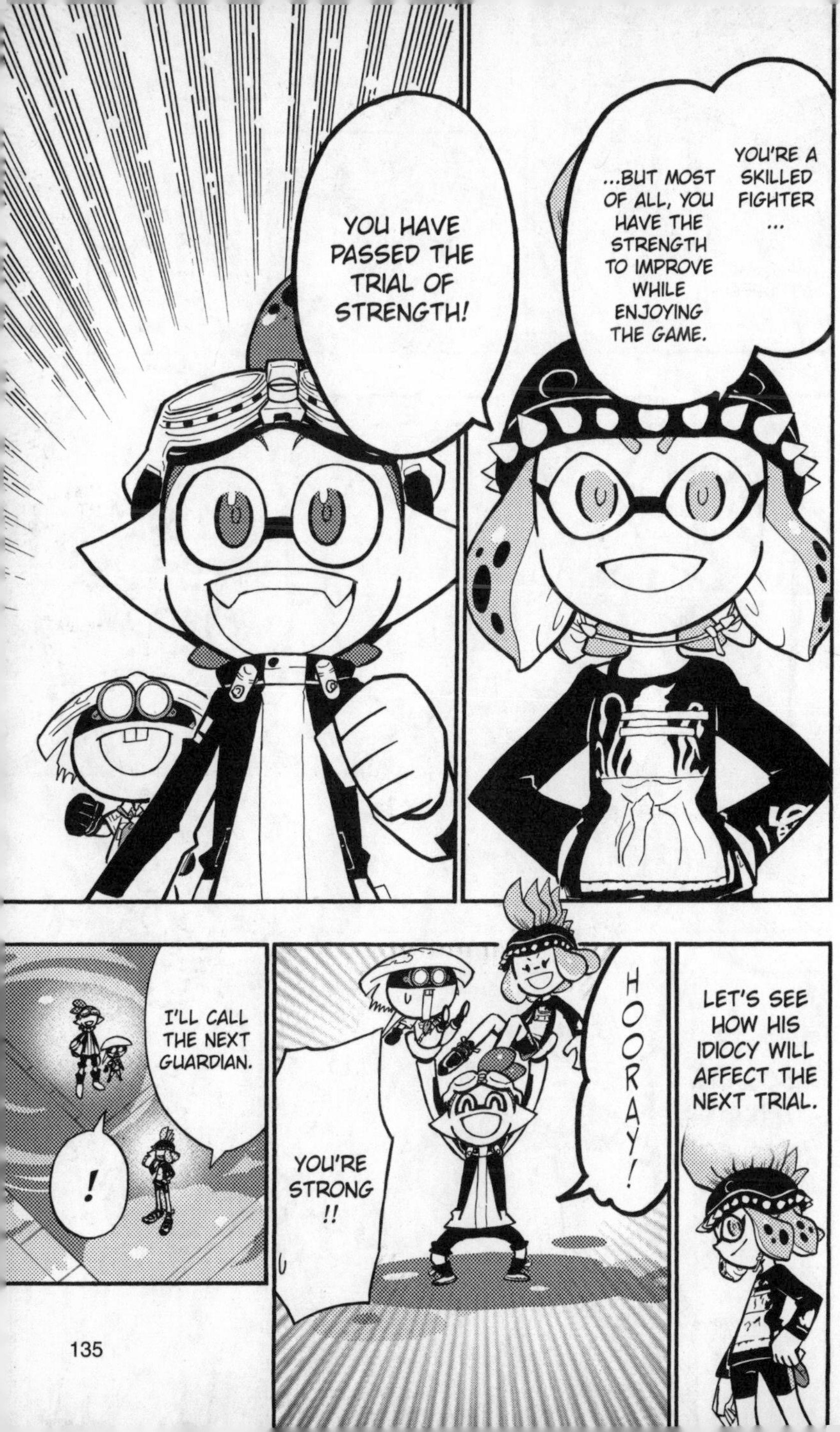
YOU'RE A SKILLED FIGHTER ...
...BUT MOST OF ALL, YOU HAVE THE STRENGTH TO IMPROVE WHILE ENJOYING THE GAME.
YOU HAVE PASSED THE TRIAL OF STRENGTH!
LET'S SEE HOW HIS IDIOCY WILL AFFECT THE NEXT TRIAL.
HOORAY!
YOU'RE STRONG !!
I'LL CALL THE NEXT GUARDIAN.
!

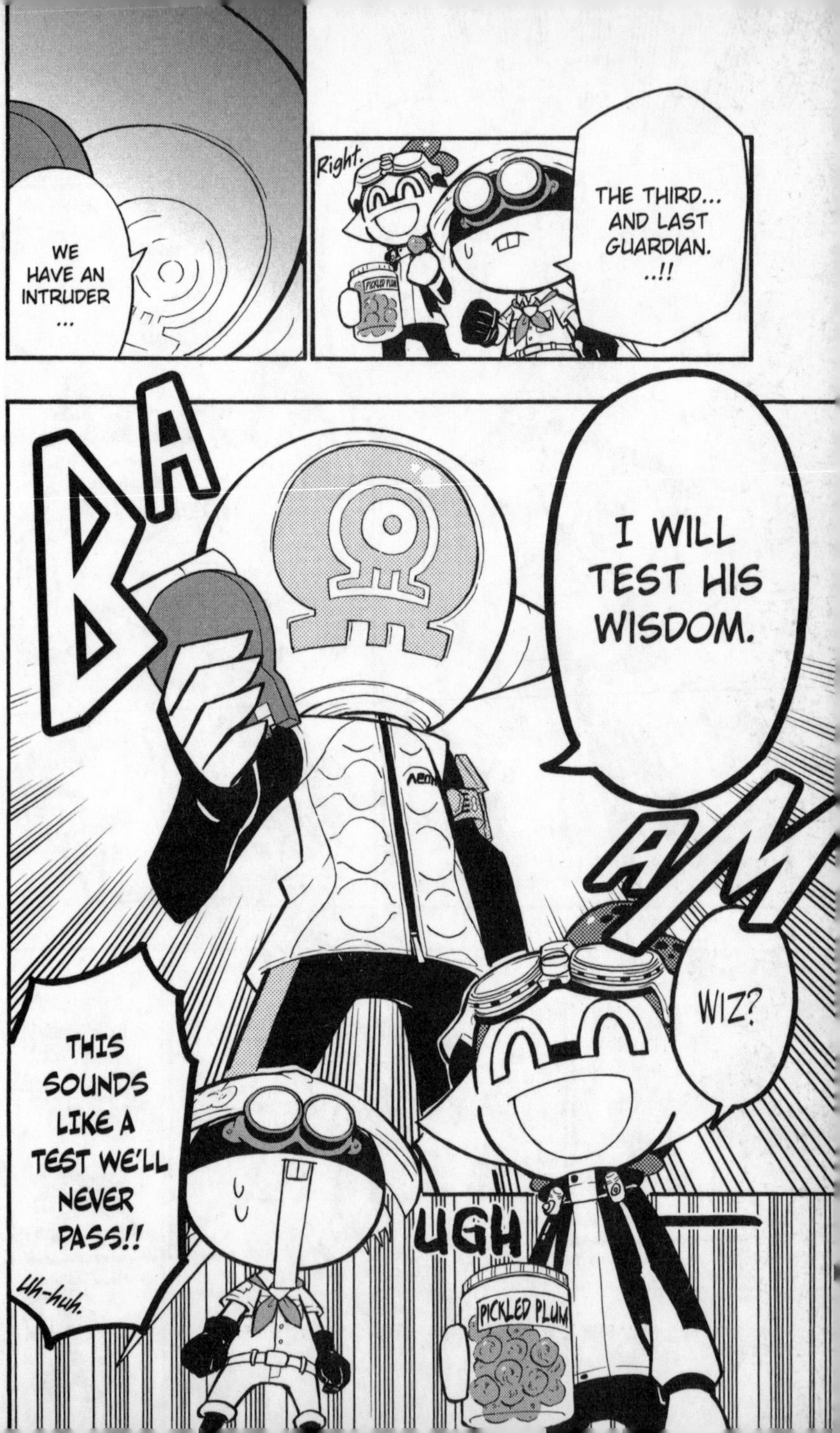
THE THIRD... AND LAST GUARDIAN. ..!!
Right.
WE HAVE AN INTRUDER ...
I WILL TEST HIS WISDOM.
BA
AM
WIZ?
THIS SOUNDS LIKE A TEST WE'LL NEVER PASS!!
UGH
Uh-huh.

SPLATOON VOLUME 12 END / CONTINUED IN VOLUME 13

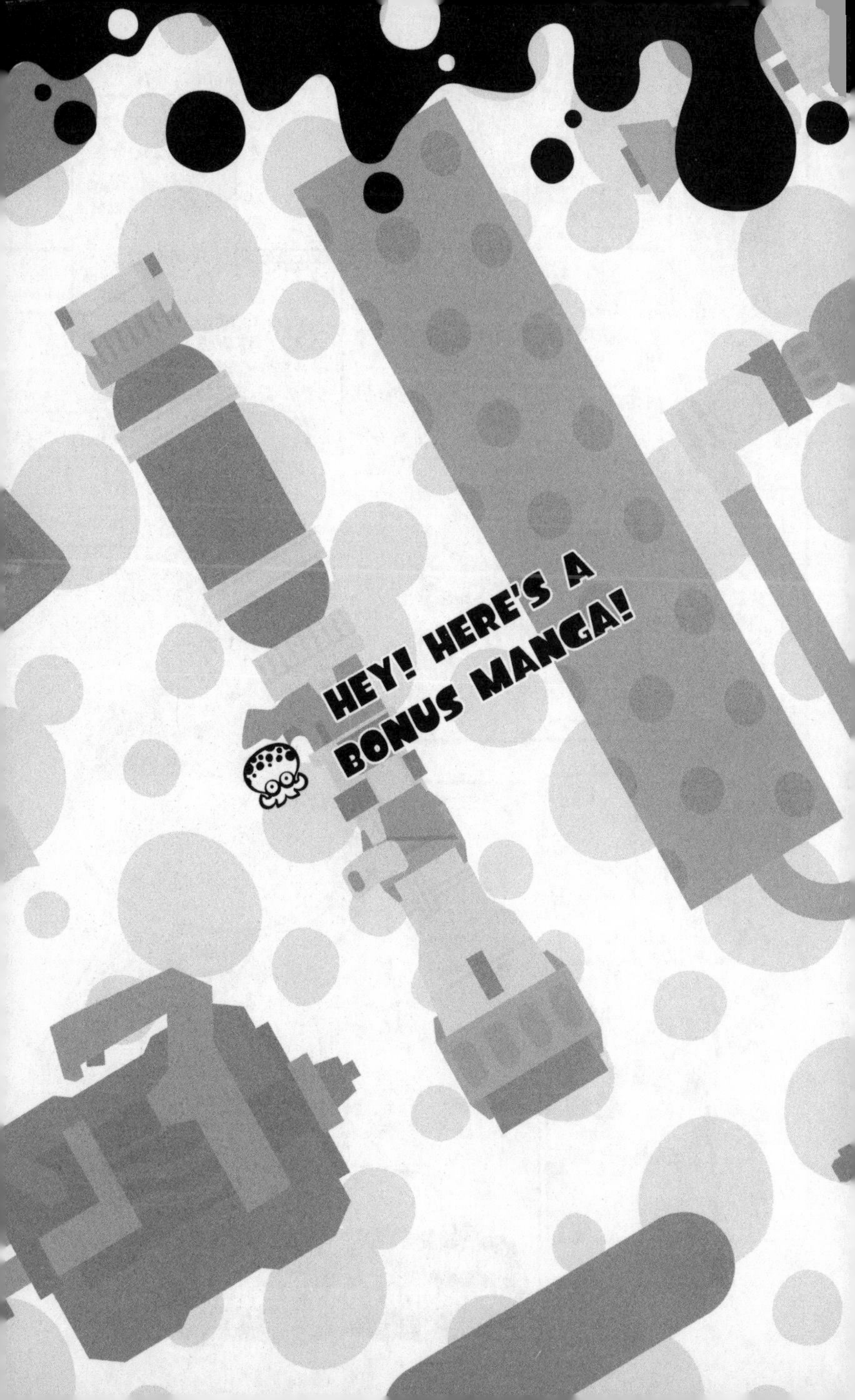
HEY! HERE'S A
BONUS MANGA!

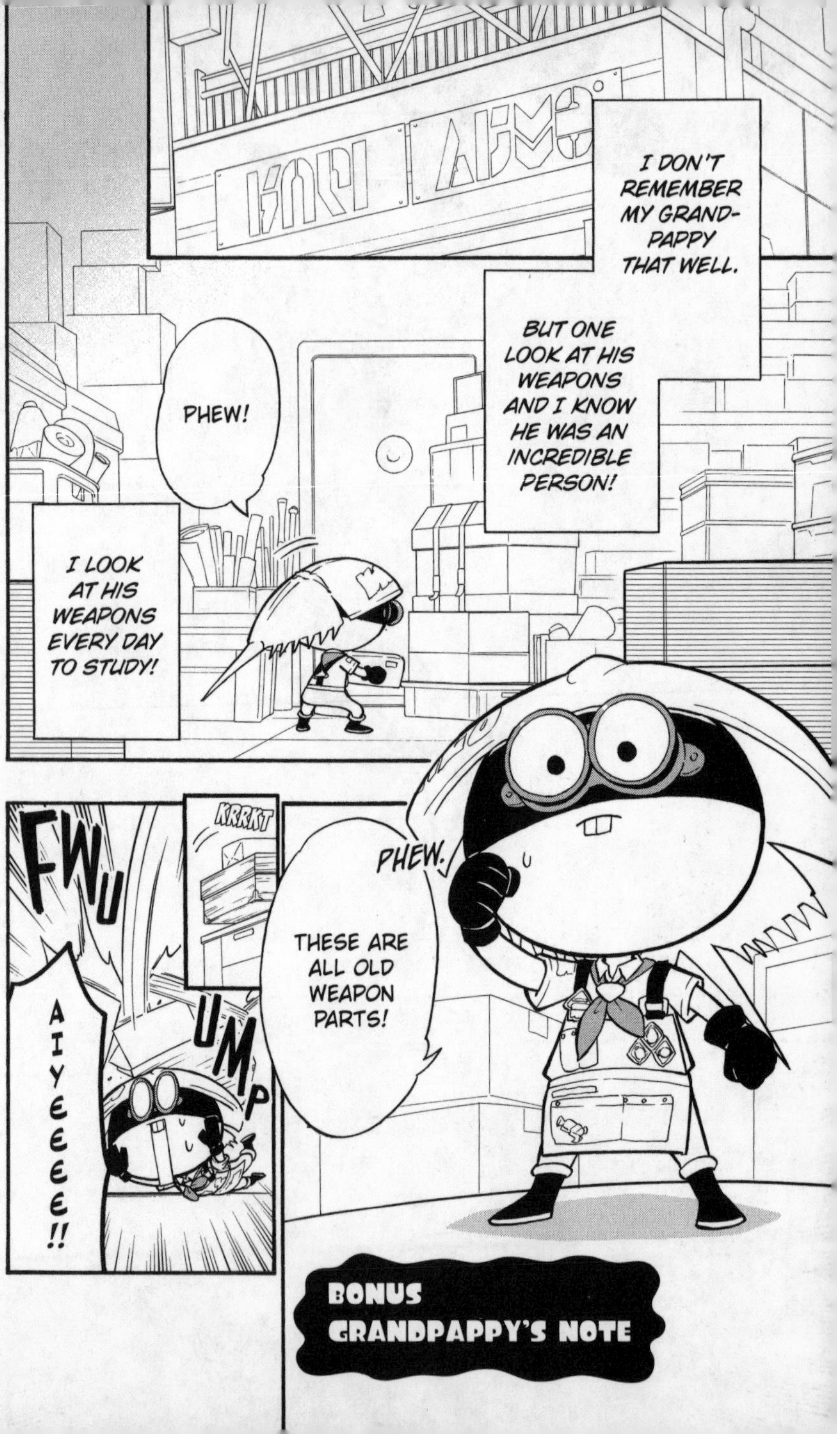
I DON'T REMEMBER MY GRAND-PAPPY THAT WELL.
BUT ONE LOOK AT HIS WEAPONS AND I KNOW HE WAS AN INCREDIBLE PERSON!
PHEW!
I LOOK AT HIS WEAPONS EVERY DAY TO STUDY!
PHEW.
THESE ARE ALL OLD WEAPON PARTS!
KRRKT
FWUUMP
AIYEEEEE!!
BONUS
GRANDPAPPY'S NOTE

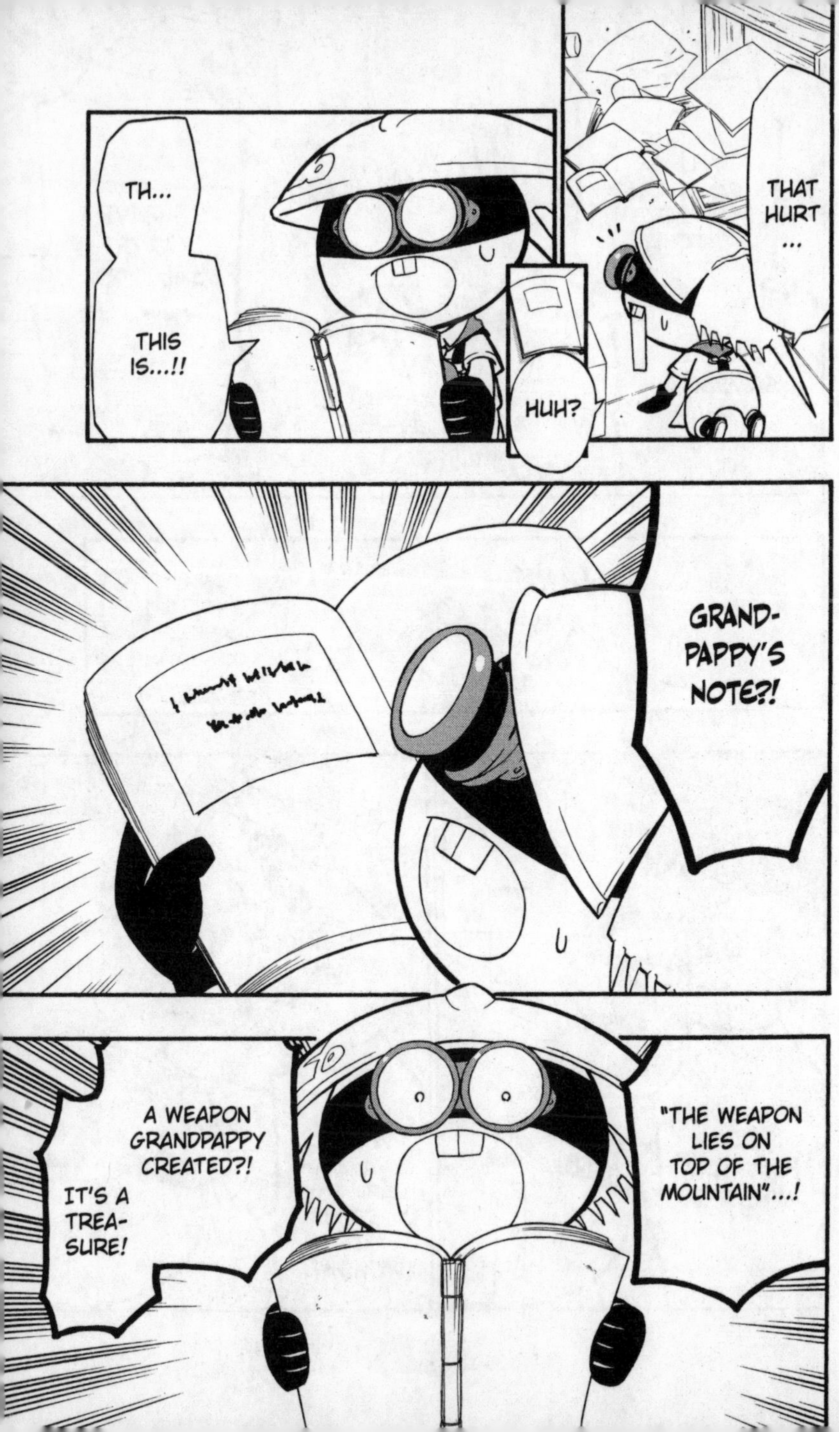
THAT HURT ...
HUH?
TH...
THIS IS...!!
GRAND-PAPPY'S NOTE?!
"THE WEAPON LIES ON TOP OF THE MOUNTAIN"...!
A WEAPON GRANDPAPPY CREATED?!
IT'S A TREA-SURE!

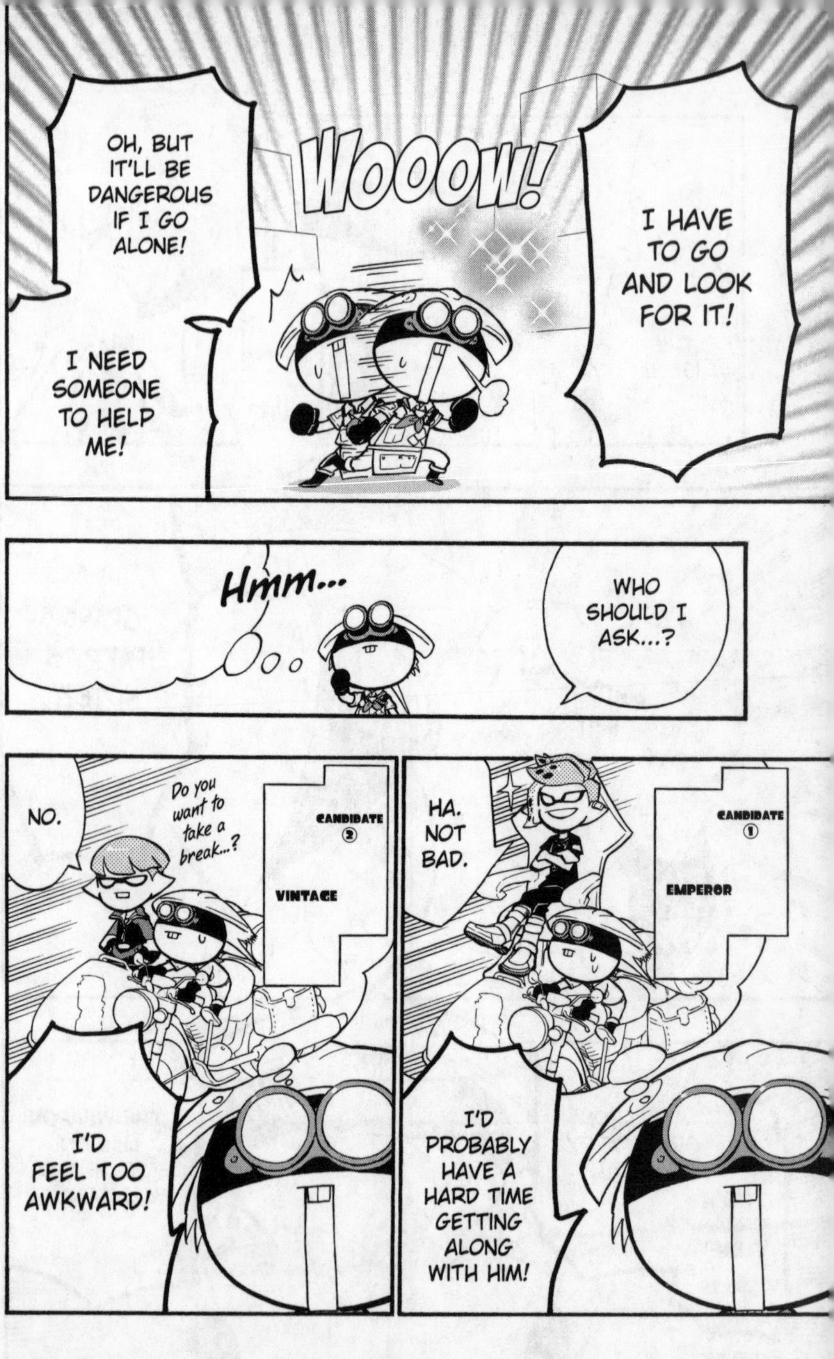
I HAVE TO GO AND LOOK FOR IT!
WOOOW!
OH, BUT IT'LL BE DANGEROUS IF I GO ALONE!
I NEED SOMEONE TO HELP ME!
WHO SHOULD I ASK...?
Hmm...
CANDIDATE ① EMPEROR
HA. NOT BAD.
I'D PROBABLY HAVE A HARD TIME GETTING ALONG WITH HIM!
CANDIDATE ② VINTAGE
Do you want to take a break...?
NO.
I'D FEEL TOO AWKWARD!

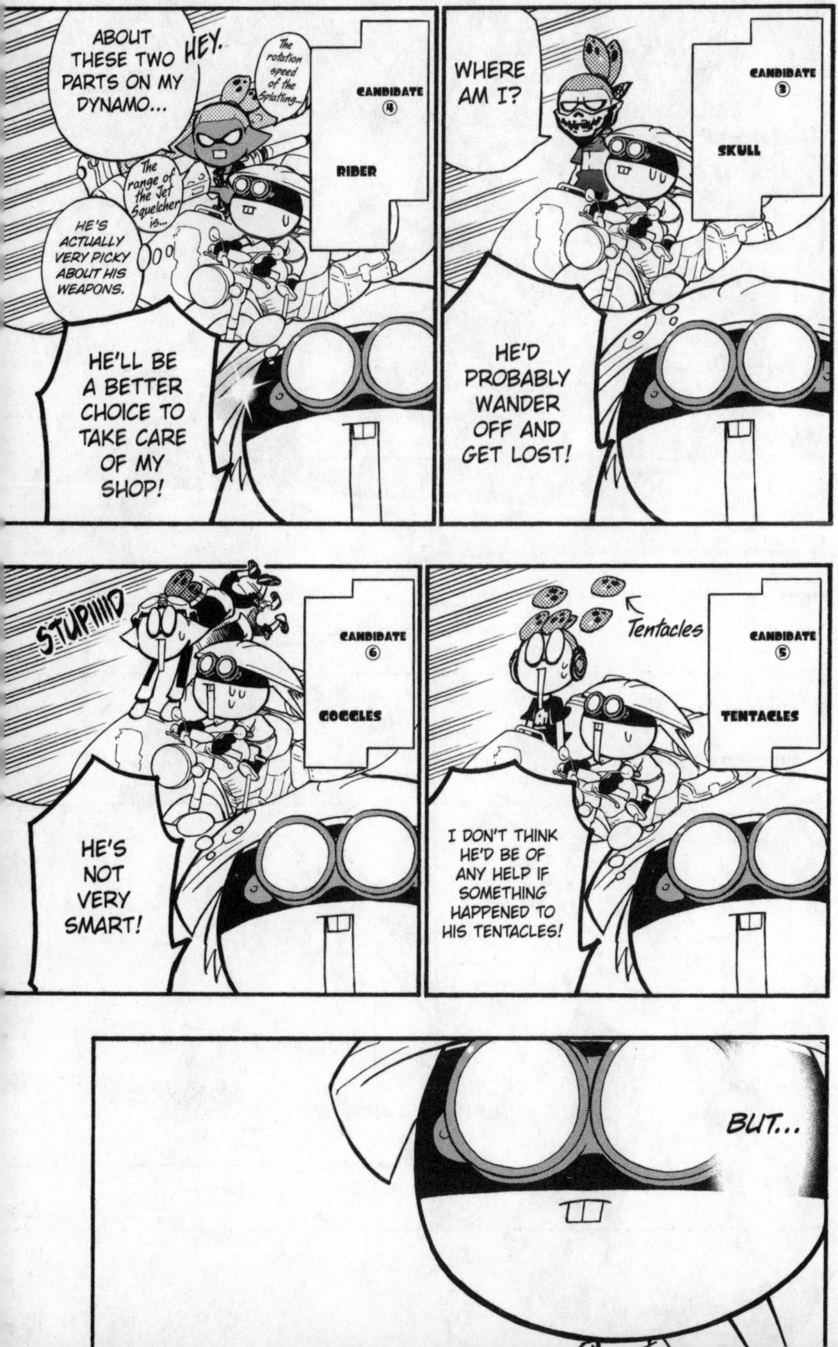
CANDIDATE ③
SKULL
WHERE AM I?
HE'D PROBABLY WANDER OFF AND GET LOST!
CANDIDATE ④
RIDER
The rotation speed of the Splatling...
HEY.
ABOUT THESE TWO PARTS ON MY DYNAMO...
The range of the Jet Squelcher is...
HE'S ACTUALLY VERY PICKY ABOUT HIS WEAPONS.
HE'LL BE A BETTER CHOICE TO TAKE CARE OF MY SHOP!
CANDIDATE ⑤
TENTACLES
Tentacles
I DON'T THINK HE'D BE OF ANY HELP IF SOMETHING HAPPENED TO HIS TENTACLES!
CANDIDATE ⑥
GOGGLES
STUPIIIID
HE'S NOT VERY SMART!
BUT...

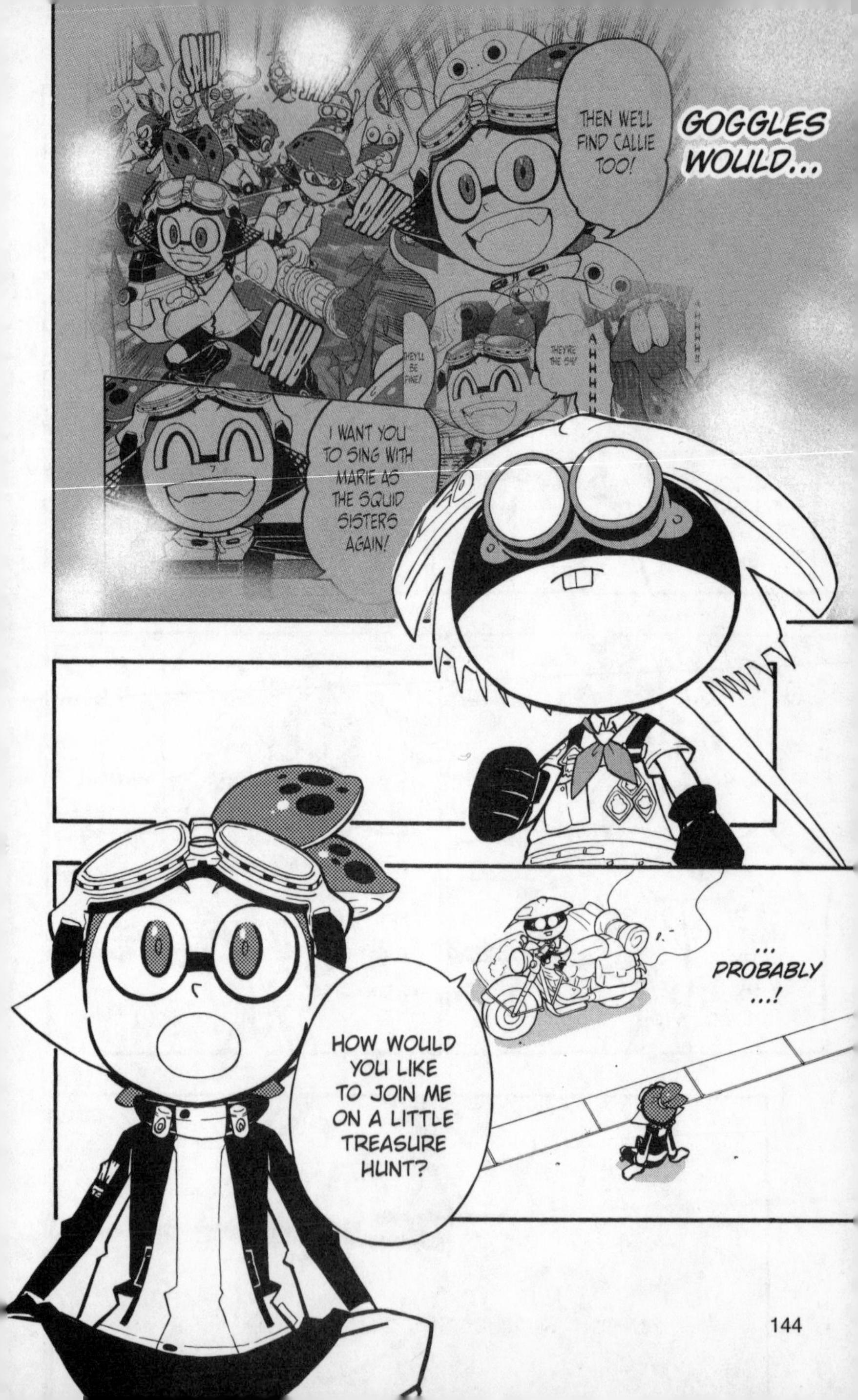
GOGGLES WOULD...
THEN WE'LL FIND CALLIE TOO!
AHHHHH
THEY'RE THE SH!
THEY'LL BE FINE!
I WANT YOU TO SING WITH MARIE AS THE SQUID SISTERS AGAIN!
... PROBABLY ...!
HOW WOULD YOU LIKE TO JOIN ME ON A LITTLE TREASURE HUNT?

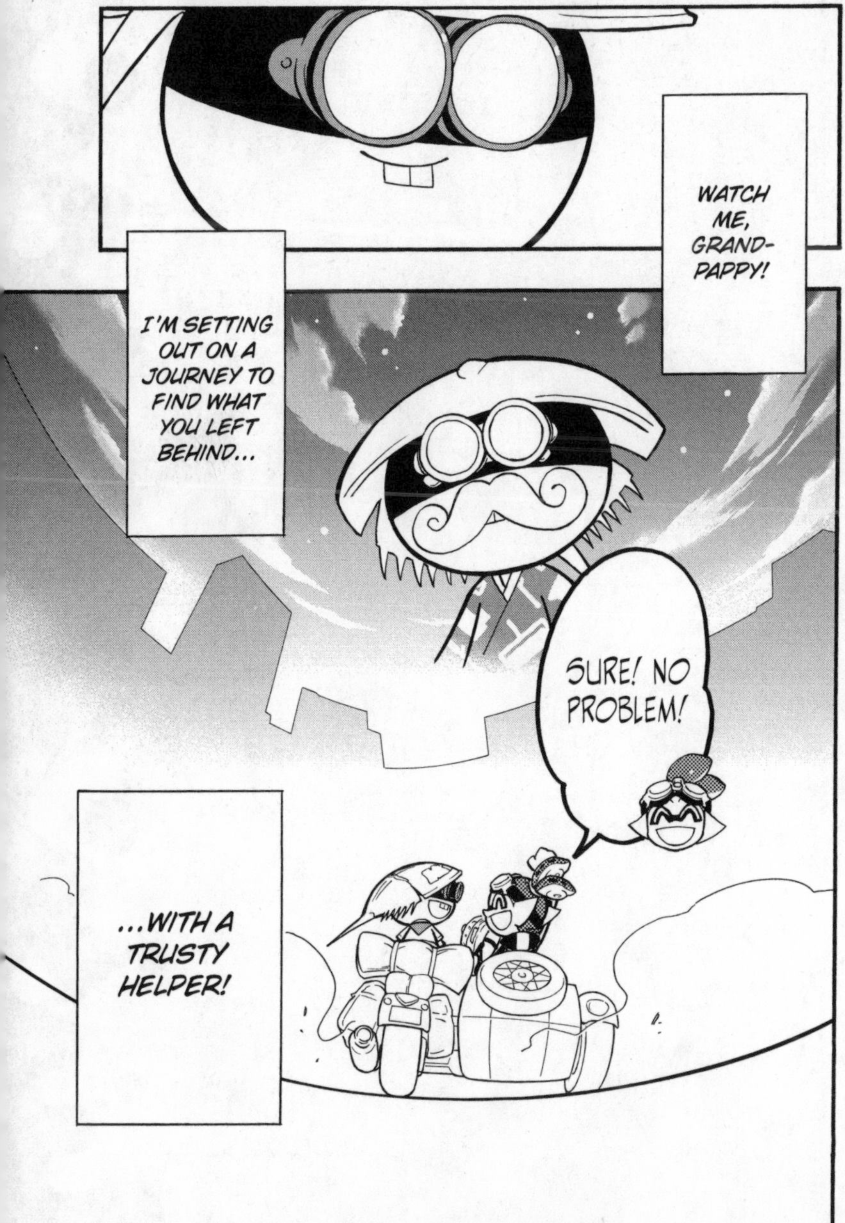
WATCH ME, GRANDPAPPY!
I'M SETTING OUT ON A JOURNEY TO FIND WHAT YOU LEFT BEHIND...
SURE! NO PROBLEM!
...WITH A TRUSTY HELPER!

(BONUS: GRANDPAPPY'S NOTE END)

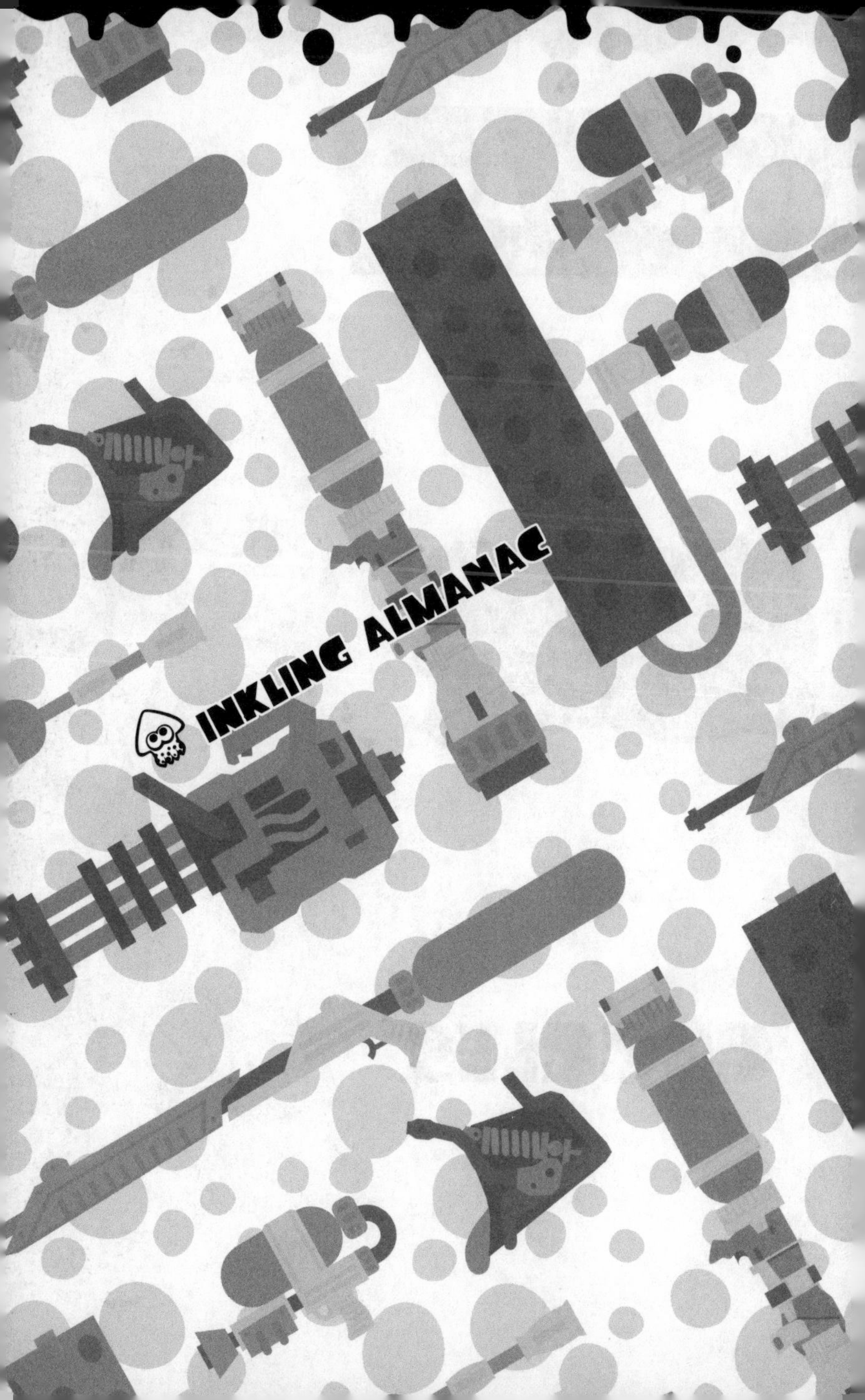
INKLING ALMANAC

MODE 2 ARC

Weapon: Hero Shot
Headgear: Pilot Goggles +
           Hero Headphones
Clothing: Hero Hoodie
Shoes: Hero Snowboots

GOGGLES

HERO

Weapon:	Hero Dualies
Headgear:	Hero Headphones
Clothing:	Hero Hoodie + Black V-Neck Tee
	Gloves
Shoes:	Toni Kensa Black Hi-Tops

GLOVES

MODE 2 ARC

Weapon: Hero Charger
Headgear: Skull Bandana +
Hero Headphones
Clothing: Hero Hoodie
Shoes: Hero Snowboots

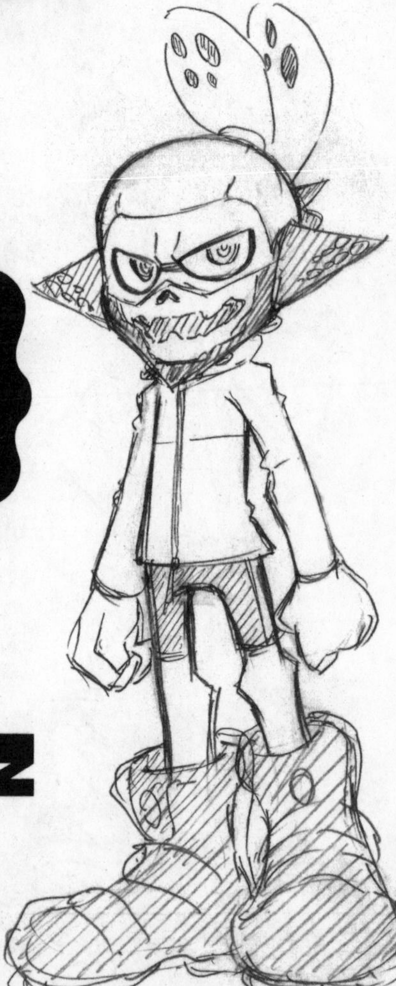

SKULLZ

HERO

Weapon: Hero Spatling
Headgear: Hero Headphones
Clothing: Hero Hoodie
Shoes: Hero Snowboots

VINTAGE

TEAM GLASSES

FULL MOON GLASSES

Weapon: Luna Blaster
Headgear: Full Moon Glasses
Clothing: Squidmark Sweat
Shoes: Punk Yellow

AVIATORS

Weapon: L-3 Nozzlenose
Headgear: 18K Aviators
Clothing: Squid Satin
          Jacket
Shoes: Choco Clogs

HALF-RIMZ

Weapon: Splatterscope
Headgear: Half-Rim Glasses
Clothing: Pink Easy-Stripe
          Shirt
Shoes: Shark Moccasins

SWIM GOGGLES

Weapon: Squeezer
Headgear: Swim Goggles
Clothing: Vintage Check Shirt
Shoes: Midnight Slip-Ons

INFO

•He has a lot of friends and he gets along well with Team Pink as well.

•He follows back on social media.

TEAM INFO

•It was Half-Rimz's idea to hold a practice match when Specs came back.

•Their group chat icons are all glasses, so they have trouble figuring out who's talking every now and then.

SPECS

GOGGLES

Weapon: Splattershot
Headgear: Pilot Goggles +
           Treasure Hunter
           (He only wears the
           Pilot Goggles in battle.)
Clothing: Eggplant Mountain Coat
Shoes: Hunting Boots

(*No Treasure Hunter during the battles.)

THE ADVENTURES

SHELDON

Front

Back

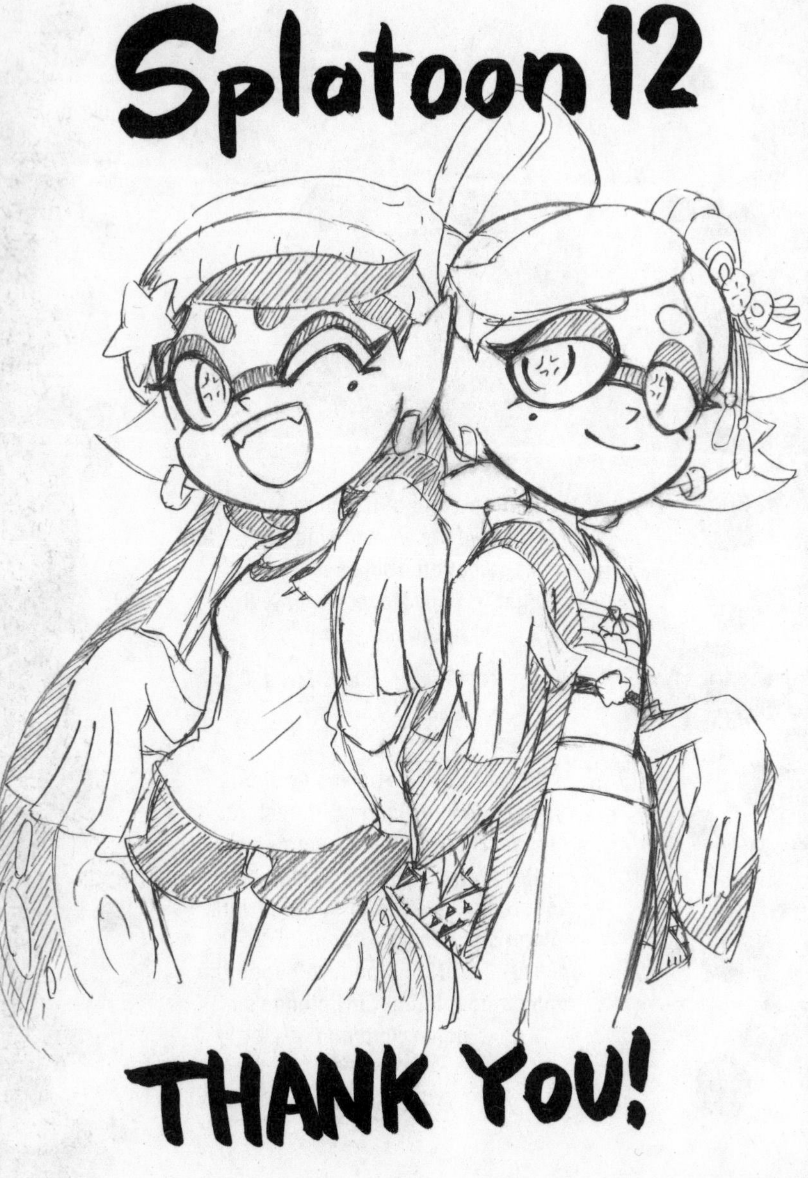
Splatoon 12
THANK YOU!

We're at the end of the Hero Mode arc!
Now that we know what kind of passion
and dedication it takes for an Inkling
to get to Hero Mode, it's time for a
brand new story!

Sankichi Hinodeya

Sankichi Hinodeya was born on
October 29 in Nagano Prefecture,
Japan. Hinodeya first emerged on
the scene in an extra issue of
Square Enix's *Gangan Powered* with
Maho Bozu Sankyu (Magical Monk
Sankyu). In 2015, Hinodeya began the
manga adaptation of Nintendo's hit
game *Splatoon*.

Splatoon™

Volume 12
VIZ Media Edition

Story and Art by
Sankichi Hinodeya

Translation **Tetsuichiro Miyaki**
English Adaptation **Bryant Turnage**
Lettering **John Hunt**
Design **Kam Li**
Editor **Joel Enos**

SPLATOON Vol. 12 by Sankichi HINODEYA
© 2016 Sankichi HINODEYA
All rights reserved.
Original Japanese edition published by SHOGAKUKAN.
English translation rights in the United States of America,
Canada, the United Kingdom, Ireland, Australia and
New Zealand arranged with SHOGAKUKAN.

The stories, characters and incidents mentioned
in this publication are entirely fictional.

Original Design **100percent**

Printed in the U.S.A.

Published by VIZ Media, LLC
P.O. Box 77010
San Francisco, CA 94107

10 9 8 7 6 5 4 3 2 1
First Printing, May 2021

VIZ MEDIA
viz.com

PARENTAL ADVISORY
SPLATOON is rated A and is
suitable for readers of all ages.

Splatoon
reads from
right to
left!

This is
the end
of this
graphic
novel.